DOS PASSOS: THE CRITICAL HERITAGE

THE CRITICAL HERITAGE SERIES

GENERAL EDITOR: B. C. SOUTHAM, M.A., B. LITT. (OXON)

Formerly Department of English, Westfield College, University of London

For a list of books in the series see the back end paper

DOS PASSOS

THE CRITICAL HERITAGE

Edited by
BARRY MAINE
Assistant Professor of English
Wake Forest University

ROUTLEDGE
LONDON AND NEW YORK

128869

First published in 1988 by
Routledge
11 New Fetter Lane, London EC4P4EE

Published in the USA by
Routledge, Chapman & Hall, Inc.
29 West 35th Street, New York, NY 10001

Set in 10/12 Bembo
by Thomson Press (India) Ltd., New Delhi
and printed in Great Britain
by TJ Press (Padstow) Ltd
Padstow, Cornwall

Library of Congress Cataloging in Publication Data

Doss Passos, the critical heritage/edited by Barry Maine.
p.   cm.— (The Critical heritage series)
Published in association with Methuen. Inc.
Bibliography: p.
Includes index.
1. Dos Passos, John, 1896–1970—Criticism and interpretation.
I. Maine, Barry. II. Series.
PS3507. 07432573   1988
813′ .52–dc19

British Library CIP Data also available
ISBN   0–415–00229–x

General Editor's Preface

The reception given to a writer by his contemporaries and near-contemporaries is evidence of considerable value to the student of literature. On one side we learn a great deal about the state of criticism at large and in particular about the development of critical attitudes towards a single writer; at the same time, through private comments in letters, journals or marginalia, we gain an insight upon the tastes and literary thought of individual readers of the period. Evidence of this kind helps us to understand the writer's historical situation, the nature of his immediate reading-public, and his response to these pressures.

The separate volumes in the *Critical Heritage Series* present a record of this early criticism. Clearly, for many of the highly productive and lengthily reviewed nineteenth- and twentieth-century writers, there exists an enormous body of material; and in these cases the volume editors have made a selection of the most important views, significant for their intrinsic critical worth or for their representative quality—perhaps even registering incomprehension!

For earlier writers, notably pre-eighteenth century, the materials are much scarcer and the historical period has been extended, sometimes far beyond the writer's lifetime, in order to show the inception and growth of critical views which were initially slow to appear.

In each volume the documents are headed by an Introduction, discussing the material assembled and relating the early stages of the author's reception to what we have come to identify as the critical tradition. The volumes will make available much material which would otherwise be difficult of access and it is hoped that the modern reader will be thereby helped towards an informed understanding of the ways in which literature has been read and judged.

B.C.S.

Contents

Three Soldiers (September 1921)

One Man's Initiation—1917 (London, October 1920; New York, June 1922)

Manhattan Transfer (November 1925)

The Big Money (August 1936)

Adventures of a Young Man (June 1939)

CONTENTS

Century's Ebb (August 1975)

Acknowledgments

I should like to express my gratitude to my Wake Forest colleagues, William Moss and James Hans, for their technical assistance, and to Townsend Ludington for generously agreeing to read a draft of the Introduction.

It has not always proved possible to locate the owners of copyright material. However, all possible care has been taken to trace ownership of the selections printed and to make full acknowledgment for their use. For permission to reprint, thanks are due to the following: Edgar M. Branch and Cleo Paturis as representatives of the Estate of James T. Farrell for No. 50, reprinted by permission of the archives of James T. Farrell at the University of Pennsylvania; the Chicago Tribune Company for Nos 7, 18, and 60 (Copyrighted, Chicago Tribune Company, all rights reserved, used with permission); Condé Nast Publications Inc. for No. 1, courtesy *Vanity Fair* (Copyright © 1921 (renewed) 1949, 1977, by The Condé Nast Publications Inc.); Malcolm Cowley for Nos 34 and 46; *Daily Mail* (London) for No. 27; Editions Gallimard for No. 42, from *Situations I* by Jean-Paul Sartre (© Editions Gallimard 1947); Farrar, Straus & Giroux, Inc., and Routledge & Kegan Paul, Ltd, for Nos 49, 55, and 57, from Edmond Wilson, *Letters on Literature and Politics 1912–1972*, selected and edited by Elena Wilson (Copyright © 1957, 1973, 1974, 1977 by Elena Wilson. Reprinted by permission); Melvin J. Friedman and *The Progressive* for No. 65 (Copyright © 1961, The Progressive, Inc., reprinted by permission); John Gross for No. 66; Harcourt Brace Jovanovich Inc., and Diana Trilling for No. 40, which first appeared in *Partisan Review*, reprinted from *Speaking of Literature and Society* by Lionel Trilling (Copyright © 1980 by Diana and Lionel Trilling. Reprinted by permission); Harcourt Brace Jovanovich, Inc., for No. 52, from *On Native Grounds* (Copyright 1942, 1970 by Alfred Kazin, reprinted by permission); I.H.T. Corporation for Nos 11, 17, 24, 33, 45, 53, and 63 (© I.H.T. Corporation. Reprinted by permission); Alfred Kazin for No. 54; Louisiana State University Press for No. 43; the *Nation*

(New York) for No. 38; National Council of Teachers of English for No. 30, from the *English Journal*; the *New Republic* for No. 68 (© 1975, The New Republic, Inc., reprinted by permission); *New York Post* for Nos 3 and 9; The New York Times Company for Nos 2, 8, 12, 25, 58, 62, and 67 (Copyright © 1921, 1922, 1925, 1932, 1951, 1961, 1975. Reprinted by permission); Lawrence Pollinger Ltd., Viking Penguin, Inc., and the Estate of Mrs Frieda Lawrence Ravagli for No. 15, from *Phoenix, The Posthumous Papers* (1936) by D.H. Lawrence, edited and with an introduction by Edward D. McDonald (Copyright 1936 by Frieda Lawrence, renewed © 1964 by the Estate of the late Frieda Lawrence Ravagli); Princeton University Press for No. 16, from Paul Elmer More, *The Demon and the Absolute* (Copyright 1928, © 1956 renewed by Princeton University Press); Russell & Volkening, Inc., as agents for the author for No. 56 (Copyright © 1949, renewed 1977 by Granville Hicks); *San Francisco Chronicle* for No. 61; *Saturday Review* for Nos 13, 26, 32, 44, and 59 (© 1925, 1932, 1936, 1939, 1951 *Saturday Review* magazine. Reprinted by permission); *Spectator* for Nos 22, 28, and 37; Times Newspapers Ltd for No. 36; Gore Vidal and *Esquire* magazine for No. 6; and *Virginia Quarterly Review* for permission to reprint No. 51.

Introduction

John Dos Passos wrote more than forty books during his lifetime, including poetry, plays, travel books, political tracts, histories, and biographies. He is better known, though, for his novels, and best of all for the documentary-style fiction he wrote during the twenties and thirties. I have limited the documentation of his critical reception to the novels he is best known for, and to those others which are representative of a period in his career or of a change in political or stylistic direction. Though it is certainly true that no American writer has been more subjected to political judgment than Dos Passos has, the history of the critical response shows that what made him the most promising American writer of the thirties and a much less respected writer later on had as much to do with his art as with his politics, if indeed the two can be separated. As Joseph Epstein observed, in a retrospective on Dos Passos's career:

What is crucial to the judgment of political novels is not only the extent to which a novelist's politics are intrinsic to his work, but the extent to which in his work he is incapable of transcending them—for to that extent, if one does not share these politics, one is scarcely likely to bear to read the work.[1]

On the other hand, as the record shows, reviewers are often equally incapable of transcending *their* politics; thus the critical reception of a political writer such as Dos Passos is likely to become a complex affair. We delude ourselves, moreover, if we believe that we exist outside a historical process that plays a role in determining which literary texts we will include in the canon. A critical reception never stops developing, and neither does historical consciousness ever fully reveal itself in openly stated principles or propositions. It reveals itself more in the kinds of questions about literature that readers and critics ask than in the answers they give, and it exists, to borrow a term from Hans Robert Jauss, as a 'horizon of expectation', beyond which the reading public by and large is unable to see and unwilling to go.[2] 'A literary work', Jauss reminds us, 'is not an object which stands by itself and which offers the same face to each reader in each period.... The historical life of a literary work is unthinkable without the active participation of its audience.'[3] In other words, the reading and

I

interpretation of a literary work over time is its literary history just as surely as its genesis is.

It is often the case that contemporary reviews do not reveal what eventually become the most important critical issues. This is most often the case when an author's reputation comes into its own rather late, perhaps because of some gap between the sensibility of the writer and that of the reading public (its 'horizon of expectation') during his lifetime or during his most productive period. (In American literature, Herman Melville and William Faulkner come immediately to mind, among others.) Dos Passos's critical reputation, on the other hand, was never so great as it was during his most productive period; and one problem critics of Dos Passos did not have was learning how to read him. This does not mean they all read him correctly, only that they could read him well enough to appreciate the best (and worst) in his work. With the exception of the Joycean Camera Eye sections in *U.S.A.*, Dos Passos's work did not challenge the patience or understanding of readers the way Joyce did, or Pound, or Faulkner, for whom the contemporary response was often bewilderment if not irritation and outright dismissal. It is true that some reviewers, especially British reviewers less well-disposed toward experiments in narrative form, were perplexed or even put off by the narrative fragmentation in Dos Passos's early work, that some critics objected to its sordid subject matter, and that a good many reviewers reacted violently against its satire of American institutions. Nevertheless, and partly as a result of such strong reactions, Dos Passos's impact upon the literary scene was as sudden as it was dramatic. His work was reviewed in all the major literary periodicals in America and abroad by some of the best critics of his day: Edmund Wilson and D.H. Lawrence in the twenties; Malcolm Cowley, Lionel Trilling, Bernard De Voto, V.S. Pritchett, and Jean-Paul Sartre in the thirties; Granville Hicks and Alfred Kazin in the forties. Add to this the decline in interest in Dos Passos since the forties relative to Hemingway, Fitzgerald, and Faulkner, and the result is a contemporary response which offers some of the best criticism written about him.

One aspect of Dos Passos's work that the contemporary reaction does not show is his development as a writer in response to it. He did not change his writing habits or adjust his style to suit his critics. Few good writers do, and fewer still admit to it. Like many artists of his generation Dos Passos instinctively mistrusted the literary establishment for its conservatism. ('Don't believe *The New York Times*,' he warned a friend about the war he was soon to see for himself.[4]) Later, a conservative himself, he mistrusted its liberalism. In either case, he was less likely to respond to critics than to the advice of friends such as Hemingway, who warned him against creating 'perfect' characters, and 'telling' rather than 'showing' what he wished to get across to the reader, or Edmund Wilson, who may have been Dos Passos's best critic.[5] He does appear to have responded favourably to such advice up to a point, but most of the time he went his own way, alienating many friends and critics who had praised his early work, even to the point where, during the early 1950s, he felt as if he were 'writing from the bottom of a well'.[6]

In France in 1938 Jean-Paul Sartre regarded Dos Passos as 'the greatest writer of our time' (No. 42) and he was not alone in thinking so. That Dos Passos was rated higher than Faulkner by their contemporaries but not by us reveals less about either writer than it does about changing criteria for great literature. Sartre preferred Dos Passos to Faulkner because he believed the latter's characters lived unnaturally in the past, as if looking out of the rear window of a moving car, and thus the premise behind his work was a 'false metaphysic'.[7] Dos Passos's characters in U.S.A., on the other hand, were always looking ahead, even as they showed us a capitalist society in which men and women did not have lives, but 'only destinies'. In other words, Sartre placed a high premium on social realism. In America, readers and critics alike during the Great Depression looked for someone to explain the relationship between the present and the past, to explain what had gone wrong. Faulkner, the more confirmed modernist, proved to be of little help in this regard because he showed in *The Sound and the Fury* and in *Absalom, Absalom!* that all order, historical sequence and causality included, is arbitrary and subjective. While it may seem at first that Dos Passos is saying the same thing in the fragmented narrative of U.S.A., this is clearly not so. He expected his readers to read between the lines and to make the connections between past and present and between individual and society which the characters themselves are unable to make. They are unable to make such connections because Dos Passos believed participation in a historical process to be, for most people, largely unconscious. That does not mean that a historical process is not at work or cannot be identified. Marxist criticism of the sort that judged a novel by its revolutionary content was much more in the mainstream during the thirties than it is now, and the Marxist critics who saw no value in literature as literature, but only as a tool for revolution, rejected Faulkner out of hand and embraced Dos Passos. When it became clear later on that his commitment to a specifically Marxist view of history had never been what the leftist critics had hoped for, they rejected him as well. Even so, Dos Passos answered the call for social realism in the thirties and answered it better than anyone else.

Dos Passos's conservative politics in his later novels is much more in the mainstream today than it was when he wrote them. Does that mean we will see renewed interest in them in the years ahead? Though not out of the question, it seems unlikely, for as the contemporary response indicates, Dos Passos perfected his art in *U.S.A.*, and defended his politics at the expense of his art in the novels thereafter, and to students of literature that may always seem a waste of talent.

THE 1920s

Dos Passos's first novel, *One Man's Initiation—1917*, a thinly disguised autobiography of his disillusioning war experiences, was written from diaries he kept as a volunteer overseas in the Norton-Harjes Ambulance Corps, the Red Cross, and eventually, the American Army. It was published in London by Allen & Unwin in the fall of 1920. Dos Passos was forced to help pay for its publication and to tone down some of the language which the printers (who in England were held liable) found offensive. The novel sold only sixty-three copies in six months.[8] The London critics ignored it completely. *Three Soldiers*, his next novel, was refused by fourteen publishing houses before George H. Doran in New York agreed to risk it.[9] Most Americans were ready to put the Great War in Europe behind them, so publishers were understandably reluctant to take a chance on a war novel. The language used by Dos Passos's soldiers presented another obstacle. Doran's acceptance of the manuscript was conditional upon Dos Passos's deleting sacrilegious and obscene words, despite his defence of these in the name of realism. He made the changes reluctantly.[10] Dos Passos left New York deliberately—with E.E. Cummings back across the Atlantic—when the date of publication approached. He was to repeat this pattern throughout most of his life, perhaps not so much to avoid the critics (for he did read them) as to put each book behind him and go on to something new. Hence his novels were often followed by travel books, as *Three Soldiers* was followed by *Rosinante to the Road Again*, a collection of impressionist essays about Spain.

No one could have anticipated the storm of controversy *Three Soldiers* raised over the American military, and Dos Passos could not have been more delighted.[11] Not since Stephen Crane's *The Red Badge of Courage* had an American novel stirred such heated debate. Whereas Dos Passos's first novel had yet to be reviewed at all, *Three Soldiers* was written up in all the major newspapers and literary journals in America, and most noticeably on the front page of the *New York Times Book Review*—twice. Dos Passos, like Fitzgerald before him and Hemingway soon after, became famous overnight. Coningsby Dawson (No. 2), who had served in the Canadian forces, got the debate off to a rollicking start by proclaiming that Dos Passos's depiction of the American enlisted man's service in the army overseas was either 'a base libel or a hideous truth'. One reviewer after another—and some soldiers too—took a turn at saying which it was. Dawson condemned the book for its 'calculated sordidness' and 'blind whirlwind of rage which respects neither the reticences of art nor the restraints of decency'. He claimed Dos Passos must have exaggerated the misuse of military discipline and the disaffection, complaints, petty recriminations, and demoralized spirit of the American infantryman. 'If the picture is false', he concluded, 'the crime of presenting it is unpardonable', and he called upon American veterans to verify or denounce it. He got his wish two weeks later in the same forum in Harold Norman Denny's 'One Soldier on *Three Soldiers*'. Denny characterized Dos Passos's assertion that American soldiers were idealists crushed by the machinery of war as 'tommyrot'.[12] Other soldiers concurred. One veteran (No. 5), writing for *Foreign Service*, the offical organ for American veterans of foreign wars, angrily denounced Dos Passos as a liar, while another (No. 7), writing for the *Chicago Tribune*, attacked the book as Communist propaganda and an 'affront to every just and decent principle upon which society is founded and organized business and government maintained'. The more liberal literary journals, on the other hand, heaped praise on the book. James Sibley Watson, under the pseudonym of W.C. Blum, lauded the novel in the *Dial*, as did Henry Seidel Canby (No. 3) in the *New York Evening Post Literary Review*.[13] John Peale Bishop (No. 1) hailed Dos Passos as a 'genius' for capturing 'the very stuff and breath' of the American Army overseas. He also praised his ability to move so many minor characters on and off the stage. Francis Hackett (No. 4) was similarly impressed by the collectivist approach in the novel and by Dos Passos's ability to substitute character and description for direct authorial statements about the war. Heywood Broun writing for *Bookman* (New York) flatly declared, 'Nothing which has come out of the school of American realists has seemed to us so entirely honest.... It represents deep convictions and impressions eloquently expressed.'[14] Impressionism or realism? There was no resolving the issue, for the novel elicited condemnation or praise depending upon one's experience in the war (a young war veteran's copy carried the inscription, 'This is the truest damn book ever written'[15]) or one's politics back home. Dos Passos's 'impression' was no doubt an honest one; but this was not the last time the representative quality of his experience was questioned by critics who did not share his political views whether they were liberal (in this case) or conservative (later on). H.L. Mencken (No. 6) contended—in excess of probable impact—that *Three Soldiers* had 'changed the whole tone of American opinion about the war'.

Hoping to capitalize on the success of *Three Soldiers*, the George H. Doran Company published an American edition of *One Man's Initiation—1917* the following year, a collection of Dos Passos's travel essays (*Rosinante to the Road Again*), a volume of poetry (*A Pushcart at the Curb* (1922)) and his next novel, *Streets of Night* (1923). The reviewer for *Bookman* (No. 10) referred to *One Man's Initiation* as 'more a memoir than a novel' and a 'prelude' to *Three Soldiers*. Lloyd Morris (No. 8) praised the immediacy of its descriptive passages, which he also found 'poetic in feeling and conception', although he maintained that Dos Passos's response to experience was emotional and aesthetic rather than intellectual. This same romantic sensibility, he continued, rather than any clear understanding of the war's causes, accounted for his anti-war sentiments. Constance Black (No. 11) praised his painter's eye for detail (Dos Passos was, it so happens, an amateur painter) and his ear for American speech, especially slang. She predicted that he might one day write 'the still unwritten great novel of modern America'. The critics were less kind to *Streets of Night*, an awkwardly self-conscious and in many ways immature novel about the sterility of Harvard aesthetes in comparison to the vigour and vitality of the working classes. Begun at Harvard before he had been overseas to see the war, *Streets of Night* is easily Dos Passos's weakest novel. Nevertheless, the choice it offers between a physically active and passively intellectual life would become an important choice for many of Dos Passos's later characters; we also find, as

Robert Rosen has pointed out, Dos Passos clinging to the 'notion of the virtuous and vital lower classes,' a notion which 'lies somewhere behind the radicalism of *U.S.A.*'[16]

Manhattan Transfer, Dos Passos's next novel, was published by Harper & Brothers in November 1925. Dos Passos fought another battle over language and was forced to cut what Harpers considered blasphemous. Despite the cuts, Paul Elmer More, speaking for the genteel tradition, referred to the book as 'an explosion in a cesspool' (No. 16) and other reviewers as well objected to the sordidness of the setting and characters. Henry Longan Stuart (No. 12) believed Dos Passos had focused too much attention on the unpleasant, but the real flaw, he pointed out, was that he had ignored the extent to which the human mind can shut out what is 'bewildering' or 'disheartening'. In other words, life was not so bad or so desperately unhappy or even so chaotic for most New Yorkers as Dos Passos made it out to be. (The tendency to judge what might very likely have been intended as satire by standards of social history is not uncommon in reviews of Dos Passos's work.) But the novel found its champions too, and mostly among other writers. D.H. Lawrence (No. 15) admired the dizzying pace and overwhelming diversity Dos Passos had captured in 'a breathless confusion of isolated moments'. Allen Tate praised his 'swift, vigorous, dynamic' prose style.[17] F. Scott Fitzgerald wrote Max Perkins to say the novel was 'astonishingly good'.[18] Sinclair Lewis (No. 13) went even further, predicting that *Manhattan Transfer* might inaugurate 'a whole new school of novel writing'. He noted the influence of the cinema in the speed and editing of the narrative. He claimed *Manhattan Transfer* was more important than anything written by Gertrude Stein, Marcel Proust, or James Joyce because Dos Passos had placed their 'experimental psychology and style' in the service of a good (and readable!) story. This comparison may only reveal Lewis's limitations as a writer and reader, though it is certainly true that Dos Passos seems to have been influenced by Joyce. New York City is as much the subject as it is the setting of *Manhattan Transfer*, much like Dublin was in Joyce's *Dubliners*, and Dos Passos, like most serious writers of the twenties, had also read *Ulysses*. He may have borrowed some of his expressionistic devices from Joyce, though they more likely reflect his keen interest in experiments with technique in painting, sculpture, literature, and film.[19] Lewis completed his encomium by concluding that Dos

Passos had captured the 'beauty and stir of life' in New York City better than Whitman, Howells, Wharton, or James before him. If this is true, it may be so only because Whitman alone had taken a collectivist approach to the city and included the full range of social classes in his portrayal of it, and because *Manhattan Transfer* was the only truly 'modern' novel about twentieth-century New York. Mike Gold, writing for the *New Masses*, the radical Left's mouthpiece in America, praised the experimental (and hence anti-traditional) style of the novel, and also compared Dos Passos to Whitman for managing to get all of New York's diverse peoples, nationalities, and occupations into his 'poem'. Dos Passos had captured *what* happens in New York City better than anyone before him, Gold concluded, but he had not explained *why* it happens. The 'hero' of *Manhattan Transfer* (Jimmy Herf) is, Gold contended, a 'baffled young middle-class idealist' who wants to escape from the evils of American commercialism but doesn't know how, because Dos Passos himself doesn't. Gold urged Dos Passos to throw his lot in with the radical branch of the labour movement to escape his bewilderment. This was an appeal made regularly to Dos Passos by the radical Left during the twenties and thirties. Dos Passos, however, was an observer, not a joiner; in an early letter to a friend written during his wartime service overseas he wrote, 'Organization is Death.'[20] In the *New Masses* he responded to Mike Gold's assertion that he was only a 'bourgeois intellectual' by arguing for intellectual independence and autonomy rather than thinking as the party line thinks. 'Intellectuals of the World unite: you have nothing to lose but your brains!' he is reported to have proclaimed at a dinner party.[21]

Even so, Dos Passos's political activity increased during the late twenties and early thirties. He wrote up for the *New Masses* an eyewitness account of a textile strike in Passaic, New Jersey during the spring of 1926.[22] He expressed his discomfort and embarrassment in that piece over being a privileged outsider, a middle-class spectator. Nevertheless, his association with the *New Masses* deepened his commitment to radical politics and strengthening the political side of his writing. If one could point to a single event that galvanized his disillusionment over the prospects of legal and economic justice in a capitalist society, it would be the trial and execution of Sacco and Vanzetti in Massachusetts. He covered the trial for the *New Masses* and immediately felt a kinship with these two soft-spoken men of deep convictions who he believed were charged with murder only because they were immigrants and anarchists (and, therefore, undesirables). In *Facing the Chair*, a pamphlet he wrote for the Sacco-Vanzetti Defense Committee, he wrote that if such men were executed, 'what little faith many millions of men have in the chance of Justice in this country will die with them'.[23] The division of America into the 'two nations' of *U.S.A.* began here, even though the division he drew between the empowered and unempowered 'classes' was more rhetorical than factual. Dos Passos himself did not know how to bring the exploited and their exploiters together into one nation, but he did yearn to reject his class background (Choate, Harvard) and assert his immigrant heritage. He had begun work on 'a very long and difficult novel', *U.S.A.*, that would show America what had gone wrong with her experiment in democracy.[24]

Before completing the first volume of that trilogy in 1930, he became involved in an experimental theatre group committed to revolutionary drama for the masses, and for which he wrote several plays himself. He continued to travel widely, including a trip to Russia (which he found full of contradictions), and he continued to write incendiary pieces for the *New Masses*. Concerning his attitude toward capitalism, Dos Passos was accused on several occasions by several critics of 'damning the sufferers along with the disease'. It is important to note, however, as Lionel Trilling (No. 40) has, that Dos Passos saw the sufferers as bearers of the disease. The fault with capitalism lay in the opportunities it afforded individuals to exploit others. Human nature was to blame, and the closer he got to the radical Left during the early thirties the more disaffected he became with it, because it brought him closer to the realization that human nature was the cause of society's ills, not its economic system or form of government. Yet believing in the importance of free choice, he defended individualism from beginning to end against all forms of bureaucracy, from the military in *Three Soldiers* to big labour unions in *Midcentury*. What most concerned him was the individual's role in shaping his society, a role which could be superseded by society's power to shape him. For that reason all his novels have a rhetorical dimension aimed at educating the reader about the forces in society that shape him, and inciting him to resistance and action in his own and in his society's behalf. The role that the individual plays in history was to become the central focus of *U.S.A.*

THE 1930s

The 42nd Parallel was published in February 1930. Dos Passos fought another battle with Harper & Brothers over such words as 'crissake' and 'sons of bitches'. He insisted these words were essential to the authenticity of his characters' speech, and he was popular enough now to get what he wanted. A British edition came out later that year. The publisher, Constable, had wanted to delete the Newsreel sections (a montage of newspaper headlines, news stories, and popular song lyrics for each year) and the Camera Eye (fragments of impressionistic autobiography) but Dos Passos had refused. (British critics were not so pleased with the experiments in narrative form, either. Allan Angoff had written off *Manhattan Transfer* in the *Times Literary Supplement* as no more than an impression of chaos.[25] The reviewer of *The 42nd Parallel* for the London *Spectator* (No. 22) observed that Dos Passos might be a good picaresque novelist if he abandoned experimental style and left biography and history to themselves.) Within a year the novel had been translated into French, German, Spanish, Italian, Swedish, Norwegian, Czech, and Russian, indicating the great interest in Europe not only in American fiction but in radical politics and the experiments in narrative form that gave expression to it. The greatest foreign interest in Dos Passos's work was probably in Spain and Russia. In Spain he was admired for his leftist politics and his interest in Spanish culture (as in *Rosinante to the Road Again)*; in Russia, he was regarded as the American novelist most likely to work towards a Communist revolution in the United States.

American reviewers were frustrated by the lack of cohesion in the novel and by the noticeable absence of closure. Upton Sinclair (No. 20) objected to the enigmatic impressionism of the Camera Eye and the slight connections between the characters in separate narrative sections. Though he acknowledged Dos Passos could 'write circles around' Theodore Dreiser, he could learn from Dreiser how to tell a story straight without all the jazzed-up special effects. Like many other reviewers, though, Sinclair believed Dos Passos had the potential to become the greatest of American novelists. Edmund Wilson (No. 19) called *The 42nd Parallel* a 'striking advance' over *Manhattan Transfer* because Dos Passos had captured 'the minds and lives of his middle-class characters' with astonishing realism, and made us see America through their eyes. He noted that Dos Passos was the first American writer 'to have succeeded in using colloquial American [speech] for a novel of the highest artistic seriousness'. He was particularly impressed by his ability to tell so much about a character so quickly entirely without authorial intrusion or commentary, though he noted that occasionally the characters became 'two-dimensional caricatures of qualities or forces which [Dos Passos] hates'. Yet Dos Passos seemed to be 'the only novelist of his generation who is concerned with the large questions of politics and society', and for that reason, the completed work 'may well turn out to be the most important novel which any American of Dos Passos's generation has written'. On the political Left, Granville Hicks (No. 23) wrote that 'Dos Passos catches, as no other author has done, the peculiar quality of life in our era—the new forces and their effects on men's thoughts and actions.' Like most critics on the Left, however, he believed at this point that Dos Passos's promise was greater than his achievement and awaited the commitment to revolution that they looked and hoped for.

1919, the second volume of the *U.S.A.* trilogy, was published by Harcourt Brace in March 1932.[26] It received excellent reviews. Malcolm Cowley in the *New Republic* called it a 'landmark of American fiction'. Henry Hazlitt in the *Nation* thought it was better than *The 42nd Parallel*, which he had rated as the best American novel of 1930. In the *Chicago Tribune* Fanny Butcher claimed Dos Passos had captured better than anyone else the 'pulse', 'tempo', and 'throb' of life in modern America. *1919*, the review concluded, 'is the kind of book a reader never forgets'.[27] John Chamberlain (No. 25) saw *1919* as something akin to social history, like Mark Sullivan's *Our Times* or Frederick Allen's *Only Yesterday*, only Dos Passos did a lesser job of showing what happened and a more thorough job of showing what effect the news, and the men and women who made the news, had upon typical Americans. Chamberlain also noted that while Hemingway continued to work out his personal problems in his fiction, Dos Passos had cast a much wider net. He did express one concern, however, which was fast becoming a common one among Dos Passos critics: the characters seemed 'flat' at times and very 'transparent' as symbols. Few of the characters were memorable, and as the product of yesterday's headlines, they could become yesterday's news. Matthew Josephson (No. 26), on the other hand, praised the collectivism of *1919* and the Marxist view of history which he believed the novel revealed. He saw the characters as 'driven beasts' in accordance with it, yet he noted as a limitation the behaviouristic approach to character which permitted no inward glances and no authorial comment, apparently unaware of the fact that the behaviouristic approach was largely responsible for making the characters seem like 'driven beasts'. The review is a revealing one because it shows, on the one hand, how eager critics on the Left were to find a Marxist thesis in Dos Passos's work, and, on the other hand, how unwilling some of them were to embrace a theory of literature that placed art in the service of propaganda.

Two Russian editors of the journal *Literature of the World Revolution* penned an open letter (No. 29) to Dos Passos expressing their support of his work even though they found it ideologically weak and warned him against seeking refuge from political realities in art. They were destined to be disappointed by Dos Passos's final volume in the trilogy which did not endorse a communist revolution. *1919* would be his last work made available to the Russian reading public for a long time to come.[28] It marked the high watermark in his career from the perspective of Marxist critics in America as well. As Granville Hicks saw it, 'the concept of the class struggle and the trend towards revolution, deeply realized in the emotions and translated into action [in *1919*], has given Dos Passos a greater sensitiveness to the world about him... has shown him the relations between apparently isolated events and enabled him to see the fundamental unity beneath the seemingly chaotic complexity of American life'.[29] Unlike Faulkner, 'spinning complex melodramas out of his neuroses', or Hemingway, 'with his twin opiates, drink and bull fighting', Dos Passos had not succumbed to the modern causes of their despair: 'whatever place the future may grant his books', Hicks concluded in his Marxist study of American literature since the Civil War, 'he cannot be denied the historical importance of having been a challenge to a generation that considered itself safely lost.'[30] Mike Gold (No. 30) also continued to praise Dos Passos as the best writer in America, believing that all Dos Passos lacked was, significantly enough, Walt Whitman's faith in the masses.

In 1934 Dos Passos signed an open letter to the Communist Party printed in the *New Masses* protesting against their violent disruption of a Socialist Party meeting held in Madison Square Garden, New York City, on 16 February. He believed such squabbles over ideological differences hurt the revolutionary movement, but his 'fellow travellers' on the Left saw his signing of the letter as an indication of his losing faith. Never one to follow 'the party line', Dos Passos would go his own way in *U.S.A.* despite all the pressure from leftist critics to make a clear political statement. Hemingway, on the other hand, reminded his friend that 'there was no left and no right in writing.... There is only good and bad writing.' His advice to Dos Passos regarding characterization (no 'noble communists' and 'keep them people, people, people, and don't let them get to be symbols') revealed a limited understanding of Dos Passos's art.[31] His characters are always representative types. Hemingway need not have worried about 'noble communists', however, for Dos Passos was about fed up with Communist Party politics.[32]

Dos Passos's picture appeared on the cover of *Time* magazine the week *The Big Money* was published, and in the cover story he was compared to Tolstoy, Balzac, and Joyce for choosing the contemporary history of his country as his subject in fiction.[33] The reviews were, again, overwhelmingly favourable despite some recurring criticisms held in common. J. Donald Adams cited Dos Passos's greatest strength as 'his range of close acquaintance with American types, groups, and classes' which was 'probably wider than any other well-known American novelist'. He noted, however, as others had previously, that some of the characters never emerged as individuals—instead they embodied 'a set of sympathies'. He also believed Dos Passos's portrait of America was too pessimistic. 'We are not a lost people', he argued, for there are plenty of people in America who live 'with integrity, with purpose and by standards which are not for a day'.[34] The reviewer for the London *Times Literary Supplement* (No. 36) registered the same complaint, even while hailing the novel as an outstanding contribution to American literature. Goronwy Rees (No. 37), writing for the London *Spectator*, speculated that Dos Passos might be a better historian, sociologist, and reporter than novelist. Dos Passos is more interested in 'telling the truth', he argued, 'in explaining a historical process, in expressing certain moral values, than in creating works of art'. (This was a perceptive and even prescient criticism which confirmed (or seconded) Hemingway's fear that Dos Passos was becoming a polemicist.) On the other hand, Rees argued, the fact that Dos Passos's characters are more the product of history than imagination encourages the reader to look beyond the self-governing world of fiction to the actual world of historical events. (It is easy to see why Marxists were so enamoured of Dos Passos from the beginning, and felt so betrayed by him later on, for he clearly placed art in the service of history instead of the other way around.) Rees ended his review by comparing Dos Passos's vision of America to Whitman's, concluding that Dos Passos saw defeat of American democratic principles everywhere Whitman had seen victory and promise. Horace Gregory (No. 33) pointed out that the political thinking behind U.S.A. was closer to Thorstein Veblen than Karl Marx, and that cinematic influences were more in evidence than literary ones where the narrative technique was concerned. Malcolm Cowley analysed the narrative technique of the novel with respect to what he took to be Dos Passos's intentions, which were to show 'that life is collective, that individuals are neither heroes nor villains', and 'that their destiny is controlled by the drift of society as a whole'. The only hero in the trilogy was the nation itself, which stood defeated at the conclusion. In a follow-up article, he complained that this defeat was premature and inaccurate, for there were still many (like himself, presumably) who carried on the struggle.[35] All Dos Passos had managed to express was his own disillusionment.

Granville Hicks (No. 41), responding to what he and other leftist critics regarded as an out-and-out betrayal in The Big Money, found precedent for its lack of commitment in Dos Passos's travel books, which revealed 'a deep emotional unwillingness to face the intellectual implications of things seen and heard'. Dos Passos had 'sympathies' but no 'convictions' because he seemed unwilling 'to think his way through' to them. Hicks believed the despair in U.S.A. was unearned because Dos Passos had forsaken his responsibility as a writer to use his intellect as well as his powers of observation. According to Hicks, Dos Passos achieved clarity of thought only during those years he was closest to Communism.

The further he got from it, the more 'stupid', 'banal', and 'naïve' his political thinking became. Hicks predicted a decline in the quality of Dos Passos's work on political and intellectual grounds. Mike Gold (No. 39) deduced simply that Dos Passos, like the French novelist Celine, 'hates Communists because organically he seems to hate the human race'.

There were some critics who saw weaknesses in Dos Passos's art more significant and potentially more damaging than any weaknesses in his political thinking. Bernard De Voto (No. 32) believed Dos Passos's vision of human experience was too constricted, too narrowly pessimistic, crabbed, and humourless. The characters lacked depth enough 'to engage one's sympathies', and the rigorous behaviourism made them act like 'lobotomized automatons'. We remain untouched by them. When Harcourt Brace brought out a one-volume edition of *U.S.A.* in 1938, it became an occasion for more praise, but also some of the same criticisms. Delmore Schwartz (No. 43) agreed that Dos Passos had succeeded in showing only one side of the truth about America. Believing literature ought to distinguish itself from history and journalism, Schwartz argued that the flaw in Dos Passos's artistic conception might not be the paucity of inner life for his characters (which might be true-to-life) or the absence of any historical dialectic (which might be true-to-life as well), but rather an excessive 'naturalism' in the form of behaviourism which left out all human potential. T.K. Whipple (No. 38), writing for the *Nation*, agreed. Whereas the subjects of the biographical sketches in *U.S.A.* had 'minds, consciousness, individuality, and personality', the fictional characters seemed 'devoid of will or purpose' and appeared to have no power to choose. He could only conclude that there was a flaw in the narrative technique. Edmund Wilson, on the other hand, saw this technique working to Dos Passos's advantage since what he attempted to show, Wilson presumed, was how swept along by the currents of social change most Americans were. In a letter to his friend upon first reading *The Big Money* he had written:

One of the things which you have done most successfully—which I don't remember any novelist's doing—is show people in those moments when they are at loose ends or drifting or up against a blank wall—such as a passage in the first volume which stands out in curious relief in my mind, when Moorehouse has washed up in Pittsburgh and simply lies on the bed for several days, not knowing what he is going to do next—moments when the social currents, taking advantage of the set of the character, will sweep the individual in. These moments and the purposive careers of your eminent men and women are the positive and negative poles of your book, between which you probably allow for more of life, cheat less on what real human experience is like (the principal exception to this is that I think you strip away too much the glamour and exhilaration of the good time which the Americans thought they were having during the Boom), than any other radical writer.[36]

Lionel Trilling (No. 40) agreed with the prevailing view that *U.S.A.* 'confirms but does not advance, summarizes but does not suggest', but he believed Dos Passos's portrait of America was 'consciously selective' and 'consciously corrective' of the cultural tradition of the intellectual Left: 'he is almost alone of the novelists of the Left... in saying that the creeds and idealisms of the Left may bring corruption quite as well as the greeds and cynicisms of the established order'. The justification for his political stance would, Trilling believed, show itself in future history. Trilling defended the selectivity of *U.S.A.* on the grounds that the trilogy did not 'falsify' existing conditions in America. The class struggle, for instance, was portrayed as an internal battle fought by all the characters as they tried to improve their material circumstances. Even so, Dos Passos's main concern throughout the trilogy, Trilling contended, had been moral integrity rather than social class: 'The national, collective, social elements of his trilogy should be seen not as a bid for completeness but rather as a great setting, brilliantly delineated, for his moral interest.' If Dos Passos is a social historian, he is so only 'to be a more complete moralist'. For Dos Passos, Trilling concluded, 'the barometer of social breakdown is not suffering through economic deprivation but always moral degeneration through moral choice'. Society and history are shaping influences but not determining ones. The rest is up to character.

The Spanish Civil War became a *cause célèbre* for most liberals in America during the mid-to-late thirties, for whom the struggle was a clear-cut one between the Fascists, military dictatorship, and class privilege on the one side, and the Loyalists, social and economic justice, and popular rule on the other. Dos Passos and others wanted to make a documentary film (eventually entitled *The Spanish Earth*) about the horrible sufferings of the people living in the villages brought on by Franco's revolt against the Republic.

Along with Hemingway, he sailed for Europe more than a little uneasy about the strong Communist presence in the Loyalist camp. When he arrived in Spain, he discovered that his long-time friend José Robles (who had translated *Manhattan Transfer* into Spanish) had been arrested by police working for his own (Loyalist) side. Dos Passos feared that Robles's commitment to the Republic had been interpreted as a threat to Russian Communist designs on Spain. Soon he learned that his friend had been executed, presumably for talking too loosely about military plans, or so ran the official explanation. Dos Passos was so dismayed by Robles's execution, and by what appeared to him as a Communist takeover of the Loyalist cause, that he backed out of the film project and returned home to America.[37]

The incident proved to be a crucial one, for it marked the final break between Dos Passos and the radical Left. He usually translated his political experience into fiction, and this time was no exception. In his next novel, *Adventures of a Young Man*, the solitary (as opposed to collective in *U.S.A.*) hero, Glenn Spotswood, listens to his conscience and leaves the Communist Party when he realizes the Party cares more about the revolution of the future than the striking miners in Harlan Country, Kentucky. (Dos Passos himself had aided strikers there in 1931.) When he attaches himself to the Loyalist cause in Spain, he is assigned a suicide mission by the International Brigade, which suspected him of being a Trotskyite.

The reviews of *Adventures of a Young Man* were mixed as Dos Passos anticipated (expecting to be crucified by the liberal press). One of the kindest reviews was turned in by John Chamberlain (No. 44), who submitted that Dos Passos had in this latest novel made up for assigning 'too little importance to the human will' in his earlier books, for Spotswood does make a choice which decides his destiny, whereas so many of the characters in *U.S.A.* had seemed driven to theirs by historical forces. He correctly sensed that Dos Passos's intention was to satirize the American radical movement now dominated by Communists. The dilemma Dos Passos explores through Spotswood is 'how to keep the political struggle for power from conquering or corrupting the humanity to which all reformers and revolutionists should aspire'. In other words it was a novel about ends not justifying the means. Not unjustifiably, Malcolm Cowley (No. 46) accused Dos Passos of allowing personal feelings to overcome what should have been intellectual commitment. Dos Passos's idealism, he claimed, was too lofty to embrace or respect any sort of political activity. But politics aside, he believed the novel was Dos Passos's weakest since *One Man's Initiation*, because it lacked the technical innovations of *U.S.A.* and Glenn Spotswood was 'simply not interesting or strong enough to carry the burden of the story'. Writing for the *New Masses*, Samuel Sillen (No. 48) predictably derided *Adventures* as a 'rotten' book, a 'bald political tract' which slanders 'everything decent and hopeful in American life'—echoing the rhetoric of attacks upon *Three Soldiers* by conservatives during the early twenties. (It is ironic that leftist critics such as Sillen objected to the polemical character of *Adventures* when what they had complained about all along was its absence in his earlier work—they didn't get the polemic they wanted.) Sillen found the characters static, and the development pitifully programmed or missing altogether. He compared the novel unfavourably to Steinbeck's *The Grapes of Wrath*, published the same year.

On the other side of the political fence, Wilbur Schramm (No. 51), writing for the more conservative *Virginia Quarterly Review*, saw nothing inconsistent in Dos Passos's work. He 'is a friend of the underdog', Schramm wrote, 'and a hater of "money culture", as he always has been. He is not a Stalinite—and probably never was—simply because he fears a heavy centralization of governmental power.' He claimed the book was much better than the liberal press would allow and he admired Dos Passos for his courage in writing it. James T. Farrell (No. 50), another lapsed leftist, took Cowley and others to task for allowing their liberal politics to affect their judgment. Like Trilling before him, Farrell saw 'moral integrity' as the issue Dos Passos addressed in all his works. The flaws of *Adventures*, he argued, were the flaws of Dos Passos's writing in general: stereotyped characters, routine description, and a bad ear for dialect. Edmund Wilson (No. 49), however, was not so willing to praise the new novel at the expense of *U.S.A.* In a letter to his friend he was frank about his disappointment in *Adventures* and perceptive (as usual) in his analysis of its failings. What was missing was the 'organic connection' between character and description that made *U.S.A.* one of the great novels of the century. In that work the reader saw the world through the characters' eyes whereas the description in *Adventures* remained just that—description with no internal reference point in character.

Dos Passos was by and large correct about the situation in Spain, but so were the critics about this latest novel. He seemed less interested in art than in defending his politics.

THE 1940s AND AFTER

Not surprisingly, given the polemical nature of his most recent fiction, and his loss of faith in Marxist revolution, Dos Passos looked for an ideal to replace it with, and found one in early America's 'storybook' democracy. He began writing historical essays, biographies, and narratives about the colonial and revolutionary periods, hoping to discover in the past what was missing in the present.[38] In the meantime he continued to travel widely at home and abroad during World War II, which affected him oppositely from World War I: he began to see America and her democracy as civilization's only hope.[39]

He also continued to write fiction, more conscious than ever of his role as social reporter and chronicler of his times. His next novel was *Number One* (1943), a satire on the contemporary abuses of democracy responsible for electing demagogues such as his central character, Chuck Crawford, modelled on Huey Long. The narrative technique, aside from some prose poem inter-chapters, was conventional as in *Adventures of a Young Man*, and this latest novel was more favourably received if only because it was more expected. Horace Gregory called it 'one of the best... I have read in the past two years'.[40] Stephen Vincent Benét (No. 53) praised the novel for its realism, claiming many a Chuck Crawford could be found in the 'Congressional Record'. In spite of this, however, he felt the novel lacked the depth of characterization and the range and scope of the *U.S.A.* novels. Alfred Kazin (No. 54) was less generous, complaining that the novel lacked any rootedness in character or setting. The style was as fresh as ever, but Dos Passos, Kazin argued, had tried too hard to convert his readers to his way of thinking. In a more recent study of Dos Passos's politics, Robert C. Rosen summed up this phase in his career as follows: 'Unable to reconcile his idealized vision of America, drawn largely from his studies of its past, with the actuality of its present institutions, Dos Passos would increasingly tend to substitute moral exhortation of individuals for a thorough, critical analysis of their society'.[41] One could argue that the 'moral exhortations' had been there all along in Dos Passos's work, but one could scarcely deny the weakening justification for them in the world of his fiction. Finally, *Number One* might have fared better over the years if Robert Penn Warren had not written a much better novel on the same subject (*All the King's Men* (1946)).

Dos Passos's next novel, *The Grand Design* (1949), about the bureaucratic centralization of power put into place by Franklin D. Roosevelt's 'New Deal' administration, prompted a heated debate, not only about this novel, but about the value of Dos Passos's work in general, and the politics of reviewing it. Most of the reviews were negative. Maxwell Geismar and Vance Bourjailly attacked the point of view as narrow and distorted. Lloyd Morris dismissed the novel as a political tract. Henry Morton Robinson observed that its weakness proceeded from Dos Passos's inability to discover or reveal 'the complex nerves of passion and motive underneath' his characters. George Miles concluded bluntly that the characters are no longer characters and 'the revelations are no longer revelations'.[42] Even his friend Edmund Wilson (No. 55) took Dos Passos to task for his 'unconvincing characters'. Some friends and critics rose to his defence. John Chamberlain stressed Dos Passos's importance as a social reporter, and maintained that he had consistently expressed his faith in the human individual and his intolerance for any power that threatened to rob him of his autonomy. J. Donald Adams protested that critics were treating the book unfairly for they had not learned 'to value writers for what they are' instead of what they wanted them to be. Dos Passos's strength had never been 'the creation of character', but descriptive writing and social reporting. He also implied that critics had allowed their politics to affect their judgment.[43] Granville Hicks (No. 56) countered that political bias was 'not a vice peculiar to the left', and Malcolm Cowley denied that Dos Passos had ever been a good social reporter because his pessimism was subjective and personal. As for the politics of reviewing, Cowley insisted that there was little else to review in the novel except for its author's political opinions. As for Chamberlain's contention that Dos Passos had kept his faith in the individual, Cowley saw few individuals in Dos Passos's work 'to love or hate or admire'. 'As a novelist—and in life too,' Cowley observed, 'he is always moving, always hurrying off to catch a taxi, a bus, a train, a plane or a transatlantic steamer; and he tells us as much about people as a sensitive and observing man can learn in a short visit.'[44] This may seem like an unfair basis for criticism, but at the very least it suggests a logical and inevitable concession Dos Passos had to make in his life—and in his art—if he were to become, as he clearly wanted to be, the chronicler of his times.

In 1952 Houghton Mifflin brought together and published as a single volume a second trilogy composed of Dos Passos's last three novels under the title *District of Columbia* (since American politics and specifically the nation's capital figured in all three).

Dos Passos's next novel, *Chosen Country*, a more autobiographical and in some ways more sentimental novel than the harsh satiric portraits of America he had been turning out since the twenties, appeared in 1951. The title indicated his political shift from radical opponent to passionate advocate of the American way of life and system of government. Archibald MacLeish, a long-time friend, wrote to tell him it was his best book.[45] Arthur Mizener (No. 58) agreed. Edmund Wilson (No. 57) found it a difficult novel to judge since he recognized so many of the originals upon whom the characters were modelled, and tended to rate the performance accordingly. Harrison Smith (No. 59) saw it as a novel about America's gene-pool, its racial and national identity. Mizener and Smith both praised its panoramic sweep, geographically and temporally, though Smith found the ending, in which Lulie Harrington and Jay Pignatelli are married, 'as slick and as artificially embroidered as a banal love story in a mass circulation magazine'. In *Chosen Country* Dos Passos filled in the national origins of his representative figures in the present, and was (not surprisingly, given his Henry Adams-like preference for the past over the present) considerably kinder to past generations of Americans than to the present one.

Dos Passos wrote two more novels during the 1950s in addition to collections of historical and political essays, and a biography of Thomas Jefferson. Both *Most Likely to Succeed* (1954), an exposé of the Communist infiltration of Hollywood, and *The Great Days* (1958), a collective novel about Americans fighting in World War II, were panned by the critics. Meanwhile, Dos Passos had been steadily at work on a novel of grand proportions that would gather in all the most important social forces in the two decades since the end of the 1920s, where *U.S.A.* had left off. In 1961 he completed *Midcentury*, which he had laboured over for fourteen years. Because it marked a return, with a few modifications, to the narrative technique of *U.S.A.*, *Midcentury* was hailed as marking the triumphant return of its author from the purgatory his critics had consigned him to. By returning to the collectivist techniques of *U.S.A.* (including thumbnail biographies of public figures, documentary collages culled from the popular press, and fictional narratives about representative Americans), Dos Passos had repeated the performance he was most remembered for. The book stayed on the *New York Times* best-seller list for fifteen weeks.

The book did little to silence his most serious critics, however. Granville Hicks found the authorial stance behind the book 'tired and fretful'.[46] Others, such as Gore Vidal (No. 64) and Richard Horchler, saw Dos Passos's imitation of himself as nothing more than an embarrassment. Horchler found the biographies 'crude' and 'sophomoric', and the fictional narratives 'transparent propaganda'.[47] Vidal claimed Dos Passos was irresponsibly naïve and facile in his politics. (James J. Kilpatrick, writing for the politically conservative *National Review*, disagreed, and praised Dos Passos for 'telling it like it is' in his best book ever.[48]) Vidal also pinpointed a central weakness in all of Dos Passos's work since *U.S.A.*: 'Dos Passos tells us this and he tells us that, but he never *shows* us anything.' Vidal attacked Dos Passos for his 'sour and mean, and finally, uncomprehending spirit'. Milton Rugoff (No. 63) also felt that the novel was but 'a hollow imitation' of *U.S.A.*: 'all the apparatus and techniques but little of the vision or insight'. And unlike *U.S.A.*, Rugoff continued, *Midcentury* was informed, not by principles or ideals, but by 'rancor and prejudice'. Most damaging of all, Rugoff noted, was the subject of the novel—labour unions—which was too narrow for its form and apparatus. The result was 'thinly disguised propaganda' in which 'the message strangles the art'. Melvin J. Friedman (No. 65) agreed that *Midcentury* was better social history than fiction, and he accounted as a loss the absence of the Camera Eye, which had given *U.S.A.* 'a poetic foundation'. Richard Chase found it ironic that the negative attitude expressed toward the labour movement in *Midcentury* was exactly the opposite of the strong support for it Dos Passos had voiced in the *U.S.A.* trilogy.[49] R.A. Frazier (No. 61), writing for the *San Francisco Chronicle*, reminded his readers that 'to say that

Dos Passos' viewpoint has changed and nothing else would be to deny him the interdependence of the individual and society he so clearly postulated in *U.S.A.*' In other words, the labour movement *had* changed since the early days of the I.W.W., and probably for the worse, if we accept Dos Passos's thesis that 'power corrupts and organization breeds power'.[50] And perhaps America *had* suffered a loss of individualism during the fifties. Frazier complained that no one seemed to be taking Dos Passos's criticisms seriously. It seems probable that this was so at least partly because he no longer spoke for the Left.

Dos Passos continued to be a prolific writer until he died of heart failure in 1970. In addition to his historical narratives about the early years of America's democratic experiment (referred to by some historians and literary critics as 'a mountain of pious Americana')[51], he wrote essays for the *National Review* attacking, among other things, the liberal press, Communist infiltration of the government and civil rights movement, and 'the rank criminal idiocy of the younger generation' opposed to the war in Vietnam.[52] (Ever since the execution of his friend José Robles in Spain, Dos Passos had been looking for Communists under every bed—and finding them, or so he believed.) He also worked intermittently on one 'last forlorn Chronicle of Despair'.[53] *Century's Ebb* was published posthumously by Gambit in 1975 in unfinished form. But Dos Passos's intentions could not have been clearer: a sweeping indictment of American culture and society, in which the honest 'working stiff' and the Apollo space programme offered the only glimmers of hope. The book was not widely reviewed, because its author had been all but forgotten. Malcolm Cowley (No. 67) pointed out that the influence of Walt Whitman upon Dos Passos's work was never more explicit than in this last novel. *Century's Ebb* began with a biographical sketch of the poet followed by a collective portrait, following the pattern of *U.S.A.* and *Midcentury*, of the frustration and defeat of every hope for America Whitman had expressed in *Democratic Vistas*—except for the technological one. Townsend Ludington (No. 68), editor of Dos Passos's letters and working on his biography, delivered a eulogy over this last book by Dos Passos which brought down the curtain on his 'remarkable effort throughout his literary career to convey the panorama of 20th-century society'. Joseph Epstein surveyed that career in a retrospective in *Commentary* and offered the following explanation for Dos Passos's decline: the pamphleteer in Dos Passos had steadily but surely won over the novelist, who had lost interest in his characters except as 'targets' for his rage.[54]

Many of the most important critical issues regarding Dos Passos's work—the political ideology behind the novels, their completeness and accuracy as social history, the depth of character development—were raised and debated in the contemporary response. But despite many excellent monographs, book chapters, and journal articles which have since taken up these issues, some remain unresolved.[55] The most crucial unresolved questions concerning Dos Passos's work are by and large questions of genre. Dos Passos wrote in many genres, but the distinction between, for example, the novels and the histories, is a difficult one to draw, because the former offer the better histories of the periods they cover. And the meaning we derive from the novels depends a great deal upon how we choose to read them—as realistic fiction, for example, or as satire, or as social history. As Townsend Ludington and Arthur Mizener both have pointed out, depth of character is not a top priority for the satirist. 'If a writer sees people', Mizener claims,

as do writers like [Ben] Jonson and Dos Passos, not as 'characters,' full of charming eccentricities, but as representative cases each of whom contributes in his way to our understanding of the community's life, and if he sees them thus with passion and intelligence, then he will produce neither romance nor tragedy but the most serious kind of satiric comedy.

The heroes of *District of Columbia*, Mizener contends, are all Gullivers, all victims of 'the forces of compromise and corruption in... society'. Finally,

[t]o say that the talk and the feelings of Dos Passos' people is commonplace is to miss completely the governing irony of his work: one might as well say that Polonius or The Citizen in *Ulysses* is not always so intelligent or original as he might be. To say that Dos Passos' judgment of our world is the application to it of perfectly familiar values is to omit what makes *District of Columbia* the imposing indictment it is; that is the passionate sincerity of Dos Passos' hatred of our failure, or humanity's failure, to be what it professes—and what it ought—to be.[56]

The same could be said, of course, about *U.S.A.* with even greater justification. In *U.S.A.* individual choices based on perceived self-interest become, collectively, social and economic forces. Dos Passos fashions satire into historical commentary by exposing the inevitable consequences of such choices. The failure of so many Americans to accept the responsibilities of freedom, to respect and uphold the democratic principles upon which their nation was founded, or to see beyond their own self-interest—this is the collective moral failure which can be said to underlie all historical causality in *U.S.A.*[57] On the other hand, if we read the novel, as some have, as an example of literary naturalism, we subordinate free choice to social and economic circumstances.[58] The issue of genre remains problematic.

Of course any definition of genre is necessarily a floating one, since the shared features of literary texts which compose it are always in the process of revision as new texts are written and new genres defined. In spite of objections to genre classifications by post-structuralist critics such as Frederic Jameson, Michel Foucault, and Jacques Derrida, who argue, variously, that they are untenable because no text can be so classified without violating its indeterminacy, subordinating one set of features to another, or positing a set of features that exists only in the abstract, the concept is still a useful one, especially if we acknowledge that a text's generic traits are non-essential, that is, imposed upon a text by readers or critics searching for the most sensible or most satisfying (which are very often not the same) way to read it.[59] In practice genre theory may encourage a pigeon-holing of texts to fit a thesis, and this is much to be regretted. If, however, genre is, as Jameson has argued, no more than a contract of sorts between a writer and his audience, an unspoken agreement which specifies 'the proper use of a particular cultural artifact,'[60] then, at the very least, we can regard Dos Passos's declining reputation during his lifetime as the result of a broken contract—though we cannot say who broke it. All we can assert with any confidence is that most readers and critics expected one thing, and got another. There is always the chance, of course, that as new genres are defined to suit our purposes in reading, a new contract will be made by a future generation of readers less put off by Dos Passos's politics than past readers have been.[61] Even so, the relationship between the political distance Dos Passos travelled from Left to Right and the quality of his fiction independent of the politics behind it is another issue yet to be fully resolved.

One side of that story—Dos Passos's politics—is an old story, and to many, a sad one. Robert C. Rosen has expertly traced in a recent study the distance and direction Dos Passos's political opinions travelled during his lifetime.[62] But less attention has been paid to how political ideology manifests itself in the style, point of view, characterization, and structure of his fiction. Barbara Foley and John P. Diggins have addressed the issue to some degree with regard to *U.S.A.*[63], but little has been done to account for the declining quality of Dos Passos's later fiction beyond the suppositions of a failing imagination or a loss of interest altogether in how to write good fiction—suggesting a kind of mirror image in reverse of the Marxist devaluation and subordination of literature to politics. If there is a necessary connection between unconvincing characters, for instance, and right-wing politics, it has yet to be discovered or demonstrated. Nor has anyone really wrestled with the effect of the politics of the humanities as a discipline, which are still quite left of centre, upon critical reputations.

We are far more likely to concern ourselves with the effect of a dominant critical methodology upon an author's reputation or place within the canon (less aware, perhaps, than we ought to be of the political implications of every critical approach). The gradual shift in focus since the 'New Criticism' from literary history and historical context to close readings of individual texts has done much more to enhance Faulkner's critical reputation, for example, than it has Dos Passos's. (Delmore Schwartz once observed that the Great Depression had probably helped Dos Passos and hurt Faulkner—suggesting a relationship between the pressing demands (often political) of the moment and the reception of authors who do or do not meet them.)[64] This is not to suggest that Dos Passos's work does not hold up under close examination and analysis, but only that his novels may display less of the rich texture and intricate complexity of theme, language, and point of view, that contemporary criticism is wont to explore and explain. This is certainly true of his fiction written after *U.S.A.* On the other hand, whatever has been or might be said about the excesses of deconstructionism as a critical orientation towards literary texts, it has brought back into focus the changing interpretations of and demands upon literary texts over time. In other words, the role of historical context has been reasserted by the hermeneutic approach, and perhaps Dos Passos will be among the beneficiaries. But aside from what attention to Dos Passos's work such a shift away from the 'New Criticism' might bring, there is one aspect of Dos Passos's work which has gone largely unexamined: his prose style. Most critics of Dos Passos's fiction have understandably focused their attention and analysis on structure and the experimental narrative devices he invented. But when it comes to the fictional narratives of *U.S.A.*, for instance, the emphasis almost universally shifts to characterization and plot simply because the style or narrative technique here does not call attention to itself. As Sartre, one of the few critics to pay close attention to the art behind Dos Passos's prose style, once observed, he, like Hemingway, offers an alternative to intellectual analysis as a way of telling a story— namely, telling the story from the outside.[65] Sartre's richly suggestive analysis of style in his review of *1919* (No. 42) has not been extended or amplified by later critics. Another largely unexplored topic is the influence of Dos Passos's style on other writers. Malcolm Cowley claimed that American writers owed a greater debt to Dos Passos than they realized, and in his *An American Procession*, Alfred Kazin claimed that 'Dos Passos was a writer whom other writers will always imitate without knowing it.'[66] But the distinguishing features of what Kazin calls Dos Passos's 'tight-lipped national style' have yet to be fully defined, let alone its influence upon other writers demonstrated or confirmed. Edmund Wilson (No. 55) complained that Dos Passos's characters tended to talk in clichés. But surely that seems deliberate on Dos Passos's part, and I wonder how close Dos Passos came in *U.S.A.* to achieving one of the goals of American literature that Whitman announced in *Democratic Vistas*: to find in speech an expression of culture.

If there is a consistent thematic focus in all of Dos Passos's work, it is what Alfred Kazin has identified as 'not merely [his] fascination with the total operations of society, but his unyielding opposition to all its degradations'.[67] Whatever fluctuations occur in Dos Passos's reputation in the years ahead due to new definitions of genre, new critical methodologies, or changes in political climate, one thing seems clear: *U.S.A.* is likely to continue to occupy the pre-eminent position in the Dos Passos canon and will continue to inspire further critical studies. The reasons for this are many and varied, but one is paramount. Joseph Epstein has explained it this way: 'So furious is its energy, so passionate its sympathies and hatreds, that it is all but impossible not to be swept up by it, captivated, hypnotized, enthralled. In later years one may forget the characters and the working out of its five separate plots, but one never forgets its impact. It is the kind of book that changes people's lives.'[68]

NOTES

1 Joseph Epstein, 'The Riddle of Dos Passos', *Commentary* (January 1976), 63.

2 See Hans Robert Jauss, *Toward an Aesthetic of Reception* (Minneapolis: University of Minnesota Press, 1982). See also Steven Mailloux, *Interpretive Conventions: The Reader in the Study of American Fiction* (Ithaca: Cornell University Press, 1982).

3 Hans Robert Jauss, 'Literary History as a Challenge to Literary Theory', *New Literary History*, ii (1970), 8, 10.

4 Townsend Ludington (ed.), *The Fourteenth Chronicle: Letters and Diaries of John Dos Passos* (Boston: Gambit, 1973), 74.

5 Carlos Baker (ed.), *Ernest Hemingway: Selected Letters, 1917–1961* (New York: Scribner's, 1981), 354.

6 Letter to Max Eastman, 25 December 1953, in Ludington (ed.), *The Fourteenth Chronicle*, 605.

7 Jean-Paul Sartre, *Literary and Philosophical Essays*, translated by Annette Michelson (London: Rider, 1955), 79–87.

8 Townsend Ludington, *John Dos Passos: A Twentieth Century Odyssey* (New York: Dutton, 1980), 192–3, 195.

9 John Dos Passos, *The Best Times: An Informal Memoir* (New York: New American Library, 1966), 85.

10 Ludington, *Twentieth Century Odyssey*, 204.

11 Ludington, *Twentieth Century Odyssey*, 213–14.

12 Harold Norman Denny, *New York Times Book Review*, 14 October 1921, 1.

13 W.C. Blum, *'The Dial'*, lxxi (November 1921), 606–8.

14 Heywood Broun, 'A Group of Books Worth Reading', *Bookman*, liv (December 1921), 393.

15 Virginia Spencer Carr, *Dos Passos: A Life* (New York: Doubleday, 1984), 187.

16 Robert Rosen, *John Dos Passos: Politics and the Writer* (Lincoln: University of Nebraska Press, 1981), 40–1.

17 Allen Tate, *The Nation*, cxxii (10 February 1926), 160–1.

18 Andrew Turnbull (ed.), *The Letters of F. Scott Fitzgerald* (New York: Scribner's, 1963), 196.

19 John Dos Passos, 'What Makes a Novelist', *National Review*, 16 January

1968, 29–32; and *The Theme is Freedom* (New York: Dodd, Mead, 1956; reprint edn, Freeport, N.Y.: Books for Libraries Press, 1970), 41. It is important to note that Dos Passos himself treated the subject of influences rather cavalierly, perhaps because the influences were not direct or at least not clear to him while he was writing.

20 Quoted in Ludington, *Twentieth Century Odyssey*, 170.

21 Malcolm Cowley, *Exile's Return* (New York: Viking, 1951), 223.

22 John Dos Passos, '300 New York Agitators Reach Passaic', *New Masses*, i (June 1926), 8.

23 John Dos Passos, *Facing the Chair: Story of the Americanization of Two Foreignborn Workmen* (Boston: Sacco-Vanzetti Defense Committee, 1927), 127.

24 Ludington, *Twentieth Century Odyssey*, 256–7, 281.

25 Allan Angoff, *Times Literary Supplement*, xxvi (3 February 1927), 74.

26 Harper & Row had insisted that Dos Passos cut the 'House of Morgan' sketch from the manuscript. Morgan had rewritten some notes for debts outstanding which, if called in, would hand the publishing house over to Doubleday. Dos Passos refused, and found another publisher, (Carr, 286).

27 Malcolm Cowley, *New Republic*, 27 April 1932, 303–5; Henry Hazlitt, *Nation*, 23 March 1932, 344; and Fanny Butcher, *Chicago Daily Tribune*, 12 March 1932, 10.

28 See Deming Brown, *Soviet Attitudes Toward American Writing* (Princeton, New Jersey: Princeton University Press, 1962), 83–108, and Yury Kovalev (ed.), *20th Century American Literature: A Soviet View* (Moscow: Progress Publishers, 1976), 331–50.

29 Granville Hicks, *The Great Tradition* (New York: Macmillan, 1935), 290.

30 Hicks, 292.

31 Baker, 354.

32 Ludington, *Twentieth Century Odyssey*, 331.

33 'Private Historian', *Time*, xxviii (10 August 1936), 53.

34 J. Donald Adams, *New York Times Book Review* (16 August 1936), 2.

35 Malcolm Cowley, 'Afterthoughts on Dos Passos', *New Republic*, lxxxviii (9 September 1936), 134.

36 Edmund Wilson, *Letters on Literature and Politics, 1912–1972*, ed. Elena Wilson (New York: Farrar, Straus & Giroux, 1977), 279.

37 For a full account of the incident, and the breakup of Hemingway's friendship with Dos Passos over it, see Ludington (ed.), *The Fourteenth Chronicle*, 495–8, 600–1, and *Twentieth Century Odyssey*, 363–74, 390–1; Carr, 363–72; and Baker, 463–5.

38 See, for example, *The Ground We Stand On: Some Examples from the History of a Political Creed* (New York: Harcourt Brace, 1941); *The Head and Heart of Thomas Jefferson* (Garden City, N.Y.: Doubleday, 1954); and *The Men Who Made the Nation* (Garden City, N.Y.: Doubleday, 1957).

39 See, for example, *State of the Nation* (Boston: Houghton Mifflin, 1944) and *Tour of Duty* (Boston: Houghton Mifflin, 1946).

40 Horace Gregory, *New York Times Book Review*, 7 March 1943, 1, 18.

41 Rosen, 105.

42 Maxwell Geismar, *New York Times Book Review*, 2 January 1949, 4, 13; Vance Bourjailly, *San Francisco Chronicle*, 9 January 1949, 11; Lloyd Morris, *Weekly Book World of The New York Herald Tribune*, 2 January 1949, 3; Henry Morton Robinson, *Saturday Review of Literature*, xxxii (8 January), 8–9; and George Miles, *Commonweal*, xlix (8 January), 402.

43 John Chamberlain, *New Leader*, 29 January 1949; and J. Donald Adams, *New York Times Book Review*, 13 February 1949, 2.

44 Malcolm Cowley, 'Dos Passos and His Critics,' *New Republic*, cxx (28 February 1949), 21–3.

45 Ludington, *Twentieth Century Odyssey*, 455.

46 Granville Hicks, 'Of Radicals and Racketeers', *Saturday Review*, lxiv (25 February 1961), 25–6.

47 Richard Horchler, *Commonweal*, lxxv (29 September 1961), 13–16.

48 James J. Kilpatrick, *National Review*, x (22 April 1961), 252–3.

49 Richard Chase, 'The Chronicles of John Dos Passos', *Commentary*, xxxi (May 1961), 395–400.

50 Dos Passos's notes for *Midcentury* reveal that he relied extensively on newsclippings, industry newsletters, and interviews (some his own) with union men. ('*Midcentury* Materials—1960—Documentary' in The Dos Passos Papers, Alderman Library Collection, University of Virginia.)

51 John P. Diggins, *Up from Communism* (New York: Harper & Row, 1975), 267. See also Irving Howe's 'The Perils of Americana', *New Republic*, cxxx (25 January 1954), 16–17.

52 Ludington (ed.), *The Fourteenth Chronicle*, 643.

53 Ludington (ed.), *The Fourteenth Chronicle*, 643.

54 Epstein, 66.

55 See John P. Diggins, 'Visions of Chaos and Visions of Order', *American Literature*, xlvi (November 1974), 329–46, and Barbara Foley, 'The Treatment of Time in *The Big Money*: An Examination of Ideology and Literary Form', *Modern Fiction Studies*, xxvi (Autumn 1980), 444–67, on political ideology in Dos Passos's work; Linda Wagner, *Dos Passos: Artist as American* (Austin: University of Texas Press, 1979), on social history; and Blanche Gelfant, 'The Search for Identity in the Novels of

John Dos Passos', *PMLA*, lxxvi (March 1961), 133–49, on character development.

56 Arthur Mizener, 'Introduction' to *District of Columbia* (Boston: Houghton Mifflin, 1952), ix–xii.

57 See also Barry Maine, '*U.S.A.*: Dos Passos and the Rhetoric of History', *South Atlantic Review*, l (January 1985), 75–86.

58 See Charles Walcutt, *American Literary Naturalism: A Divided Stream* (Minneapolis: University of Minnesota Press, 1956), 289.

59 The arguments voiced by post-structuralist critics against genre classifications deserve a better summary and more critical scrutiny than I can give them here. See Frederic Jameson, *The Political Unconscious: Narrative as a Socially Symbolic Act* (Ithaca: Cornell University Press, 1981); Jacques Derrida, 'The Law of Genre', *Critical Inquiry*, vii (Autumn 1980), 55–81; and Michel Foucault, *The Archaeology of Knowledge* (London: Tavistock Publications, 1972).

60 Jameson, 106.

61 A case in point is the 'rediscovery' of Dos Passos as a forerunner of the so-called 'New Journalists'. See Barbara Foley, 'From *U.S.A.* to *Ragtime*: Notes on the Forms of Historical Consciousness in Modern Fiction', *American Literature*, l (March 1978), 89.

62 See also Daniel Aaron, *Writers on the Left* (New York: Harcourt, Brace & World, 1961), 343–53; and John P. Diggins, *Up from Communism*, 74–117, 233–68.

63 See above.

64 Robert Phillips (ed.), *Letters of Delmore Schwartz* (Princeton, New Jersey: Ontario Review Press, 1984), 286–7.

65 Jean-Paul Sartre, 'American Novelists in French Eyes', *Atlantic Monthly*, clxxviii (August 1946), 115.

66 Malcolm Cowley, 'Dos Passos and His Critics', *New Republic*, cxx (28 February 1949), 22; and Alfred Kazin, *An American Procession* (New York: Knopf, 1984), 382. Sartre and Solzhenitsyn both have acknowledged their debt to Dos Passos's collectivist approach and invention of narrative devices. (See Sartre, 'American Novelists in French Eyes'; and Michael Scammell, *Solzhenitsyn: A Biography* (New York: Norton, 1984), 789.)

67 Alfred Kazin, *On Native Grounds* (New York: Harcourt Brace Jovanovich, 1942), 342.

68 Epstein, 64–5.

THREE SOLDIERS

September 1921

1. John Peale Bishop, Review, *Vanity Fair*

October 1921, 9

Bishop (1892–1944) was an American 'lost generation' poet, novelist, and critic. Educated at Princeton, where he was a classmate of F. Scott Fitzgerald and Edmund Wilson, Bishop became friends with Dos Passos in New York during the early 1920s. His *Collected Poems* were edited by Allen Tate in 1948. In addition to Dos Passos's first novel, Bishop reviewed F. Scott Fitzgerald's *The Beautiful and Damned* and Stephen Vincent Benét's *The Beginning of Wisdom* as the best work yet written by young writers of his own generation.

Seeing how these two studies of army life stand out by sheer honesty from previous attempts, it is difficult to speak calmly of John Dos Passos' *Three Soldiers*. However viewed, whether as a novel or as a document, it is so good that I am tempted to topple from my critical perch and go up and down the street with banners and drums.

Here, once and for all, is the very stuff and breath of that strange thing which was the American Army of 1917-1919. The burdensome discipline of the training camps, the unutterable boredom of billets and hospitals, the filth and terror of fight, the dizziness and gay abandon of spring in Paris. He has evoked the American soldier, alive and individual for all the effort to press him into a mould, a young man with the helpless, lovable charm of a child and the uncontrolled viciousness of an animal. His speech is here, with its unceasing obscenity and its hatred of affectation.

Three Soldiers is a story of Fuselli, an Italian of the second generation from San Francisco, eager to adapt himself and to get on

32

in the army; of Chrisfield, a wild-angered, lovable boy from an Indiana farm, and of the Eastern John Andrews, insurgent in thought and passion, but outwardly tamed. The background is filled with figures—officers, soldiers, French peasants, Y.M.C.A. workers, cocottes, Parisian aristocrats. I know of no American novel of this generation in which so many minor characters, each unforgettable and perfectly placed, appear and disappear without confusion. Mr. Dos Passos, realizing that two of his principals at least were unusual characters going toward unusual fates, has contrived to silence criticism by placing against his protagonists, in each crucial moment, an ordinary soldier with quite normal reactions. Despite the technical difficulties of carrying three major characters the book has the firm structure of steel.

If it were only that *Three Soldiers* is the first complete and competent novel of the American Army it would deserve great praise, but it is more than that, for, in Mr. Dos Passos' hands, the army becomes a symbol of all the systems by which men attempt to crush their fellows and add to the already unbearable agony of life. Here is more than an honest record of young men's lives: here are the tears of things, the shadows of the old, strong, unpitying gods lying across the paths of men; anger, and hate, and lust are here and laughter and the manly love of comrades, and at the end, resignation and despair, the return of a bloody and hateful thing done in an autumn wood, the beautiful proud gesture of a man going down in defeat before life. And this is why I say that John Dos Passos is a genius.

2. Coningsby Dawson, 'Insulting the Army', *New York Times Book Review*

2 October 1921, I, 16–17

Dawson (1883–1959) was an Anglo-American author of steamy romances (such as *The Garden Without Walls*, a best-seller in 1913) and patriotic war novels (including *The*

Glory of the Trenches 1918). He served in the Canadian Expeditionary Forces during World War I as a lieutenant of field artillery.

This is the kind of book that any one would have been arrested for writing while the war was yet in progress. It purports to be the 'Now It Can Be Told' of the enlisted man in the American armies. It is either a base libel or a hideous truth. It is so savagely explicit in its accusations that it deserves no quarter at the hands of the reading public. You must be either for it or against it. If the statements which it makes can be proved to be varacious, it ought to raise the roof.

Under the flimsiest of fictional disguises *Three Soldiers* would appear to be the record of indignities and injustices very intimately experienced and witnessed. The story is told brutally, with calculated sordidness and a blind whirlwind of rage which respects neither the reticences of art nor the restraints of decency. Nothing that Barbusse[1] set down in *Under Fire* is more resentfully tragic than this exaggerated picture of American youth wantonly humiliated by the callous misuse of military discipline. If the picture is false, the crime of presenting it is unpardonable. Whether it be false or true will not take long to discover, for there are millions of men from the Atlantic to the Pacific who have the knowledge either to brand it as a lie or to acclaim it as a heroic revelation.

For myself, I am in no position to judge of its value as a historic document, as my service was with the Canadian Forces. In the light of that experience. I should be inclined to say that *Three Soldiers* tells not what men thought while they were in uniform, but what the least worthy of them think they thought, now that they're free to wag their tongues and have had time to brood over their grudges. If the heroes of Chateau-Thierry and the Argonne had gone into battle believing themselves to be the cheated slaves whom these pages portray, the western front would have been lost and the Kaiser would be permanent President of the United States. One of the characters expresses the book's spirit in a phraseful 'Fellers don't seem to think about beatin' the Huns at all, they're so busy crabbin' on everything.' If the shocking incidents which crowd the chapters of *Three Soldiers* were facts, one wouldn't wonder that the unhappy victims became so absorbed in crabbing that they lost some of their sense of duty. One is surprised, however, to find them lapsing into contented moral rottenness. One of them murdered a wounded American officer when he ought to have been attacking the enemy. Another lost the clean pride of his manhood through dissipation. The third, on the last page of the book, is arrested and carried off to life imprisonment as a deserter. Three such weak failures hardly form a trustworthy foundation on which to build such a grave indictment.

The book is very thorough. Starting with the training camp in America, it describes accurately the hours of enlistment:

[Quotes from *Three Soldiers*, 21–2.]

It goes on to describe in a series of vivid pictures how the individual freedom which men had surrendered for the saving of humanity was ignorantly abused in the early stages of training:

[Quotes from *Three Soldiers*, 23.]

So from the very first day the 'crabbing' commenced at the infringements of personal likes and dislikes which were of necessity the lot of every man who enlisted in whatever army. The hope of the reader is that somewhere as the front is neared a sense of the heroism of the undertaking will dawn in the men's souls and make their burden lighter. But no. Here's the frame of mind in which three soldiers went aboard the transport that was to carry them to the place of sacrifice:

[Quotes from *Three Soldiers*, 43–4.]

But it was when they got to France that the real torture started, according to John Dos Passos. There authority felt itself safe from public sentiment and exceeded all limitations. A typical instance of the kind of proof offered is the following:

[Quotes from *Three Soldiers*, 121–3.]

Besides this, as a companion sample of the kind of brutality which *Three Soldiers* would have us believe to be typical, place the following. The war is ended and Andrews, still in uniform, has been permitted to study music at the Sorbonne. He has not yet been demobilized and, in order to please a French girl, having foolishly omitted to obtain a leave-warrant, has accompanied her for a day's outing to Chartres. There he has been picked up by the military police and is awaiting in the guardhouse the arrival of an officer.

[Quotes from *Three Soldiers*, 357.]

Villianies of the kind depicted above may have occurred, as they occur in peace life, and probably did occur in single instances in all armies; but the moment they were discovered they were punished. They were emphatically not a part of any army system. Mr. John Dos Passos seems to have either imagined or remembered every exceptional example of abuse of authority on the part of subordinates, and has pasted them together into a moving picture which he labels a novel. Though the isolated cases quoted in this book may have taken place in scattered instances, the effect of them when joined up into one long film is unspeakably dreary and unconvincing. The spirit of the book is all wrong. It implies that every man in uniform above the rank of private was a bully; that in the army between men and officers there was never any bond of loyalty— only a gulf of hate: that the man in the ranks who went to France to fight, went as a slave, with a dull anger in his heart; that whatever his initial patriotism and idealism, it had all been battered out of him long before he reached the battle line. Most of this is untrue on the face of it; for it was the man in the ranks who won the war. Moreover, it is a dastardly denial of the splendid chivalry which carried many a youth to a soldier's death with the sure knowledge in his soul that he was a liberator.

I remember a discussion which I had with a Russian who had served in the French Foreign Legion, as to what the individual man who had been part of the war had got out of it. On the one hand, you had Barbusse declaring that all that war did to a man was to deprave him. On the other hand, you had Alan Seeger[2] and a throng of idealists of all nations declaring that they had found the purpose of their lives in the sacrifice. What was the explanation of these irreconcilable points of view? My Russian gave an answer that was very true. 'Men got out of the war,' he said, 'what they brought to it. The hero found heroism: the coward found cowardice. Except in rare instances the war did not recreate men; it only made emphatic in them tendencies that had been latent. Now that the war's ended, bad men are a little worse for their experience;

honorable men are a little more good.'

The men depicted in *Three Soldiers* got out of the war what they brought to it—low ideals and bitterness. They would have got the same out of life if there had been no war. They were spineless, self-centred weaklings, with a perpetual chip on their shoulders— deserters in spirit from whatever duty beckoned. In the battle of ordinary civilian life their record would have been equally disastrous. They knew nothing about playing the game. They were born trouble-makers, who would always have refused to pull their weight and would always have recognized in a superior a tyrant.

The book fails because of its unmanly intemperance both in language and in plot. The voice of righteousness is never once sounded; the only voice heard is the voice of complaint and petty recrimination. There are scenes in it which are tragic and powerful as a storm, but the intention of all this wealth of energy is dismal vituperation. If the purpose of Mr. John Dos Passos in writing *Three Soldiers* was to expose what he considered to be a nation-wide injustice, he seems to this reviewer to have achieved a nation-wide insult.

NOTES

1 Henri Barbusse (1874–1935), a French novelist and essayist, served in the French army and wrote an anti-war novel (*Le Feu*) based on his experiences.
2 Alan Seeger (1888–1916), an American poet and soldier, died a hero's death in France.

3. Henry Seidel Canby, 'Human Nature under Fire', *New York Evening Post Book Review*

8 October 1921, 67

Canby (1878–1961) was an American critic and literary historian. Author of biographies of Thoreau and Whitman, he also served as literary editor for the *New York Evening Post*

(1920–4) and founded the *Saturday Review of Literature* in 1924, serving as its editor until 1936. Canby helped to organize the *Yale Review* and was editor-in-chief of the Book-of-the-Month Club (1926–58). In his autobiography, *American Memoir* (1947), he wrote: 'Dos Passos invented a kind of literary television, calculated to put the new background of noise, movement, and confusion against which Americans were living, into a novel like a motion picture but without its plot. He made a sensation in Europe, for this was the way America looked to them in photographs and sounded in American newspapers. But I doubt whether his books have enduring quality. There is too much of the "stunt" in them; too much of the visual and auditory; too little depth and wisdom' (342–3).

In the strait between Lakes Erie and Huron is a narrow channel fringed on either side with summer houses set upon piles in the water. When the great steamers go through, the inhabitants, young and old, pile into boats and take the great swells that after a while coming rushing towards them. So, with the war. It has passed, but its wake is rocking us. And this book will rock many boats.

There have been many books expressing the reactions of war upon a sensitive civilized mind. Barbusse's *Le Feu* was perhaps the most important and is spiritual grandfather of the series. *Three Soldiers*, however, is the first for America written with sufficient passion and vividness of detail to count as literature, and is therefore of more than passing importance. Whether or not it is a masterpiece, there is no question that it is an intense, a skilful, and an utterly sincere expression of throbbing human nature, and therefore real literature, to be discussed respectfully as such.

I very much fear that it is not going to be discussed as literature. Like *Le Feu*, it will be regarded as propaganda against war, and its implications supported or refuted as if they were arguments, whereas the precise character of the creative skill involved is really much more important.

John Andrews, Fuselli, and Chrisfield are the three soldiers. Chrisfield is an Indiana farm boy, slow and thick, with a devil in him that has been roused just once in the past. The war gives it power over his spirit. He kills with a grenade the officer who bullies him, is haunted by fear, not remorse, deserts, and comes—one guesses—to a bad end. Fuselli is a second-generation Italian with no particular qualities except an ambition to stand well with his friends. He breaks down because hard luck keeps him from being a corporal, and winds up in the K.P. with disease and a wrecked morale—not that there was much to wreck. John Andrews—through whose eyes the book is seen—gives the dominant motive of the story. A Virginian and a college man, intensely musical, and on the eve of creation, the draft makes a slave of him. At first he takes it cheerfully, having a mind that can escape. But this cannot endure. The petty tyranny of discipline wears his nerves till they begin to thrill just when others are deadening. He is wounded, held in routine after the armistice, released for the paradise of school training in Paris, caught on leave without absence, and thrown into the labor gang. He deserts by diving into the Seine, wanders back to love and music, is caught and flung again under the wheel that was crushing him—and the story ends. It is the story of the caged lark.

Now to build up an argument against the A.E.F. and the conduct of the war out of materials like this is manifestly absurd. Not all 'loots' were pink-faced debauchees, as they appear in this story, not all 'sarges' barbarians, not all Y.M.C.A. men hypocrites or snobs with parchment faces. Nor are Fuselli, Chrisfield, least of all John Andrews with his artist's soul and notable lack of common sense in crises (he invariably forgets to salute when he wishes to ask a favor), typical of the doughboy.

On the other hand, it is useless to criticize this book by saying that the war was inevitable, ruthless discipline essential for the army, the fight a fight against tyranny. War is a curse, not the less when it seems inevitable; the discipline of the army when applied to men not made to be soldiers (which means very many men) a harmful, not a helpful, experience, as any one with eyes can see today; and liberty of soul, the most valuable of all possessions, far more likely to be jeopardized than safeguarded in a 'war for freedom'. We know these things are true. They have little or nothing to do with whether we should or should not have entered the war, circumstances being what they were, although they have much to do with the future. Therefore it does not help criticism to call this a pacifist book. Every sensitive man put under the stress of modern war is a pacifist, if protesting with all his soul and strength against it makes him a pacifist. If he says differently, he is either abnormal or insincere. Mr. Dos Passos's book is the story of such a man, broken by the war. The opinions are of less importance than the experiences. To call it a pacifist book and then attack pacifism will make easy reviewing but worthless criticism of a passionate study of human nature under fire.

Let us therefore hang up philosophy and read this novel for what it is, a transcript of war experience in which an attempt is made to give all that happened behind some of the impassive faces we watched so often on parade. It is not a pretty narrative. No one of our three guardsmen was in any true sense immoral; indeed, they stood apart from their fellows, two of them at least, by impulses to stay clean. Nevertheless, the story of what happened in France does not read like the letters to 'Dear Mable' or diaries published in the *Atlantic*. Mr. Dos Passos is not licentious in his art. The censor will have no reasonable excuse for attacking this volume. But he writes in the Latin rather than the American tradition. He calls a spade a spade, although never brandishing it. Dainty readers will now and then be shocked.

But fastidious readers will find that the intellectual honesty which does not omit the hours between midnight and morning also assures such a picture of France that has not been found in any recent book. It is an incidental, not a made-up picture, and that is why it is so vivid. My own memory of war-time France is vivid because of the brevity of my experience. It responds to this book and lives for a while in 1918. The trenches, the front lines generally, figure little in the story, as they figured very little in the life of the A.E.F. abroad. But Paris, Chartres, a hundred little 'courts', roads, cafés, smells, human contacts—it is marvellous how the man has got them all, how admirable his bits of description, such as the Cathedral of Chartres 'rising nonchalantly, knee deep in the packed roofs of the town'. He gets them because he is an artist and these are merely the background touched to intense vividness by the intensity of his theme.

As for this theme—no Frenchman, no Englishman could have done it justice, and, to be fair, only a few Americans. *Le Feu*, which protests the war in its most hopeless moment, is far more objective, more philosophical. The practical French mind sees all the poilus. His book is a sociology of the trenches, to be philosophized afterwards into a socialistic theory well documented. The English poets protested the ugliness of war, but they were bitterly on the defensive for England. The lovely English country which was being guarded so crudely, so bloodily, was at the back of their verse. We alone went to war without the biting urge of immediate self-defence. We alone were primed with other people's sayings of the war, with phrases, some true, some merely sentimental; none of which were made really our own. The second fact cancelled the first. In the brief months, which for most Americans made the war, there was time to unlearn our taught psychology, but not find a new one. We entered inexpressive because all had been told us, and emerged singularly inexpressive because we were not sure yet of what we had found. The silence of intelligent youth upon what they found in the war has been the marvel of those who have dealt with them since. Now the ice is beginning to break.

Not that I think John Andrews is spokesman for his generation. Decisively he is not. He is artist, not spokesman. He was one of those rare Americans who, being an individualist, a dreamer, an artist, went into the war with the absence of intense personal motive which characterized most Americans, yet completely free from the ideas of duty, loyalty, group patriotism which inspired them. That was his misfortune. It was also his advantage. For it enabled him to see his own problem clearly and truly from the beginning. He had shared the personal freedom of America—the widest in the world—freedom from caste, freedom from obligation to the State, financial freedom, freedom of opportunity. This he shared with others; but while they, scarcely knowing what was the matter with them, were only beginning to grudge and strain under the yoke, his burning love for the kind of life that war makes impossible, unrestrained as it was by loyalty, patriotism, or duty, made him long for martyrdom while they were still in the mood of self-sacrifice or revenge.

Nothing was clearer in 1918 than that the civilized men in the French and British armies were of three categories—the dull and broken and usually degraded, the rebellious or vindictive, the resigned who had profited in the Christian sense by misfortune and become nobler in spirit whatever their sins of the flesh. This was apparent to those prophets who, guessing that in Germany the facts were not otherwise, foretold an early end of the war, and the prophets were right. Into all of these three categories the Americans would have drifted, and they would have drifted there more quickly than had the others because their nervous tension was higher. Into which class most abundantly, let those who know them judge. The three soldiers went too rapidly; John Andrews, dreamer and individualist, most rapidly of all.

I find the materials of this story so interesting, the grip upon imagination so powerful, that the task of criticism is unusually difficult. I feel, however, that, as with *Main Street*,[1] discount must be made for the timeliness, the 'news' value of the subject. I think that the book is too long. I am sure that, after the manner of the younger realists, it is overcrowded with incident, far too photographic in its method. It is a less skilful book than *Le Feu*, chiefly because too little is left out. The art of selection is not a gift of youth, but Mr. Dos Passos must grasp it. His intensity too often wastes itself in masses of words. A novel cannot be a diary, unless the diary is written as a novel—and this book is, very often, not so written. The characterization, too, is still weak: Fuselli, Chrisfield, Genevieve, even John Andrews, are too much argued. The author seems again and again to say they *did* say this, *this* is what they were always doing. The fine line drawn between exposition and description of character is hard to see but immutable. The novelist must stay on the further side.

In short, this is by no means a perfect book, but it is a very engrossing one, a first-hand study, finely imagined and powerfully created. Its philosophy we may dismiss as incomplete; its conception of the free soul tortured, deadened, diseased by the circumstances of war, we cannot dismiss. It is convincing, even though partial. In character study, in form, in incisiveness, Mr. Dos Passos may do better later. But he may never again have such fresh and interesting material, and he will do well in the career that awaits him if he succeeds in telling a story as interesting in spite of its mass, so tragic in spite of its special pleading. Among the books of youth, after the war, this one is perhaps preeminent.

NOTE

1 *Main Street* (1920) by Sinclair Lewis. See No. 13.

4. Francis Hackett, 'Doughboys', *New Republic*

5 October 1921, vol. xxviii, 162–3

Hackett (1883–1962) was born in Ireland and emigrated to the U.S.A. in 1901, where he eventually became the first literary editor of the *New Republic* in 1914. He compares the novel favourably with Stephen Crane's *The Red Badge of Courage*, and sides with Dos Passos's implicit condemnation of conscription as undemocratic.

Many of the young men who went to France in 1918 returned to civilian life hopelessly incommunicative, and some of them saying, 'you can never know.' Mr. John Dos Passos's novel breaks silence with corresponding sharpness. It is unlikely that it will find great favor with the American Legion, or that it will seem entirely just and salubrious to those who worked at G.H.Q. or with the intelligence corps. It should certainly infuriate the Y.M.C.A. But it is written of the common soldier by a common soldier out of a full heart and an extraordinarily quickened spirit, and, now that the world has been made safe for democracy, we can afford to look at one man's version of the great crusade.

It is, if you like, rather bitter, rather morbid, rather self-centred. The John Andrews of the story had no stomach at all for the war. But since the United States wished 'selective service' or what crude people call conscription on its young men, it was inevitable that youths with no stomach for the war should have been jammed into it, in the name of democracy, and the actual results of this deliberate military enslavement are now part of our priceless heritage.

Andrews was apparently a young American of the more highly organized and sensitive kind who happened to take the war 'subjectively,' as they say. He brought to the army certain large assumptions of the American sort about justice and freedom and equality and consent. Nothing prepared him emotionally for the dirty work of the war—the work of killing, to which he was consigned. Not being emotionally prepared either by the circumstance of his education for the work of killing, not having a sense of necessity or a natural aptitude or any patriotic exaltation, he found in the army an institution particularly revolting. Had it been the army of the Civil War rather than the army of machine process he might not have liked it much better. But this army, at any rate, sickened his soul. He was the type of Crusader who discovered in the American machine a school of intolerance, brutality and self-seeking, violating everything he had ever been taught of equality and freedom and consent and all the other shibboleths of democracy. So long as he kept his faith in these shibboleths, which he did to the end, he was a sick soul, with the Y men and the officers as the worst emetics of all. And naturally, not trying to get out of the dirty work by those arts of favor or bluff or solicitation to which most people stoop under duress, Andrews never did acquire that full appreciation of the arduous tasks of the G.H.Q., those difficult and delicate activities of the Crillon, those brow-knitting agonies of the intelligentzia, with which so many publicists have sympathy. Andrews kicked against the pricks. He resented cleaning windows, drilling, handling garbage, chasing cooties. He felt affronted by the sweet Y man, the whining Y man, the jolly-'em-along Y man, the Christly Y man. He never completely grasped the importance of saluting instantaneously, of giving orders with gusto, of taking orders with equanimity. He had, on the whole, that attitude toward war which is reasonable as regards culture and unserviceable as regards the modern state. We like it when Tolstoi has it, concerning a war a hundred years old.

Granted that many men just as highly organized and just as sensitive as Andrews took their experience in an entirely different spirit—some of them being even willing to go through with it again rather than have Hohenzollern Germany on top—the fact remains that we have in *Three Soldiers* a remarkable vivification of a significant experience. Mr. Dos Passos has the great sense to embody his theme in his characters, to let them speak and act from their own centres. Consequently our attention is never transferred to the abstract consideration of the author's position. It is passionately absorbed in his presentation of fact. He gives us a drama of war that has the movement, the living light, of *The Red Badge of Courage*, and that never flags except in a few places where, in the Sorbonne period, the author indulges in the rhetoric of beauty. Outside this occasionally cloying lyricism, the story is strikingly clear and unaffected in expression, extremely rich in racy episode and sweeping in its progress from the enlistment well up beyond the armistice. Its account of Andrews's desertion is as exciting as any so-called action story in the all-too-human magazines.

What keeps one most interested is the sense of multitude with which Mr. Dos Passos fills the novel, especially in the earlier part. The fatigue, the monotony, the toadying, the humiliation, the olive-drabness, are woven out of many lives, with Fuselli, an Eyetalian, and Chris from Indiany, as the two simpler friends of John Andrews. Even though Andrews is a man who wants to write music, who goads himself 'not to let himself sink too deeply into the helpless mentality of the soldier,' he is boyishly at home with the child-like Fuselli and the untamed Chris. And through the voyage overseas, the encampment, the journey up to the front, one has innumerable glimpses of the army in being—with the sergeant whom Chris murders, the poilu who eats glass, the boy who dies of fright, the sage Eisenstein who is 'disciplined,' the wild Irishman who brags in the cabarets, the complaisant women, the crazy man back from the front. Some of these glimpses are grossly drawn— the Irishmen, for example, talking a perfectly traditional brogue. But the talk on the whole is astoundingly real, with a good dash of verbal paprika and a few verbal cooties hopping about.

And, in the midst of the subordinations with which this soldier's life is poisoned, there comes an assuaging memory or a lovely perception, as for example when Chrisfield is maudlin in a café:

[Quotes from *Three Soldiers*, 143.]

Such passages, with an emotion singing through them, are common throughout the book. Majors may pass on the word that prisoners are easier to kill than to ration, sergeants may be falsely jovial or greedily on the make, the young undertaker in hospital may be sardonically perceived or the Y man may be seen lividly, but it is impossible for Mr. Dos Passos not to make pictures and poems as he proceeds. Is he too imagistic? For my part, yes, but it is probable that the criminal brutality shown to Andrews as a military prisoner is thrown into relief by the very fact that he whispers 'la reine de Saba, la reine de Saba' in his adolescent soul.

The adolescence of Andrews, cropping out as it does in the romantic picture of Henslowe in Paris and in the collegiate cabaret-unconventionalities of Heineman, is really an element in intensifying the tragedy of *Three Soldiers*. One feels that the war, for various reasons, was not the best experience for the generation born in the nineties. The officer who starts a man-handling with, 'Don't you know enough to salute? One of you men teach him to salute,' may in reality be no more brutalized than a certain type of New York policeman. The American major who suggests that prisoners be killed, the Y man who sings '"we're going to get the Kaiser"—now once more, and lots of guts in the get and lots of kill in the Kaiser'—these subservient creatures may be no worse than corresponding figures in the ordinary America from which they were recruited, but the flooding of young life with so much of this sewerage seems to have poisoned a great many of the millions who were enlisted. A conscripted army, in and of itself, is not compatible with the democratic assumptions. To educate men for the army is to denature them for democracy, if there is not willing cooperation on a military basis. And a democracy that goes in for conscription—that is a contradiction in terms, unless one is satisfied with a cleverly bamboozling phrase like 'universal voluntary involuntariness' or 'universal enforced consent' or 'the nationalization of adolescents.'

It is this vileness of conscription that gives so much force to *Three Soldiers*. The A.E.F. contained its high proportion of young men who should never have been soldiers. But as one sees the machine working, with obedience its watchword and Fort Leavenworth or court-martial casting its shadow over the scene for the rebellious, the marvel is that so much rebellious spirit was retained as informs this seething novel. And that, after all, is the best part of it. Mr. Dos Passos's young man is indubitably self-centred, morbid, bitter, but his resistance is a fine thing. If great states cannot launch great wars unless they mobilize public opinion, then the sooner we learn to realize that our one hope of freedom is variety of independent opinion the better. The young men I know personally who went through the war did not all suffer as John Andrews suffered. Some of them went out rather bumptious and came back deeper and more humane. But apart from its brilliant expressiveness and its beauty *Three Soldiers* should be welcomed for its candor. It shows what sins have been committed in this country's name.

5. Norman Shannon Hall, 'John Dos Passos Lies!', *Foreign Service*

November 1921, vol. x, 11–12

Hall rose through the ranks of the American Expeditionary Force from buck private to second lieutenant. He paid tribute to the heroes of the Great War in a 'biography' of flying ace Frank Luke, published in 1928 as *The Balloon Buster*.

'With a passion for truth-telling that burns with a white flame through all his pages, John Dos Passos states the case for Youth in rebellion against the Established Order—particularly the case of Young America, generous, open-minded, spiritually alive, courageous idealists, caught and crushed in the great stamping machine of war.'

Gibberish!

Bunk!

Nonsense!

The above quotation is taken from the paper cover of *Three Soldiers*, by John Dos Passos, a piece of contemptible falsehood published by the George H. Doran Co.

It should read this way:

'With a passion for distorting the truth that burns with a yellow flame through all his pages, John Dos Passos states the case of a biased, embittered youth against the Established Order—particularly the case of a young American who was neither generous, open-minded, spiritually alive, nor blessed with courageous ideals when caught in the great equalizing machine of war.'

That is a perfectly correct one paragraph summary of *Three Soldiers*.

Had Dos Passos written it three years ago he would have been classed with Bergdoll and locked up. The classification is of minor importance, but he should be locked up. Unfortunately or fortunately—there are two viewpoints—Dos Passos is abroad. That removes the source of the odor a little way. He is urged to remain abroad. America wants bigger men.

Three Soldiers purports to be the story of three typical American soldiers. That is the unforgivable feature. Dos Passos has twisted and distorted every line he has written to make these despicable characters, Andrews, Chrisfield and Fuselli, typical. There were soldiers like them, just as there is a Bergdoll.[1] But is every man taken in the selective draft comparable to Bergdoll? Does any man dare say Grover Cleveland Bergdoll is typical of American youth?

There were deserters. There were men who would shoot a wounded American officer, and there were degenerates who looked upon service in the American Expeditionary Forces as an opportunity for an endless debauch at the expense of the United States Government and the respect of their fellow-soldiers. Thank God this type was rare. The A.E.F. didn't want them, would have repudiated them gladly had it been possible, and the A.E.F.—the A.E.F. we loved and worshiped and cried over, resented with hard-knuckled blows the intimation that the Andrews and Chrisfields and Fusellis of *Three Soldiers* were typical.

We all know Andrews. His name appears on the sick report the greatest number of times, he always had to have his pack carried on a long march, and he was the first under shelter in the line if he hadn't managed to wheedle a transfer to some base detail before his unit 'went in.'

We have known Chrisfield, too. Chrisfield, the braggart, drunkard, roisterer. The man who always brayed of physical prowess, but never lifted a hand unless it was to strike a smaller man in the dark and from behind. Chrisfield is the same, whether you put him in France in O.D., or put him on the street corner ogling women and terrifying children.

And Fuselli. There were Fusellis, as well.

Cringing, whining, boot-licking every man whose authority superseded theirs, and grinding those beneath them relentlessly with a cruel under-handed cunning which defied detection. Outwardly, they preserved a demeanor of loyal courage, but within they were slinking cowards, without honor and without shame.

According to Dos Passos these men are typical of the A.E.F. Dos Passos specializes on Andrews. He gives Andrews whole pages in which to talk of his 'soul.' Andrews, we believe, says what Dos Passos lacks the courage to say in his own name. If that be true, and the entire book creates that impression, then we have nothing but pity for Dos Passos. Pity, because we know how he must have suffered whenever it seemed likely that his precious 'soul' would be emancipated from his trembling body. Pity, because even now, three years after the cessation of hostilities, he creates an imaginary character to carry his message of bitterness and hopelessly distorted facts. I believe Dos Passos has deliberately waited until now to publish his book. I believe he has watched with glee the increasing disappointment and bitterness among former service men and, believing that wave of dissatisfaction to be at its height, has floated his book in the hope that the bitter ones will pick it up as a daring declaration of truth. Bitterness there is, and many are justly bitter, but their disappointment is displaced by anger after reading three chapters of *Three Soldiers*. Soldiers don't like lies, and *Three Soldiers* is nothing else.

Throughout the entire book you cannot find a commissioned officer nor a non-commissioned officer who isn't a red-faced, swaggering bully, who delights in felling the men of his command with a blow. In the whole damnable document there isn't an enlisted man that doesn't cringe or that isn't driven into action by the fear of what will befall him if he follows the dictates of his 'soul.'

Stern officers there were, and 'hard' non-coms. Men, he men, who exacted the most in obedience and the maximum of effort. But they were men. Men who knew the magnitude of the things they demanded, and loved the soldiers in their command because they met each demand willingly, gladly, and with a good-natured yell. It was a hard game, the hardest game thousands of them ever played, but it was a game in which they had elected to play a part, and, John Dos Passos to the contrary, they played it as no other men on earth could.

Kick? The whole A.E.F. kicked. That's a soldier's privilege. You might as well take an infantryman's rifle as forbid him to grumble. But they didn't whine. Dos Passos lies when he says they did.

I've been a buck and I've been a shavetail. I've over-stayed my pass and I've sent the best corporal in my battery to the kitchen for two weeks for over-staying his. I've collected garbage on Officers' Row, and when my shoulder bars were so new they squeaked when I walked I lit into a first-class private with nine years' service in the Regular Army because he had two buttons of his blouse unbuttoned. I didn't whine, and I didn't boot-lick. Neither did the corporal I sent to the kitchen nor the private whose dress I criticized, and, although I haven't the slightest idea where that corporal and private are now, I know any one of us will cheerfully thump Dos Passos if he says we did.

I claim to know the average man of the A.E.F. about as well as anyone, and *Three Soldiers* is true of but mighty few of them.

I've kicked with them and 'bawled them out' for kicking. I've known battery commanders who were always good for at least five francs to any man in the battery, and there is a certain Army Nurse who has eaten more than one meal only because one Bacon—the second best side-car driver in the A.E.F.—had had a good night with the galloping dominoes the night before.

I know a Captain who went out and sat in front of two 75's while German shells made the immediate surrounding country as near like Dante's inferno as anything I care to see. He did it because he couldn't withdraw his guns and their orders were to stand to for action. He did it because he felt he had to run as big a risk as the gun crews who were ordered to stick to their pieces; and he isn't wearing a D.S.C. for it, either.

I know—I know so darn much more than Dos Passos about the A.E.F. that it is foolish to talk any more about it. I know they were not like Andrews and Chrisfield and Fuselli.

Dos Passos can write. He paints a strong picture, and he paints it vividly. But who wants a picture that lies? Who wants to wade through 400 pages of the most unjust misstatements that ever went unpunished? Who wants to hear the men who lie in Romagne called 'cringing cowards,' 'moral degenerates' and 'driven slaves'? That is what John Dos Passos claims in *Three Soldiers*. He would have his readers believe that men of such stamp took Bouresches Woods, Chateau Thierry and St. Miehel. John Dos Passos would have his readers believe that every man who wore a chevron or a

Sam Browne was a 'Hard Boiled Smith.' And John Dos Passos Lies!

NOTE

1 Grover Cleveland Bergdoll, an American draft evader arrested and tried in Philadelphia.

6. H.L. Mencken, review, *Smart Set*

December 1921, vol. lxvi, 143–4

Mencken (1880–1956) was an American journalist, editor, essayist, and critic. A self-appointed enemy of Puritanism in American thought, he was co-editor with George Jean Nathan of *Smart Set* from 1914 to 1923, author of *The American Language* (1919), and editor of *American Mercury* from 1924 to 1933.

Published three years ago, or even two years ago, John Dos Passos' *Three Soldiers* would have been suppressed out of hand, and the author hurried to Leavenworth or Atlanta, with a Federal judge bawling obscene farewells to him from the bench. Even as it stands, it shows the marks of a good deal of discreet trimming; in fact, the publishers admit openly, over their sign manual, that they induced Mr. Dos Passos to tone it down somewhat before he departed for Europe and safety, and that they themselves continued the process after he had left. Nevertheless, the thing still has enough frankness to make it stand clearly above the general level of American novels. It is a serious attempt to picture the war, not as it appeared to newspaper editorial writers denouncing the Hun, or to bankers' committees forcing Liberty Loans on the yokels at a personal profit of 3 or 4%, or to sentimental women parading the streets in grotesque uniforms, or to four-minute spellbinders in movie parlors, but to three young men who actually served in it, as the author did himself. It is a picture somehow disconcerting. The theory of the time was that service would be of great spiritual and intellectual benefit to the conscripts, whatever the risk to their skins—that it would elevate and mellow them to be parts of so knightly an organization as the Army, and to take part in so noble a cause as the struggle to preserve democracy, the Word of God, and the French and English loans. But the fact seems to be that the Army quickly acquired the tone, not of a crusade of Geoffrey de Bouillons, but of a Billy Sunday revival, a chautauqua, a convention of Rotary Clubs, a women-flogging session of the Ku Klux Klan. In other words, most of the efforts of its managers were devoted, not to making the conscripts gallant and brave, but simply to making them swallow all sorts of childish piffle about the enemy. The aim, it would seem, was to augment their resolution by scaring them to death—by trying to make them believe that if they ever fell into the hands of that enemy they would be relieved of their ears and teeth, beaten with clubs, and boiled in oil. The ideal soldier, by this system, was the one who most quickly acquired the imbecility of a Y.M.C.A. secretary or a college professor working for the Creel-Wilson-Hog Island press bureau.

It is an unfortunate fact—to be deplored, I hope, by future historians—that the American people got so little of spiritual value out of the war. I am a firm believer in war, and regard it as the most effective of all antidotes to the sickly sordidness of Christian civilization. It lifts men above all their usual puerile fears and uncertainties, and gives them something to be genuinely afraid of; it brings out qualities of a rare and lofty variety, wholly obscured by the daily routine of life. But it must be obvious that it is possible to enter even a great and brilliant war in a manner so discreditable that all of the advantages of the enterprise will be lost. It was in this way that the United States entered the war of 1914–1918. We hung back for three long years, meanwhile robbing the Allies in a manner unparalleled in history. We hid behind a neutrality that was dishonest and knavish. Then we marched in against a foe already beset by odds of at least two to one, and gave him the *coup de grâce* at odds of at least four to one. Meanwhile, the great majority of Americans who were liable to military duty tried to get out of it, and those who succeeded devoted themselves riotously to plunder. Not only the so-called profiteers fought for the loot; the honest laboring man, within the limits of his opportunities, was just as eager. And over all we had a *Kriegherr* who drenched the world with streams of pious balderdash so sickening that even our allies began to gag. In brief, a war with no more gallantry in it than a lynching, and no more dignity than an auction sale. Is it any wonder that its chief psychic effect has been the horizontal degradation of the whole American people, so that they become bywords in the world for hypocrisy and sharp–dealing, and so far forget the ideas the Fathers of the Republic fought for that they accept any invasion of their old liberties, however gross, with scarcely a protest?

Mr. Dos Passos takes three young Americans, each typical of a large class, and shows their progress through this great machine. It is not a pleasant picture; I do not recommend the book for lazy reading on a Sabbath afternoon. But a passion for the truth is plainly there, and with it an imagination that makes that truth live.

7. Unsigned review, 'Blow at Americanism', *Chicago Tribune*

13 March 1922, 1C

The author has remained anonymous. In this diatribe against Dos Passos's first novel, which he brands 'a textbook and bible for slackers and cowards', he identifies himself only as 'a member of the First Division, a Legionnaire, a father, and a citizen'. What follows is approximately the first third of the review.

The review of this story—*Three Soldiers*, by John Dos Passos—is written by a legionnaire who bases his attitude toward the book on a deep sense of justice to those who endured the hardships, suffered broken health and maimed bodies, and who made the supreme sacrifice; it is written as a father would write to counsel his son and

53

the generations of youths he represents to avoid being inoculated with the poison of this story by consuming the capsules of cowardice and selfishness, sugar coated with finely painted word scenes and sentimentalism; the reviewer writes as a citizen of a state to warn his countrymen of the anarchistic, bolshevistic doctrine running through this story, and to call their attention to the book's affront to every just and decent principle upon which society is founded and organized business and government maintained.

Mr. Dos Passos' book, to the thoughtful student, and certainly to the citizen soldier who could sacrifice, suffer, and meet hardships for a high purpose, will be considered of great evidential value in establishing what the author least expected, that the army which he characterizes as a 'treadmill of slavery,' a breaker of spirits, and a destroyer of individuality, is the greatest institutional asset in our republic.

The author, in his vicious attempt to attack the army, has defined it as a machine operating on human beings like the hopper and grinder, a funnel shaped device for feeding material into a machine where it is crushed into identical particles, instead of considering the hopper as a receiver of material attached to a separator by means of which the undeveloped or unfit specimens are segregated and thrown into the waste heap, while those that meet the required high standards are carried on into the fulfilment of a higher destiny....

Mr. Dos Passos, the 'Dos pesos, oro net,' is a small price for your book, if our countrymen will read it in the light that it has a real mission and not for its tear producing effect. If so read this is the finest story in the decade in support of universal military service.

Regardless of all ethical or academic discussion of the right or wrong of war, America was in the war. Her millions in money were being expended daily and the blood of her young men was being spilled on the scattered battle fields from 'Switzerland to the sea.' The German menace was well known to our people.

The restrictions of the army that the author's heroes held in horror would have been a child's kindergarten regulation compared with the iron hand of the German war lords if the American youth had not stopped them on the western front. And think, Mr. Author, if our treadmill army had been filled with your heroes, who knows but what a considerable percentage of the publisher's

'Two dollars net' would have been given towards America's tax burdens imposed by the Hindenburg-Ludendorff firm?

To you who have given favorable criticism to this story, what would have been your thoughts and your feelings had you been able to see and to hear Chrisfield and Andrews in their boxcar ride to the front. I know that you would have longed for a treadmill that would have separated these weaklings and assigned to them missions in the home 'knitting squad,' where, in all probability, removed from hardships and suffering, their tender hands may have produced socks and sweaters for the men at the front.

That America's effort was successful is the living evidence that the Chrisfields, Andrews, Fusellis, and the other miserable characters of this story were in such small numbers that those misfits and their kind could be thrown aside in this great purpose towards which the life and courage of the nation was directed. There can hardly be that proverbial shadow of doubt but that these men were all failures, opinionated with that ego, who resented group life and mass action and such concentration of effort as would cause them to contribute some of their personal rights and freedom for the benefit of others.

The sacrifice of individual action that can only be attained by the concerted power of the group was unknown to these 'liberty lovers' who probably never knew that the liberty for which they craved had been purchased by the blood and sacrifices of the men of the revolution, and made eternal by the

> Men of the blue of the windswept north
> Who fell on the fields of our south!
> And the men of the grey of the sun-kissed south
> Who fell on the fields of our north.

Evangeline Booth addressed the American soldier as 'wonderful and stalwart.' I wonder what her thoughts would have been if she had heard Dos Passos' hero, Andrews, express the thought that 'he would like to go to sleep and not wake up until the war was over,' and he could be a 'civilian again.' What our hero really meant was that he could return to his life of ease.

How different was his thought to that of the Virginia boy, coming out of the hospital, thanking God that his rest was over and that he had been privileged to again serve in this great human effort to 'win the war.'

How horribly shocked our hero would have been had he heard a mother exclaim over her dead boy, 'what a privilege it was to give him in such a cause!' And how he would have 'damned' the soldier receiving the 'distinguished service cross' if he had heard him exclaim, 'How proud my mother will be of this!'

Some gentle female soul, in the over-generousness of her sweet nature has said, referring to this book, 'It is well done.' But please, gentle women of America, give your true version of this putrid story, with its 'goddam' characters, criminals, and potential criminals, that were forced into the nation's service in the mistaken conception that beings who answered certain draft specifications were men, and in the Utopian dream that such chaff and riffraff could ever feel that fine individual responsibility for team accomplishment of a great mission.

The attack on the welfare organizations, symbolized in the 'Y' man, is in keeping with the general attack on all uplifting influences of organized effort to bring some cheer into the great 'fog of war' and 'gloom of the battlefield.' The sarcastic remarks at the great Creator, religion, and prayer are significant, if one reads between those proverbial lines in the 'Y man's' introduction of Dr. Skinner.

The reflections on the honesty of the draft boards, that have been praised so generally and so generously throughout the country for their honesty and fairness, are flung into the reader's face through the medium of the character Applebaum, all of which gross unfairness is subscribed to by the hero, who admitted that he was a 'sucker,' too.

The author drags the great fraternal order of Masonry into the story by picturing one of his characters, a Mason, as a thief, and explains 'that's why he only got five years,' meaning the misfit would have received a longer sentence but for the protection of this fraternal institution.

The veiled insinuation expressed by the character Henslowe that 'the Red Cross sent supply trains to keep them at it,' meaning that this welfare organization utilized this means to keep nations at war, is so perfectly silly that it is stupid.

The reflection on the men who enlisted voluntarily in those great bodies of regular army and national guard is demonstrative of the total ignorance of the words 'fair play' and 'square deal,' and is evidenced by this spirit of service being personified in the coward undertaker, Applebaum, who had enlisted and regretted it.

The author hates soldiers so bitterly that he pictures a dog suspicious of them and makes his hero imagine 'many soldiers would change with them if they had a chance.'

His hostility to the salute was thoroughly indicative of his ignorance of its meaning as a recognition among military men and that its rendition is as binding on the senior as on the junior who initiates the salutation. He could not understand this simple greeting, this ceremonious military form that insures the enlisted and commissioned personnel always 'speaking' to each other and fixes this responsibility in the commissioned ranks by requiring the junior to 'speak' first.

The author has certainly demonstrated his complete aversion of any and everything that smacks of 'authority.' His officers are 'pompous,' they are 'dramatic,' they are 'busy feeling their importance,' they are 'coarse,' 'their voices are metallic and shrill,' they are 'illiterate,' they are 'snarling,' 'they shout their orders with and without fury,' they are 'blue-jawed' and have the 'eyes of a crab.' They have 'savage green eyes,' they are 'red faced,' they are 'pink faced,' 'bottle nosed' and have 'red hair.' They lean back in deep cushioned automobiles, splashing mud on their juniors as they drive by. They invariably 'fastidiously' put on their gloves by 'fingers.' They live in 'white and golden staterooms' on the ships.

For some reason the author must have an aversion for red. His noncommissioned officers are hated simply on account of the authority which they represent. He describes them as being red headed, sandy haired, burly, coarse, unshaven, illiterate, and with 'rings around their eyes like a monkey.'

His M.P.'s symbols of authority, are 'red faced,' 'red cheeked,' with 'squeaky voices,' 'raw looking faces,' and 'puffy under the eyes.'

Even the paymaster and his clerks, symbols of authority, have 'red faces,' and we find that the guard who represented authority over prisoners was 'pink faced.'

Of course this is intended primarily as an attack on authority and incidentally as a reflection on noncommissioned officers, but later on the author unconsciously informs us that these coarse, uneducated, make-believe noncommissioned officers were lumbermen, baseball players, ranchmen, etc.

The description of these officers and noncommissioned officers will be a revelation to those thousands and thousands of clean cut, clear eyed, determined countenanced, physically clean men who attended our great training camps and noncommissioned officer schools in these eventful years of 1917–1918.

They will stand aghast, Mr. Dos Passos, and wonder in amazement from where you obtained your idea of 'those blue jawed fellows' and 'crab eyed figures.' Was it from the derelicts en route to Bias for 'reclassification' that you passed in 'chauffering' your ambulance in the environs of Paris?

It is a great pity, Mr. Author, that you did not have at least one officer or noncommissioned officer in this motley mob to explain to your heroes that discipline does not mean servility but the subordinating of mind and body in order to attain correctness and precision in set, in habit and in dress. Such instructions would, in all probability, have prevented their minds from working without coordination with their bodies, and the frequent movement of their bodies, without any reference to their mental sides.

It is a great pity that the mob to which they belonged was not taught one of the basic principles, that fear and cowardice comes from negative thinking, and that success and failure are results of mental action.

Let us examine the heroes of this story, study their natures from their own thoughts, analyse their characters, throw them into the spotlight just a bit, and see whether or not 'they are slaves' because 'they are in the army' and whether or not the publisher's preposterous claim is just when he states that this story is 'The Case of Young America.'

What follows is descriptive in content, derisive in tone.

ONE MAN'S INITIATION—1917

London, October 1920; New York, June 1922

8. Lloyd R. Morris, 'Dos Passos in Perspective', *New York Times Book Review*

18 June 1922, 17, 22

Dos Passos's first novel was not reviewed in its first edition and very likely would not have been reprinted or reviewed at all had it not been for the popular success of *Three Soldiers* in 1921. Morris (1893–1954) was an American literary critic and author of books on Nathaniel Hawthorne, E.A. Robinson, and William James. Half the space of this review was devoted to *Rosinante to the Road Again,* Dos Passos's collection of travel essays on Spain, which Morris found equally 'impressionistic'.

The almost simultaneous publication in this country of John Dos Passos's first and his latest books should be a source of satisfaction to an increasing number of readers interested in the work of the younger American writers. For these books not only afford a perspective of the progress of his talent, but indicate certain conclusions as to its depth and power which the much-debated *Three Soldiers* tentatively suggested but never wholly confirmed.

The dominant passions in which the whole of his work is grounded are a fierce hunger for beauty and a vigorous enthusiasm for absolute, primitive liberty. These, it may be noted, are not characteristic of the intellectualist, of the man to whom experience is a matter for logical cogitation. They are attributes primarily of the lyric temperament, exuberant in emotional response to experience, nervously aware of the shifting play of its colors on the spirit, mysteriously sensitive to every contact with the external world. A perhaps unconscious, but none the less abnormally acute, receptivity to physical sensation colors the whole of his art.

All these qualities of temperament are readily apparent in Mr. Dos Passos's first book, *One Man's Initiation*, which, although it is published as a novel, is essentially a lyric interlude, poetic in feeling and in conception, though written in prose. It is quite simply a record of Martin Howe's experiences as an ambulance driver in France during the year 1917, and one may suppose it to be largely autobiographic in content. Mr. Dos Passos gives us a series of fleeting impressions, sharp, vivid, quivering with light and largely disconnected. Curiously enough, it is this very lack of continuity which lends the book something of the urgency of reality, conveying almost without any synthesis the immediacy of a fluent stream of events.

One Man's Initiation was written before *Three Soldiers*, and its relation to that widely read novel is a matter of some interest. They have in common the background of the war, and they share the acidulated cynicism and the petulance with which Mr. Dos Passos's attitude toward the war is saturated. The difficulty is that many readers have been disposed to take Mr. Dos Passos's discussion of the war as the product of a species of intellectual reflection whereas it appears to be an expression of purely spontaneous feeling. The war, it seemed to Mr. Dos Passos, restricted, if it did not abolish, the liberty of the individual. Complete individual liberty, unhampered by any external agency, to any one but a romanticist is an unattainable and perhaps not desirable ambition; but to Mr. Dos Passos it is an ideal precious beyond any other but beauty. 'All my life,' says Martin in *One Man's Initiation*, 'I've struggled for my own liberty in my small way. Now I hardly know if the thing exists.' That is the essence of Mr. Dos Passos's feeling about the war. The romantic attitude develops in the motive which sent Martin Howe, and perhaps sent Mr. Dos Passos into the war. 'Oh, but I think it's so splendid of you to come over this way to help France,' says a peculiarly vapid girl to Martin on the steamer. 'Perhaps,' is Martin's reply, 'perhaps it's only curiosity.'

This romantic curiosity explains, I think, the powerful attraction which the exceptional and horrible in experience exercises upon Mr. Dos Passos: just as a keenly sensitive nervous system is responsible for his apparent physical recoil from these aspects of life and his reluctance to becoming subject to their evident fascination.

And the consequent turmoil of spirit results, in *One Man's Initiation*, as it did in *Three Soldiers*, in magnificently powerful descriptions of physical suffering, of torn and broken and tortured bodies, of filth and squalor, of hideous disintegration. Against this undercurrent motif is the counterpoint of Mr. Dos Passos's eager, febrile response to all loveliness of color and form and perfume. Few American writers possess so extraordinary an acuity to the impact of sensory impression; few, too, translate it into such flaming, eloquent beauty.

9. Unsigned review, *New York Evening Post Literary Review*

29 July 1922, 835

The reviewer found this apprenticeship to *Three Soldiers* to be in some ways even better, the impressions of war sharper and more vivid.

This little book, with its awkward title, was published in England before the advent of *Three Soldiers* here. It is not, like the latter book, the complete war history of the sensitive mind of the hero, but rather a series of preliminary sketches, vignettes of ambulance experiences, in which Martin Howe plays the part of the John Andrews whose career ended so disastrously in *Three Soldiers*.

A preliminary sketch for a *chef d'oeuvre* is a fair description of this book, and like many a sketch it is sharper and simpler and often more excellent than the completed work. Dos Passos's peculiar gift is for emotionalized description, and nowhere has he written more admirably than in the description of the abbey under bombardment, or put more smell, sound, fearful night, and horrid sensation into words than in his night in the Poste de Secours.

Of course. *One Man's Initiation* lacks the weight and drive of *Three Soldiers*, the pacifist thesis is undeveloped, the tragedy of a war 'like Alice in Wonderland, like an ill-intentioned Drury Lane pantomime, like all the arty futility of Barnum and Baily's Circus' is not carried to its last act in the lives of men whom it crushes. Yet, just because there is more fresh impression and less thinking over, more humor and less philosophy, and not such an over-emphasis upon dirt, despair, and dissipation, the little book is more perfect, if less important, than the big one.

Readers who saw the war in the newspapers were confused and finally bored by the infinite detail of *Three Soldiers*. They read a few chapters and then trusted to the reviews for the rest. To them, we recommend this other volume. They will finish it, if they begin, and they will be given a more vivid impression of what 'it was really-like' than is easily obtained elsewhere in American prose. The implied philosophy of protest they may disregard if they please; they may think it unbalanced, a product of hysterical moments, but it would be unwise to call it trivial. The art of the book will speak for itself, except when the author drops from narrative into stilted argument.

A sensitive soul in contact with war at its worst, this is Mr. Dos Passos's label, if we must label him, and it limits and defines his value as a witness. But it was only the sensitive souls who in any larger sense understood the war at all.

10. Unsigned review, *Bookman* (New York)

August 1922, vol. lv, 648

One Man's Initiation is not a pleasant affair, despite the beautiful simplicity with which it is written. More than from a revulsion against the intimate glimpses of the physical devastation of war, the unpleasantness of the book comes from the once forbidden expression of mental devastation so closely related to the physical horrors. John Dos Passos wrote these memoirs before he fictionized his observations in *Three Soldiers*. One is seeing the novel at a stage of its gestation, before the vitals were covered by plot. The literary workmanship is remarkably skilful as war is forced to parade in nakedness—robbed of its chauvinistic, romance-embroidered clothing.

11. Constance Black, review, *New York Herald Tribune Books*

13 August 1922, 5

Constance Black reviewed books irregularly for the *Tribune* during the early 1920s.

One Man's Initiation, by John Dos Passos was written before his widely famous *Three Soldiers* and has already been published and acclaimed in England.

It is very much like *Three Soldiers* excepting that there seems to me more passages of descriptive power and slightly less of the profanity that is so terribly omnipresent in *Three Soldiers.*

Dos Passos has some very remarkable gifts. He can write slang and make it readable, convincing, not exaggerated and extraordinarily vital. He can paint in a bit of scenery so that it stamps itself more vividly on your mind than if you had actually seen it with an eye untrained for delicate observation.

He has an amazing power of projecting a scene on his canvas not by the force of detailed analysis, but in large bold strokes, and yet to me both books are somehow unsatisfactory.

Both books seem artistically injured by the fact that the iron of army futilities and war futilities has eaten into the soul of the writer to the extent of making him too biased, though the bias is less evident in *One Man's Initiation.*

With the drawback of the war absent and with all his various abilities present, Mr. Dos Passos should be the logical man to achieve the still unwritten great novel of modern America.

MANHATTAN TRANSFER

November 1925

12. Henry Longan Stuart, review, *New York Times Book Review*

29 November 1925, 5, 10

Stuart (1875–1928) translated French novels into English and wrote several novels himself, including *Weeping Cross* (1933). He reviewed fiction regularly for the *New York Times Book Review*. The review contrasts Dos Passos's narrative technique with Joyce's, and finds his portrait of life in New York City unduly pessimistic.

A time seems to arrive in the career of nearly all of our writers of the younger school when the challenge of New York to their imagination and descriptive powers assumes the proportions of a clear duty that may no longer be shirked if self-respect is to be maintained. This piled up mass of humanity, amorphous and heterogeneous at one and the same time, is a storehouse of impressions that it is either affectation or cowardice to ignore. These canyons, twenty stories high, replete with complex creatures who have only a frail screen of plaster between themselves and the good or evil chances of close neighborhood—what endless possibilities for contacts! Streets and speedways, Babylonian palaces and shabby makeshifts in moldering brick—bite by their very contrasts. Even the configuration of the monstrous city, set on a spit of land thrust seaward like a thirsty tongue surrounded by bleak waters that seem all the more savage for the flotsam cast on their surface, imposes a sort of wild beauty on its fret and fury, the grandeur and squalor of it all, and invests the very mechanism of its daily life, the whence and whither of its transport with a kind of savage beauty. What artist shall convey the effect of its overpowering confusions? What poet in words, the novitiate of his first bewilderment and numbness over, shall rise to the heights of its inspiration? 'This thing of New York—what about it?'

John Dos Passos in *Manhattan Transfer* has made the attempt perhaps with more obvious intent and more consciously than any prose writer hitherto; hence in estimating his success or failure it is more than ever necessary to take intentions into account. Two ways will occur in which the effect of a mass of superabundant human energy compressed into a small space might have been conveyed to us through the medium of fiction. One was by showing its impact on two, three—at any rate a limited number of human destinies. These would have been linked together by something more than chance relations. They would have experienced the resistance of the mass will to the individual which Croce tells us is the essence of drama, and its intensity would have been heightened by the fact that men and women in the modern city live, move and have their being on a basis of mutual tolerance that only becomes evident in the acute moments when it is suspended. This was the method older writers would have chosen. Indeed, until Mr. Joyce cast his mokeywrench into the mechanics of the novel, it is the method they have chosen, though more and more at the mercy of the reverberations of their impressibility. It entails that old-fashioned device—a plot, and that other convention, equally démodé, a psychological apparatus.

The other way is the one Mr. Dos Passos has elected to follow. It is simpler, but must not, on that account alone, be condemned as obvious. This is to take the rhythms of the vortex into the very stuff and substance of form and matter—to become a mere instrument for registering impressions, so exacerbated that not the most fleeting is missed; to discard no episode, however trivial, since the sensitized plate records them all with a mechanical impartiality; to allow the senses their momentary function, and no more; and to note, with a toneless precision that scarcely deserves the name of zest, the sinking of a fork into an alligator pear or the frown that forebodes murder or lust; lips pursed for love or fingers poised to pull a clam out of its shell; the smell of talcum, the smell of stale bedding—or the smell of blood.

There is no vestige of plot in Mr. Dos Passos's tragic 'Trivia.' One story runs through it, however, its peripatetics taking their chance with episodes that begin and end nowhere. This is the life or career (the lady is of the stage) of Elaine Thatcher, daughter of an accountant, who has all the respectability associated with his craft. Elaine marries and divorces a sexual pervert, becomes the mistress of a millionaire's alcoholic son, marries (when he is killed) a dreamy and unpractical newspaper man in France, and leaves him, with a child—when once convinced his low earning power will not increase with the years—for an unscrupulous and forceful lawyer who has himself come to her arms at the end of a series of illicit and casual love affairs. One is doing Mr. Dos Passos no injustice in dismissing the thread of his main story so cavalierly, for there is no evidence that he considers it important himself. The real 'meat' of his strange book comes in the host of human moths, more or less singed or wilted, who flutter and swarm round the lights of Broadway and Fifth Avenue—tramps, drunkards, wastrels, homosexualists, prostitutes more or less accredited, 'Villagers,' waiters, bootleggers and ruffians, with the shadow of Jefferson Market Night Court somehow never far from their shoulders. These people are stunned by city noises (the thunder of the elevated recurs again and again like a motif in a symphony) and sickened by its smells: they crave its pleasures, yet hate the work that pays for them: they smother down their heartaches with food and drink; they cheat—themselves the oftenest; they can conceive of life nowhere else than in the prison-city that is turning their faces gray before their hair. 'The terrible thing of having New York go flat on you is that there's nowhere else. It's the top of the world. All we can do is go round and round in a squirrel cage.' Thus George Baldwin, the hard-boiled corporation lawyer, in a moment of depression, or dyspepsia.

Jimmy Herf, the young newspaper man, through whose reactions we catch the nearest thing to moral comment Mr. Dos Passos permits on all this episodic life and epidermic love, is perhaps the one sympathetic character in his novel. It may be because childish impressions reach us when the heart is virgin—or it may be some other reason. But it is the comforting fact that the hardest-boiled of the new-method-ists, the most glittering and devastatingly metallic of the super-realistic seem to forget their art when faced with the appeal of the artless. There are not many things more pathetic in this year's novels than the arrival of poor little Jimmy from overseas with his loved and frail mother and her seizure with the fell sickness that takes her from him in the big hotel that once looked over Madison Square.

[Quotes from *Manhattan Transfer*, 88–9.]

Manhattan Transfer, it may be granted at once, is a powerful and sustained piece of work. The world it shows us is a world caught 'en dishabille,' of unmade beds, littered dressing tables and dubious bathrooms—of spoiled lives reaching out for mean and momentary alleviations, of debauch at the one end and a grinding, soul-searing poverty at the other, of Dives and Lazarus reduced to a common level of disrespectability. It might be said that Mr. Dos Passos has an exasperated sense of the unpleasant. But the same has been said of the Brontës, and in any case such a comment has long ceased to be criticism. A juster estimate would perceive his work vitiated with an initial flaw that he shares with practically all the impressionists and 'super-naturalists,' American, English and foreign alike. He ignores the immunity which the imagination acquires when disheartening or bewildering impressions crowd upon it, the compensations that keep it sane and balanced under almost any circumstances that are endurable at all, the 'leakage,' to borrow a word from psychology, which enables it to keep, of all its functions and impressions, only that part in its consciousness which administers help or pleasure while consigning the rest to the realm of the purely automatic, where they are in place. Thébaides are erected in the busiest and most harassed lives. The shadow of city canyons may fall everywhere but upon the soul. For lack of a discrimination which would have permitted this very tempered optimism Mr. Dos Passos's story of war was a very partial picture of military life on active service. For lack of it here, a study that seemed designed to convey the stir and movement of multiple lives too often freezes into a set piece of horror.

13. Sinclair Lewis, 'Manhattan at Last!', *Saturday Review*

5 December 1925, vol. ii, 361

Lewis (1885–1951), the American novelist, became in 1930 the first American to be awarded the Nobel Prize for literature. His contributions to American literature include

Main Street (1920), *Babbitt* (1922), and *Arrowsmith* (1925).
Lewis and Dos Passos were both satirists, but the latter's
experiments in narrative form, and interest in radical political
and economic reform, set them apart. Lewis was attacked in
the liberal press for having invented characters who were
alienated from middle-class society but incapable of imagin-
ing an alternative. His comparisons in this review between
Dos Passos and other writers (all in Dos Passos's favour) may
be indicative of his shortcomings both as a reader and writer.

I didn't want to review the book; I was off for a vacation in
Bermuda. Now that I've read it, still less do I want to because I am
afraid that Mr. Dos Passos's *Manhattan Transfer* may veritably be a
great book. And I have come to hate all the superlatives of
book-boosting.

The professional executioners, like Mr. Canby[1], Mr. Sherman[2],
Mr. Mencken[3]—it is their official duty to jerk all the aesthetic
criminals off into eternity. But we occasional guardians of spiritual
peace, we are typical militiamen, we hate to quell literary strikes
and arrest chronic offenders, we like only to parade with roses on
our muskets, cheered by the flappers along the way. Yet violent
strike duty is really less risky than being benevolent.

Nevertheless, I am going to take the risk.

I wonder whether it may not be true that *Manhattan Transfer* is a
novel of the very first importance; a book which the idle reader can
devour yet which the literary analyst must take as possibly
inaugurating, at long last, the vast and blazing dawn we have
awaited. It *may* be the foundation of a whole new school of
novel-writing. Dos Passos *may* be, more than Dreiser, Cather,
Hergesheimer[4], Cabell, or Anderson the father of humanized and
living fiction. . . . not merely for America but for the world!

Just to rub it in, I regard *Manhattan Transfer* as more important in
every way than anything by Gertrude Stein or Marcel Proust or
even the great white boar, Mr. Joyce's *Ulysses*. For Mr. Dos Passos
can use, and deftly does use, all their experimental psychology and
style, all their revolt against the molds of classic fiction. But the
difference! Dos Passos is *interesting*! Their novels are treatises on
harmony, very scholarly, and confoundedly dull; *Manhattan
Transfer* is the moving symphony itself.

True, no doubt, that without Joyce et Cie., Dreiser and Gesellschaft, Dos Passos might never have been able to devise this channel for the river of living life. Perhaps without a Belasco[5], even a Charley Hoyt,[6] O'Neill might never have written as he does. But there is no 'perhaps' in the question as to whether one prefers *Desire under the Elms* to the glib falsities of *The Girl of the Golden West*. And for one reader there is no question as to whether he prefers the breathless reality of *Manhattan Transfer* to the laboratory-reports of *Ulysses*.

In *Manhattan Transfer*, Mr. Dos Passos does, really does, what all of us have frequently proved could not be done; he presents the panorama, the sense, the smell, the sound, the soul, of New York. It is a long book—nearly two hundred thousand words, no doubt—but almost any other novelist would have had to take a million words to convey all the personalities and moods which here are quite completely expressed. The book covers some twenty-five years of the growth and decay of not only the hundred or more characters, but of the whole mass of the city—the other millions of characters whom you feel hauntingly behind the persons named and chronicled.

Mr. Dos Passos manages it by omitting the tedious transitions from which most of us can never escape. He flings the heart of a scene before you, ruthlessly casting away the 'And so the months and seasons went by and Gertrudine realized that Augustus did not love her' sort of plodding whereby most journeymen novelists fatigue the soul. It is, indeed, the technique of the movie, in its flashes, its cut-backs, its speed.

Large numbers of persons are going to say that it is the technique of the movie. But it differs from the movie in two somewhat important details. It does not deal only with the outsides of human beings; and Dos Passos does not use the technique to acquire a jazz effect, but because, when he has given the complete inwardness of a situation, he will not, to make a tale easy to 'drool out,' go on with the unessentials.

Dickens, too, expressed the vast London of his day, Dickens, too, leapt from one set of characters to another; and I can hear (with all the classroom tedium returning, after these twenty years) some varnished pedagogue explaining to the four select young literary gentlemen and the hen-medic whom he always has in for tea on Sunday afternoon, that after all, one Mr. Dickens did in his untutored way manage to do everything that Mr. Dos Passos is alleged to have done.

Yet with all this, Dickens, who created characters more enduring than Dos Passos is likely to give us, like Mark Twain and O. Henry, doubted his own genius and, straightway after he had built immortal reality, apologized for such presumption by dragging in page on page of respectable and lying hypocrisy. That Dos Passos does not do, probably could not do, not for one phrase. There is nothing here which is not real, instinct with life as we all know it and all veil it; there is not one character without corpuscles; not one moment when Dos Passos is willing to emblazon his characters by the tricks of caricature, which, though they are considerably harder to achieve than is believed by the layman, yet are pathetically easier than authentic revelation of genuine personality. And the classic method was—oh, it was rigged! By dismal coincidence, Mr. Jones had to be produced in the stage-coach at the same time with Mr. Smith, so that something very nasty and entertaining might happen. In *Manhattan Transfer*, the thirty or forty characters either do not impinge at all or do so only naturally. Each thread of story is distinct yet all of them proceed together. Aunt Tessie McCabe of Benner's Falls may seem far from Croce of Naples, but Aunt Tessie's nephew Winthrop, who is a lawyer in Omaha, has for client a spaghetti importer whose best friend is the nephew of Croce. And to just that natural degree does Dos Passos intertwine his stories.

But the thing that really distinguishes Dos Passos is not the mechanics of technique. It is his passion for the beauty and stir of life—of people, of rivers and little hills and tall towers by dawn and furnace-kindled dusk. Many wise persons will indicate that he is 'sordid'. He is not! Scarce Keats himself had a more passionate and sensitive reaction to beauty in her every guise. He does not always express it in breakfast food, easy for the moron to digest; no suave couplets are here, nor descriptions of sky-scrapers so neat that the Real Estate Sections of the Sunday newspapers will beg to reprint them. He deals not in photography but in broken color (though never, thank Heaven, in Picasso impressionism). But there is the City, smell of it, sound of it, harsh and stirring sight of it, the churn and crunch of littered water between ferry-boat and slip, the midnight of skyscrapers where a dot of yellow betrays an illicit love or a weary accountant, insane clamor of subways in the dark, taste of spring in the law-haunted park; shriek of cabarets and howl of loneliness in hall bedrooms—a thousand divinations of beauty without one slobber of arty Beauty-mongering.

I am wondering again—I am wondering if this may not perhaps be the first book to catch Manhattan. What have we had before, what have we had? Whitman? That is not our Manhattan; it is a provincial city, near the frontier. Howells, Wharton, James? A provincial city near to Bath and the vicar's aunt. Hughes, Fitzgerald, Johnson, all the magazine reporters of the Jazz Age? Foam on the beer! O. Henry? Change Broadway to Market Street or State Street in his stories, and see whether any one perceives a change.

But, to return, the real discussion will be as to whether Mr. Dos Passos is Sordid and perhaps even Indecent. (Dear Lord, and is this to be but joking? Who was the mayor of Florence when Dante looked at Beatrice? Who was the master of the college which kicked out Shelley?)

Yes, Mr. Dos Passos will be slated as sordid. He alleges that the male persons, properly married, owning Buicks and bungalows, sometimes betray an interest in wenches who are not allied to them by matrimony. He hints that physiological processes continue much as they did in the days of Voltaire and M. le Père Rabelais. He maintains that bums on the Bowery often use expletives stronger than 'By golly.' He even has the nerve to imply that college bred journalists sometimes split infinitives and bottles of synthetic gin.

A low fellow! He does not see life as necessarily approaching the ideals of a Hartford insurance agent. He sees it as a roaring, thundering, incalculable, obscene, magnificent glory.

For whatever John Dos Passos does in this book, he finds life, our American life, our Manhattan life, not a pallid and improving affair, but the blood and meat of eternal humanity.

I have, fortunately, one complaint. I see no advantage in Mr. Dos Passos's trick of running words together as in a paralyzing German substantive; in using such barbarisms as 'millionwin-dowed buildings' or 'cabbageleaves,' 'Grimydark' does certainly give a closer knit impression than 'Grimy, dark,' but 'peppery-fragrance' 'tobaccosmoke' and 'steamboatwhistles' are against God, who invented spacing and hyphenation to save the eyes. Mr. Dos Passos does not need to call attention to himself by thus wearing a red tie with his dinner clothes. That may be left to the vaudeville intellectuals who, having nothing to say and a genius for saying it badly, try to attract bourgeois notice—which they so much despise and so much desire—by omitting capitals, running words together, and using figures in place of letters. It is necessary to collate *Manhattan Transfer* with the book which introduced Mr. Dos Passos; *Three Soldiers*. To me it seemed lively and authentic, to many it was arty and whining—whine, whine, whine—the naughty brutal sergeant, oh, the nasty fellow! I challenge those who felt so to read *Manhattan Transfer*. There is no whining here! There is strength. There is the strong savor of very life. I met Dos Passos once. I have a recollection of lanky vitality and owlish spectacles. That was many years ago, and it was not till now that I found the feather, the eagle's feather—well, I forget the rest.

NOTES

1 See No. 3.
2 Stuart Pratt Sherman (1881–1926), American literary critic for the *Nation* (1908–18) and literary editor for the *New York Herald Tribune* (1924–26).
3 See No. 6.
4 Joseph Hergesheimer (1880–1954), American novelist.
5 David Belasco (1859–1931), American playwright and theatrical producer.
6 Charles Hoyt (1860–1900), popular American playwright known for his farces.

14. Michael Gold, review, *New Masses*

August 1926, 25–6

Gold (1894–1967) was an American editor, author, and journalist who played an important role in the labour movement in the U.S.A. during its infancy. Assistant editor of the left-wing *Masses*, which was suppressed in 1918 by the U.S federal government for its opposition to World War I,

Gold helped to found the *New Masses* in 1926. Dos Passos, a frequent contributor, disagreed with Gold over the editorial policy, Gold advocating ideological conformity and Dos Passos freedom of thought.

This book of John Dos Passos would make an epic movie; and maybe in the hands of a director who was artist and genius, (where is he) it would be a magnificently popular, breath-taking, strange, barbarously poetic movie for a nation to understand.

Manhattan Transfer is a swift unreeling of New York sights and sounds and scattered chunks of drama. Thousands of faces flash by, some sad, some hilarious and bawdy, and each in its moment on the screen speaks and reveals what is deepest in one's heart.

This novel flies and hurries so, like an express train, it has such a stiff schedule to maintain, it swoops and maneuvers like a stunt aeroplane, that maybe slow and peasant-minded people cannot follow easily. The method is too new and experimental. But read the book twice and the method conveys its own emotion—the zoom of the aeroplane flight over a city.

I have always admired this gorgeous writer John Dos Passos. He has ever loved the visible world with such virgin delight. His senses are so fresh; he smells like a wolf, sees like a child, hears, tastes and feels with the fingers. I was born in New York, it is in my bones, but he has made me see and feel and smell New York all over again in this book; yes, it is nothing but a great poem of man's senses in New York city.

A hundred fine new stories could be quarried out of this book; it is as full of creative beginnings as a page of Walt Whitman.

John Dos Passos seems to know capitalists, and crooked stock brokers, and factory hands, pimps, lonely young thieves, waitresses in one-arm lunches, morbid newspapermen, army captains, manicure girls, actresses, detectives, agitators, briefless young lawyers, milk-wagon drivers, bootleggers, sailors, cabaret singers,—he knows them, the way they make a living, their slang, the rooms they live in, the food they eat, their lusts, their hates, their defeats and hopes. He knows them. Multitudes move in his book—each sharp and different. But he more than reports them—he knows them.

I do not pose as a critic and have no wisdom to offer John Dos

Passos to make him a better writer. What I want to say is I feel in him a bewilderment. The hero of his book and of his recent play and of his other books is a baffled young middle-class idealist. This protagonist is tortured by American commercialism, and always seeks some escape. But Dos Passos does not know how to help him; and the result is not tragedy, which may be clean and great, but bewilderment, which is smaller.

Dos Passos must read history, psychology and economics and plunge himself into the labor movement. He must ally himself definitely with the radical army, for in this struggle is the only true escape from middle-class bewilderment today. That is what I feel.

There are pages of keen social rebellion and proletarian consciousness in this novel, but the mass effect is that the dilemma of the young idealist in America is insoluble. John Dos Passos is too enormous a talent to be held back in his creativeness by such nihilism.

Buy and read this novel. It is education; for it extends one's knowledge of America. All writers are propagandists; and the middle-class writers sentimentalize the people of their class (see Hergesheimer, for instance) so that a proletarian can only read them with a faint disgust. But Dos Passos knows the good and the bad, and tells both. He is fiercely honest. He is accurate. He is the propagandist of truth, and truth in America leads to rebellion against the liars of Wall Street and Washington. Dos Passos suffers with nostalgia for a clean, fair, joyous and socialized America. And his is a fresh virgin mind, and through him one can enjoy a great experience—one can roam the wild streets of New York, and climb up and down the fire-escapes, and see and know all that happens in this mad, huge, fascinating theatre of seven millions, this city rushing like an express train to some enormous fate.

15. D. H. Lawrence, review, *Calender of Modern Letters*

April 1927, 70–2

Lawrence (1885–1930), the English novelist, had offered his original and insightful impressions of America's literary past in *Studies in Classic American Literature* (1923). This is an extract from a longer review of several contemporary works of American fiction including Carl Van Vechten's *Nigger Heaven*, Walter White's *Flight*, and Hemingway's *In Our Time*. Lawrence rated Dos Passos's novel highest with Hemingway's a close second.

Manhattan Transfer is still a greater ravel of flights from nowhere to nowhere. But, at least, the author knows it, and gets a kind of tragic significance into the fact. John Dos Passos is a far better writer than Mr. Van Vechten or Mr. White, and his book is a far more real and serious thing. To me, it is the best modern book about New York that I have read. It is an endless series of glimpses of people in the vast scuffle of Manhattan Island, as they turn up again and again and again, in a confusion that has no obvious rhythm, but wherein at last we recognize the systole-diastole of success and failure, the end being all failure, from the point of view of life; and then another flight towards nowhere.

If you set a blank record revolving to receive all the sounds, and a film-camera going to photograph all the motions of a scattered group of individuals, at the points where they meet and touch in New York, you would more or less get Mr. Dos Passos' method. It is a rush of disconnected scenes and scraps, a breathless confusion of isolated moments in a group of lives, pouring on through the years, from almost every part of New York. But the order of time is more or less kept. For half a page you are on the Lackawanna ferry-boat—or one of the ferry-boats—in the year 1900, or somewhere there—the next page you are in the Brevoort a year later—two pages ahead it is Central Park, you don't know when—then the wharves—way up Hoboken—down Greenwich Village—the Algonquin Hotel—somebody's apartment! And it seems to be different people, a different girl every time. The scenes whirl past like snowflakes. Broadway at night—whizz! gone!—a quick-lunch counter! gone!—a house on Riverside Drive, the Palisades, night—gone! But gradually you get to know the faces. It is like a movie picture with an intricacy of different stories and no close-ups and no writing in between. Mr. Dos Passos leaves out the writing in between.

But, if you are content to be confused, at length you realize that the confusion is genuine, not affected; it is life, not a pose. The book becomes what life is, a stream of different things and different faces rushing along in the consciousness, with no apparent direction save that of time, from past to present, from youth to age, from birth to death, and no apparent goal at all. But what makes the rush so swift, one gradually realizes, is the wild, strange frenzy for success: egoistic, individualistic success.

This very complex film, of course, does not pretend to film all New York. Journalists, actors and actresses, dancers, unscrupulous lawyers, prostitutes, Jews, out-of-works, politicians, Labour agents—that kind of gang. It is on the whole a gang, though we do touch respectability on Riverside Drive now and then. But it is a gang, the vast loose gang of strivers and winners and losers which seems to be the very pep of New York, the city itself, an inordinately vast gang.

At first, it seems too warm, too passionate. One thinks: this is much too healthily lusty for the present New York. Then we realize we are away before the war, when the place was steaming and alive. There is sex, fierce, ranting sex, real New York: sex as the prime stimulant to business success. One realizes what a lot of financial success has been due to the reckless speeding-up of the sex dynamo. Get hold of the right woman, get absolutely rushed out of yourself loving her up, and you'll be able to rush a success in the city. Only, both to the man and woman, the sex must be the stimulant to success; otherwise it stimulates towards suicide, as it does with the one character whom the author loves, and who was 'truly male.'

The war comes, and the whole rhythm collapses. The war ends. There are the same people. Some have got success, some haven't. But success and failure alike are left irritable and inert. True, everybody is older, and the fire is dying down into spasmodic irritability. But in all the city the fire is dying down. The stimulant is played out, and you have the accumulating irritable restlessness of New York of to-day. The old thrill has gone, out of socialism as out of business, out of art as out of love, and the city rushes on even faster, with more maddening irritation, knowing the apple is a Dead Sea shiner.

At the end of the book, the man who was a little boy at the beginning of the book, and now is a failure of perhaps something under forty, crosses on the ferry from Twenty-Third Street, and walks away into the gruesome ugliness of the New Jersey side. He is making another flight into nowhere, to land upon nothingness.

'Say, will you give me a lift?' he asks the red-haired man at the wheel (of a furniture-van).

'How fur ye goin'?'

'I dunno...Pretty far.'

The End.

He might just as well have said 'nowhere'!

16. Paul Elmer More, 'Modern Currents', from *The Demon of the Absolute*

1928

More (1864–1937) was an American author of many philosophical works. He served as literary editor of the *Independent* in 1901 and of the *New York Evening Post* in 1903; he was editor of the *Nation* from 1909 to 1914. Along with Irving Babbitt, he was an apostle of American 'humanism', which meant tradition, decorum, and classicism. He was opposed to all forms and expressions of 'naturalism'. His comment on *Manhattan Transfer* is extracted from *The Demon of the Absolute* (Princeton, N.J.: Princeton University Press, 1928, 63). At this point in the book More is comparing the Eastern 'aesthetes' with the Mid-western 'realists'.

As a contrast the realists who throng the left wing of the modern school come almost without exception from small towns sprinkled along the Mid-Western States from Ohio to Kansas, where for the most part they have grown up quite innocent of education in any such sense as would be recognized in Paris or London. It would not be easy to exaggerate the importance of the fact that in letters they are self-made men with no inherited background of culture. One of them, indeed, Sinclair Lewis, coming out of Sauk Center, Minnesota, has a degree from Yale University; but intellectually he is perhaps the crudest member of the group, cruder, for instance, than Theodore Dreiser who got most of his education in the streets of Chicago and from the free libraries of this and that town, or than Sherwood Anderson who apparently owes his acquaintance with the alphabet to the grace of God. Another of the group, John Dos Passos, was born in Chicago, is a graduate of Harvard, and has been influenced, one guesses, by certain French Writers and by the Spaniard Ibañez; his work is too knowing to be called crude intellectually or perhaps even artistically, but as a reflection of life it is about the lowest we have yet produced. His much-bruited novel *Manhattan Transfer*, with its unrelated scenes selected to portray the more sordid aspect of New York, and with its spattered filth, might be described in a phrase as an explosion in a cesspool.

THE 42nd PARALLEL

February 1930

17. Mary Ross, review, *New York Herald Tribune Books*

23 February 1930, 3–4

A graduate of Vassar and the Columbia School of Journalism, Mary Ross was an American freelance writer and reviewer during the twenties and thirties, and associate editor for more than a decade of *Survey*, for which she wrote on a wide range of social issues. Her review is typical of most reviews of *The 42nd Parallel*, which were generally quite favourable despite objections to the experiments in narrative technique.

From an old book on American climatology John Dos Passos draws his title. General storms, says its author, travel eastward across the United States from the Rockies to the Atlantic along three paths or tracks, of which the central corresponds roughly to the forty-second parallel of latitude. And at the end of the path, where the storms meet the ocean, rests New York. In this book, a brave experiment in dynamic fiction, Mr. Dos Passos shows the eddying currents of individual lives that ultimately blow through or into the metropolis.

Though four years have passed since the author's preceding novel, *Manhattan Transfer*, I can still feel beating in my memory its bright, sharp rhythms, the jangled, unorderly music of the Manhattan of dusty or rain-swept streets, taxis, trucks, steam riveting, jazz and symphonies. Behind its hurrying beat lay only the dim backgrounds that fed their youth into it. 'The terrible thing about having New York go stale on you,' said one of the people in *Manhattan Transfer*, 'is that there's nowhere else. It's the top of the world. All we can do is to go round and round in a squirrel cage.'

Here Mr. Dos Passos starts, not at the center of the maelstrom but out on its periphery, in small towns, on lonely farms, with flickering glimpses of Paris, London, Pittsburgh, San Francisco, Mexico, Chicago, Washington, showing the devious ways in which human atoms are finally drawn into the spinning circle.

There is Mac, who learned printing in Chicago, peddled tracts and pornography from a buggy in Michigan, fought with the wobblies on the west coast, married because he had to and made an honest try at domesticity in Los Angeles, followed revolution in Mexico and found himself running a bookstore till revolution came too realistically his way. There is Eleanor Stoddard, who swore she would die if ever a man touched her, and became an interior decorator in Chicago and a devoted (platonic) friend of a public relations counselor in New York and went to France with the American Red Cross. And then Ward Moorehouse, who started in Wilmington, promoted real estate at a Maryland beach, married the unhappily adventurous daughter of an innocent Philadelphia doctor, divorced her, rose to eminence in publicity on the fortunes of a Pittsburgh heiress and finally helped regulate the war from New York with the services of Janey and inspiration of Eleanor. And, finally, Charlie Anderson, whose mother kept a railroad boarding house near the station at Fargo, N.D., who learned to tinker with Fords, eluded matrimony by a hairbreadth, hopped and worked his way through Milwaukee, Chicago, St. Louis and finally on to New Orleans at the time of the Mardi Gras and cleared out to New York in time to join the Ambulance Corps. And about these five the multitude of people whom they passed, ate or flirted with, fought, pursued or fled from.

Behind them, by an intricate structure of breaks in the narratives, Mr. Dos Passos suggests the evolution of America from the '90s on to the start of the Great War. The book has five main sections, each in turn subdivided into sections that deal respectively with Mac, Eleanor, Janey and the rest, into a series of passages headed 'The Camera Eye,' 'Newsreel' and isolated portraits of Americans. 'The Camera Eye' in a succession of flashes, twenty-seven in all, carrying the thread of time subjectively in the recollections of a boy as he grows on from childhood through adolescence—bright fragments of memory of walks, cabs, boats, vistas and visitors, on to college, war meetings in Madison Square Garden, the steamer going to France. 'Newsreel' is another series of snatches, carried out in contemporary newspaper headlines, the doggerel of popular songs, fragments from the accounts of passing events, all jumbled together. And interspersed among these and the narratives are passages of a page or two set apart from the rest typographically on 'Lover of Humanity,' Eugene Debs, 'The Plant Wizard,' Luther Burbank, 'Big Bill' Haywood, Bryan, Minor C. Keith ('Emperor of the Caribbean'), Andrew Carnegie, Edison, Steinmetz and 'Fighting Bob' La Follette.

Such a book abandons the ordinary structures of fiction for a form as intricate as that of a symphony. It gives no satisfaction at all for those who would know how the story 'comes out.' Its main theme would seem to be nothing less than life in America through three decades, with a range from coast to coast, from top to bottom of the economic scale, from the sublime to the ridiculous in emotions. It is often excessively irritating in its demands on the reader's attention and imagination—and absorbing in the vividness and diversity of full moments of living it beckons from hither and yon. Like all of Mr. Dos Passos's writing, it has the poet's acuteness of sensuous perception—sights, sounds, smells, tastes, that fairly leap from the print to engulf you. Occasionally a whole page comes as clear and true as a lyric—for example, 'The Camera Eye (25),' the nostalgia of spring night in Harvard Square.

Yet if *Manhattan Transfer* was baffling in the almost indiscriminate richness of its texture, *The 42nd Parallel* is doubly so, in its added range of time and place, its bombardment of ideas, types, social movements and individual lives. One cannot but admire the range of perception and sympathy that makes possible such a book, the stimulating courage that essays a synthesis of time, class, geography and social theory. For I believe the author's intention is not encyclopedic, as the listing of the substance of his book implies; nor yet a self-conscious attempt to startle and impress by doing The Big Thing in a big way. Mr. Dos Passos is groping toward some new approach that would catch life whole and living without the little frames that one's individual limitations and traditions impose on it. Despite its weight of concreteness, *The 42nd Parallel* becomes in the end a search for generalization, as a spectrum whirled on a disk shows solid white. All these sights and sounds and flavors, realized so acutely, seem to be means to an end—an end which is not clear. And because of this unasked and unanswered question—the bafflement which seems to me inherent in the book itself—the reader, too, ends with a sense of confusion. In attempting through the individual to wipe out the individual, going 'round and round in a squirrel cage,' searching for an end in a circle, *The 42nd Parallel* attains a brave and often stirring futility.

18. Fanny Butcher, review, *Chicago Tribune*

1 March 1930, 15

Fanny Butcher Bokum (b. 1888) wrote for the *Chicago Tribune* for fifty years (1913–63) as a feature writer, music critic, and society and literary editor. She was one of the first influential female book reviewers in America.

John Dos Passos wrote in *Manhattan Transfer* a completely artistically successful impressionistic novel. It was a technical trick, but it was a perfect marriage of material and manner. It was a panorama of New York composed of rapid flashes, casual, vivid, intense. The individuals who jumped on to and off the screen were brilliant sketches, but it was the conglomerate massed impression, which gave the essence of a metropolis, that made *Manhattan Transfer* unforgettable.

Mr. Dos Passos has chosen the same trick for a novel of America called *The 42nd Parallel*. The book is composed of 'newsreels' as he calls them, records of 'The Camera Eye,' satirical, sketchy biographies of great Americans and short chapters about the characters of the novel. The newsreels are composed of headlines and sentences out of stories of the period. They set the back drop for the drama, flashes of fact against which the action of the play takes place.

'The Camera Eye' chapters are observations of various people (or the same one, growing from childhood to young manhood as the action of the book progresses) about various other people, not associated with the leading characters in the book, but expressing, in their own lives, reactions of the principal characters. The short impressionistic, satirical biographies of great men of their times—Eugene V. Debs, Luther Burbank, Big Bill Haywood, W.J. Bryan, Minor C. Keith, Andrew Carnegie, Thomas A. Edison, Charles Steinmetz, Robert M. La Follette, like the newsreels, add the factual furniture of the action. Against that fact and fancy, rolled like a panorama before the eyes of the audience, the lives of the principal characters are lived in the same panoramic manner.

The technique is unquestionably fascinating. The reader's impression is of the extreme hodge-podginess, the lack of direction, of modern life. But Mr. Dos Passos does not, to this reader at least, make his experiment wholly successful, as he did in *Manhattan Transfer*.

The introduction of the biographies of great men of the period, for instance, while a good idea, turns out to be a disconcerting feature. While the back drop is turning slowly as the years pass, there are flashed against it pictures of men whose lives began years before the moment which the back drop is recording and went on for years after that. The chronology is thus jerked around frightfully by Mr. Dos Passos, for—so far as we can see—no reason whatever. He lowers the vitality of his technique by it.

The principal characters of the book are done with masterly skill. Mr. Dos Passos certainly has that rare gift of telling a story—only one novelist in twenty even approaches it. But, granted that he gives the essence of the lives and trends of the nine great men he chooses to summarize in a few pages—granted that the whole pattern of a human life is what interests the rest of the world—the fictional characters in his book are picked up and set down like marionettes handled by an erratic puppeteer. Their lives, while they are on the stage, are superbly recorded. What becomes of them after their short, vivid part is played Mr. Dos Passos never says nor even hints. And it is human life, and not, as it was in *Manhattan Transfer*, the pattern of a city, that he is painting.

The 42nd Parallel is, instead of being the masterpiece which it might have been, a brilliant tour de force.

19. Edmund Wilson, review, *New Republic*

26 March 1930, vol. lxii, 156–8

Wilson (1895–1972), the American critic and author of such works as *Axel's Castle* (1931) and *To the Finland Station* (1940), joined the editorial staff of the *New Republic* in 1926. His laudatory review of *The 42nd Parallel* is preceded by a lukewarm review of Thornton Wilder's *The Woman of Andros*, and a brief but enthusiastic notice of Edward Dalberg's *Bottom Dogs*, which Wilson admired for its tough prose to match its sordid subject.

Now Dos Passos, in *The 42nd Parallel*, has consciously and deliberately worked out a literary medium curiously and strikingly similar to Dahlberg's. *The 42nd Parallel*, which it seems to me Dos Passos's publishers have made a great mistake in not announcing for what it is: the first section of a novel on a large scale, is to deal with the role of the United States in the western world during the first years of the present century; but though it is written from the point of view of an unusually internationally minded American of unusually complete culture, the author has been able to immerse himself in the minds and the lives of his middle-class characters, to identify himself with them, to a degree which must astonish any reader of Dos Passos's other novels. In this respect, *The 42nd Parallel* is quite different from *Manhattan Transfer* and marks a striking advance beyond it. *Manhattan Transfer*, after all, might almost have been written by a very intelligent and well documented foreigner: the characters are seen from the outside and, in consequence, seem sometimes scarcely human. But in his new novel, Dos Passos has abandoned all the literary baggage which encumbered his exploration of New York—there are no elaborately painted descriptions and no Joycian prose poems. Dos Passos has studied Anita Loos and Ring Lardner for the method of *The 42nd Parallel*, and he is perhaps the first really important writer to have succeeded in using colloquial American for a novel of the highest

84

artistic seriousness. This has enabled him to keep us close to the characters as we never were in *Manhattan Transfer*. Dos Passos, in *The 42nd Parallel*, is not without his characteristic moments of allowing his people to lapse into two-dimensional caricatures of qualities or forces which he hates; but, in general, he has made us live their lives, see the American world through their eyes.

The characters of *The 42nd Parallel* almost all belong to the white-collar class—almost all begin as obscure and sufficiently commonplace-appearing people who are anxious to improve their condition from the point of view of ordinary American ideals. The stenographer from Washington, the publicity director from Wilmington, the interior decorator from Chicago, have no intimation of any other values than those of the American business offices, of the American advertising game, of the American trade in luxury, where they make their salaries and conceive their ambitions. Only the nephew of the radical Irish printer finds himself discontented with the life of the white-collar class and tends to identify his interests with those of a proletariat. The author introduces each of his five main characters separately—we read the complete continuous history of each from childhood. Dos Passos has hit upon a method of swift close narration which enables him to present an immense amount of material with astonishing ease and speed—we seem to know all about his people's lives: all the members of their families, all their friends, all their amusements and periods of stagnation, all the places where they work and how much they get, all the meals they eat, all the beds they sleep in. And without any explicit commentary of the author, each of these series of incidents and details creates an unmistakable character. Eleanor Stoddard's cold-blooded shrewdness and passionate appetite for refinement, J. Ward Moorhouse's well-meaning and unconscious charlatanry, are presented entirely in terms of *things*. And when these commonplace individuals, who have been introduced independently of one another, are finally put into relation with one another, further significances begin to appear—we realize that what we have been witnessing is the making of our own contemporary society. And as Dos Passos marks in masterly fashion—always without explicit comment—the shift from one American city to another, so that we understand, without, apparently, having been told, the difference between the way people behave and feel in Chicago and the way they behave and feel in New York, in Washington, Minneapolis,

Pittsburgh or Mexico City; so—also without, apparently, being told—we finally begin to understand the national character of America. Dos Passos has sandwiched in between the sections of the life-histories of his characters 'newsreels' which are medleys of newspaper-clippings and which remind us of the American public consciousness contemporary with the private events of which we have just been hearing, and brief biographies (very well done) of eminent contemporary Americans, all hampered or perverted or stunted by that same middle-class commercial society in which the characters of the novel are submerged. And at the end of this first instalment of his story, with the entrance of the United States into the War and the introduction of the last of the characters, a young garageman from North Dakota, who in his wanderings around the country has fallen in with a rich and drunken cracker from Okechobee City and been persuaded that he ought to go over and see the fun 'before the whole thing goes belly-up'—Dos Passos, in the perfectly aimed final paragraphs, shows us this character suddenly as a symbol of the United States, provincial, adventurous, well-intentioned, immature, going out from its enormous country into a world of which it knows nothing:

[Quotes from last page of *The 42nd Parallel*.]

The 42nd Parallel, when it is finished, may well turn out to be the most important novel which any American of Dos Passos's generation has written. Dos Passos seems the only novelist of this generation who is concerned with the large questions of politics and society; and he has succeeded in this book in bridging the gap, which is wider in America than anywhere else and which presents itself as a perpetual problem to American literature and thought, between the special concerns of the intellectual and the general pursuits and ideas of the people. The task of the intellectual is to make his symbols and his ideas *seem* relevant to the common life even when they actually are—to express them in terms of the real American world without either cheapening them or rendering them vacuous. Dos Passos, who has read as much and traveled as widely as Wilder, does not always avoid spinning literature— especially in the first Huckleberry Finn section of *The 42nd Parallel*—when he should give us a first-hand impression of reality; and, in consequence, he is sometimes flimsy, where Dahlberg dealing with a similar subject, would be authentic and hard. But though in intensity and execution *The 42nd Parallel* is not superior to Hemingway, for example, from the point of view of its literary originality and its intellectual interest, it seems to me by far the most remarkable, the most encouraging American novel which I have read since the War.

20. Upton Sinclair, review, *New Masses*

April 1930, vol. v, 18–19

Sinclair (1878–1968), an American novelist and journalist, is best known for *The Jungle* (1906), his book about the Chicago stockyards, but he wrote more than sixty novels during his lifetime, many of them polemics in support of various liberal causes. Early in his education, Dos Passos had read and admired his work.

Two or three years ago I stood on a street corner in New York for half an hour, arguing with John Dos Passos about the form of the novel. It was the right sort of place, the sort he likes, with plenty of rattle of machinery, honk of automobile horns, and other evidences of mass activity. I was trying to make an impression on him. What I said was, in brief this:

'I have just been reading *Manhattan Transfer*. You have put into it the material for several great novels, and also the talent, insight, and knowledge of our times. But for me you spoiled it by that kaleidoscope form you put it into; giving me little glimpses of one character after another—and so many characters, and switching them back and forth, so fast, that I lost track of the stories, and half the time couldn't be sure which was which. It is my belief that if you would put into a plain, straightaway narrative the passion and humor that is lost in *Manhattan Transfer*, you would have a great novel.'

I didn't know if I produced any impression; so I looked into *The*

42nd Parallel with no little curiosity. What I found this time is a sort of compromise between the two forms. The jazz effects are still here, but we get larger chunks of story, and so we don't lose track of them. What we have really is five novelettes, tied together with frail and slender threads. In between the chapters is a lot of vaudeville material, some of it funny, and some of it interesting, and some of it just plain puzzling to my old-fashioned mentality. Let us dispose of this vaudeville material first.

Some of the sections are called 'Newsreel,' and consist of a jumble of newspaper headlines. All newspaper headlines are absurd, as soon as they become a year or two old. They are like our fashions: revealing a stupid and vicious people trying to appear magnificent and important to themselves. We are willing to see them ridiculed, just so soon as they are out of date—that is, when they no longer touch our present delusions. Anyone may laugh at 'Teddy' Roosevelt and at Harding; but of course he mustn't laugh at the great engineer who is curing unemployment by blowing blasts of false statistics.

Another set of interpolations tells us about some of the leaders of that time: Debs, Bryan, Burbank, Lafollette, Bill Haywood, etc. These are interesting enough, and as they are short, we don't mind them especially. But I cannot say the same about the third variety called 'The Camera Eye.' These are queer glimpses of almost anything, having nothing to do with the story or stories, and told as if they were fragments from an author's notebook, or perhaps from his dreams. Maybe they are what happened to Dos Passos himself as he grew up through this period of his novel. Maybe he will tell me some day. He hasn't told in this book.

Now for the five main stories. First, Mac, a working-boy who turns Wobbly, and gets into the Mexican revolution. Second, Janey, a girl whose home life is unhappy, and who becomes a stenographer. Third, J. Ward Moorehouse, a lad who is bound to rise in the world, and becomes a 'public relations counsel,' one of these magnificent, 'Poison Ivy' Lee creatures who for a hundred thousand dollars or two will cause the American public to believe that glycerine mixed with toilet perfume will cure pyorrhea, or that high wages are bad for public morality. Fourth, Eleanor Stoddard, a young lady seeking culture, who learns to decorate homes for the rich. And fifth, Charley, another working-boy, who goes to the war.

The ties which bind these five into the narrative are of the very thinnest. Mac sees and hears about Moorehouse while the latter is doing his stuff on behalf of the American oil crowd in Mexico. Janey is there as Moorehouse's stenographer. Eleanor does some decorating for Moorehouse, and becomes his high-minded friend. As for Charley, who comes in at the very end, all he does is to hear about Moorehouse. One can imagine Dos Passos saying to himself: 'Go to, I am sick of these closely knit novels, which are full of coincidences and improbabilities, and with everything obviously contrived. I am going to write a novel that is like life itself, in which most of the boys whom Moorehouse helped send to war don't ever do any more than just hear him mentioned.'

All right, Dos, that is according to reality. But then, I point out to you that it is also according to reality that the great J. Ward Moorehouse knows a whole lot of people, and why couldn't we have had these in the novel, just as well as those who didn't know him? The point of my kick is not any delusion about the ancient 'unities' of a work of art, but merely the fundamental fact of human psychology, that when we have got interested in a person we want to know more about him; and if, after you have got our interest all worked up, you just shunt us off to some other character, we are not clear in our minds why you should have introduced us to either one. J. Ward Moorehouse is, I venture to assert, one of the most convincing characters in modern fiction, a real creation, simply gorgeous; and I am grumbling because, instead of telling me all I want to know about him, you switch me off to Charley, who is all right too, only less so, and who comes in at the very end, when there isn't room to tell me much about him.

If Dos Passos won't take my word, maybe he will take the example of Theodore Dreiser. When it comes to writing, Dos can make circles around Dreiser—who is, I firmly believe, the very worst great writer in the world. Also Dos has a clearer mind, he knows the revolutionary movement, which puts him a whole generation ahead of Dreiser's old-fashioned muddlement and despair. Furthermore, Dos has an impish humor, a quite heavenly impishness, if you know what I mean. All these gifts ought to make him our greatest novelist, and the one reason they don't is that he is so afraid of being naive that he can't bring himself to sit down and tell us a plain straight story, that we can follow without having to stand on our heads now and then, or else turn the page upside down. Dreiser is not afraid to be naive; he is willing to take a common ordinary bell-hop, and tell us about him to the extent of some four hundred thousand words—miserably written words, many of them—and yet, at the end he gets hold of us so that he was able to make a best seller out of a story that ends with the electric chair.

While I am registering my kicks, I want to beg Dos Passos to use a dictionary. His book is full of the sort of errors which publishers and printers' readers usually take care of. Molasses gets an extra 'l' while Lafollette loses one. Such common names as Bismarck, Folkestone and Dick Whittington each lose a letter. Bill Haywood is Heywood four times and Haywood only twice. Sometimes there are errors which may be jokes, who can say? On page 79 'Mac dosed off to sleep,' and on the same page 'a dog barked at him and worried his angles.' That is the sort of thing with which James Joyce is amusing himself in his new effusion—only you have to know twenty or thirty languages, and all history, ancient and modern, to appreciate the Joyce puns—and I am never going to.

Also, I want to know, just as a matter of curiosity, why the punctuation mark known as the hyphen should be considered counter-revolutionary. I noted one or two in the book, but I think they got in by accident. Dos Passos runs his compound words together, and when first our eye lights on them, we may not sort out the syllables correctly; I didn't, and got some funny effects— such as 'riverbed' and 'gass-tove' and 'teaser-vice' and 'co-algas' and 'musicle-ssons.'

Enough with fault finding. I want Dos Passos to be the great American novelist, as he is entitled to be. I want him to 'become as a little child' again, and tell us a good, straight, bedtime story, to keep us awake all night. The reason I take the trouble to write this discourse, is because, in spite of all the handicaps he takes upon himself, he has written the most interesting novel I have read in many a long day. I happened recently to read the last volume of Paul Elmer More, in which that very august academic gentleman, leader of the so-called 'Humanist' movement, condescends to refer to *Manhattan Transfer* as 'an explosion in a sewer.'[1] Well, there is a little of the sewer in this new book also but not proportionately as much as there is in America and the lives of its people. I will conclude my review of *The 42nd Parallel* by the prophesy that they will be teaching this book in high schools in future years, when the teacher will have to go to some old encyclopedia to look up Paul Elmer More and the 'humanists,' in order to find out when they lived and what they taught.

NOTE

1 See No. 16.

21. Unsigned review, *Bookman* (New York)

April 1930, vol. lxxi, 210–11

Like *Mahattan Transfer*, this book is experimental in form. It contains four series of compositions, arranged like a scrapbook with no apparent order. These are: (1) short biographies of noted Americans, told in a form bordering on free verse, with considerable seasoning of Menckenesque irony; (2) 'news-reel'; (3) 'the camera eye'; and (4) five tales, told in excerpts, about two hobos, a publicity man, and two working girls.

The nineteen sections of the 'news-reel' are arranged chronologically within the years 1900–1917. They are pastiches of scraps of headlines and news-stories and popular songs, and must represent considerable grubbing in old files. In expressionistic style they give vivid ironical pictures of the times they represent.

In 'the camera eye' Mr. Dos Passos once again indulges in Joycean expressionism. These twenty-seven short passages present scoops from the stream of consciousness of some youth—perhaps the author?—from infancy to manhood. Here the author carefully shuns hyphens and coherency.

But these are mere interludes in Mr. Dos Passos's vaudeville program. The reader finds real interest, if anywhere, in the five tales. These are told in that carefully naive condensed, colloquial style that Ernest Hemingway, among the followers of Stein and Joyce, has most successfully affected. They are, in pleasant contrast to the interludes, perfectly coherent, and contain abundance of vivid and convincing observations of life, particularly on its seamy side. The five characters' peregrinations take them all over the North American continent, and display, on the part of the author, an extraordinary knowledge of local color, particularly that tint seen in bawdy houses and saloons.

Despite the vividness of detail, however, the total effect is disappointment. In *Manhattan Transfer* one felt a unified theme: an attempt to portray the disordered complexity of the life of a great city. The author's scrapbook technique was, in view of this theme, justified. Here there is no such justification. From the title and the opening quotation on meteorology one is led to hunt a geographical motif, and one is unsuccessful. Such a motif would seem *a priori* rather futile; and as a matter of fact the characters range from Winnipeg to Mexico City. At the end we willingly suspect the author of a not very funny joke at our expense.

Apart from the title, the characters, though some of them meet, lead unrelated and insignificant lives, and not one of their stories has, in an artistic sense, an ending. Perhaps the author has given himself to that naturalistic creed which denies the existence of ends in life, and hence refuses to make endings in fiction. It remains a fact about human nature, however, that readers most enjoy stories which, in Aristotle's phrase, have a beginning, a middle—and an end. Finally, the very absence of any coherent scheme and of any explicit underlying idea, coupled with the author's bitter naturalism, yields an impression of futility. One must conclude that here again we have a sample of the naturalistic pessimism and spiritual anarchy which mark our age.

22. V.S. Pritchett, 'The Age of Speed', *Spectator*

27 September 1930, vol. cxlv, 421–2

Pritchett (b. 1900), the English critic, has held visiting appointments at many British and American universities. He is author of more than thirty books, both fiction and non-fiction, including several collections of essays and books on Balzac, Turgenev, and George Meredith. His review of *The 42nd Parallel* is excerpted from a review essay which also covered new novels by Phyllis Bentley, Rosamond Lehmann, and Heinrich Mann. All four novels, Pritchett noted, were conspicuous for their lack of direction and slow pace. Where narrative technique was concerned, Pritchett felt Dos Passos ought to abandon 'mechanical stunts and devices'.

The 42nd Parallel is about everything—everything that happens in the America of labour agitators, underdogs, men 'on the bum,' spurious Big Business men, their wives, mistresses and secretaries. Not only everything that happens in America, for there are interpolated tape-machine extracts from the news of the world. The book is divided mainly between six life stories which converge eventually in the Great War, but there is no emotional unity to it, for once the convergence is vaguely effected, the narratives peter out. The first life story, that of a young printer and labour agitator, who eventually drifts into Mexico; and the last, that of an underdog who gropes blindly through the squalor and violence of the slums to the War, are the best. The Business Men are tedious. Mr. Dos Passos is, like all the modern American realists, a reporter, a community singer, who is obsessed with the idea that he has got to shout the whole history of the United States since 1900 through a megaphone. He has no emotions, only moods: moods of revulsion, satire, lyricism, sensuality. He writes with startling, kaleidoscopic vividness. He has vitality. The opening chapters suggest that, if he abandons mechanical stunts and devices, and leaves American history and biography to look after themselves, he has the makings of a first-class picaresque novelist—American literature's greatest present need. At the moment he is like a man who is trying to run in a dozen directions at once, succeeding thereby merely in standing still and making a noise. Sometimes it is amusing noise and alive; often monotonous.

23. Granville Hicks, 'Dos Passos's Gifts', *New Republic*

24 June 1931, vol. lxvii, 157–8

Hicks (1901–82) was an American Marxist critic and literary historian. Author of *The Great Tradition* (1933), a Marxist study of American literature since the Civil War, and *John Reed: The Making of a Revolutionary* (1936), Hicks became a Communist Party member in 1934. This is the third and last essay in a series Hicks wrote for the *New Republic* about novels that dealt with industrial life in America. The first two essays were on John Hay and Robert Herrick, respectively.

After the Civil War, most novelists devoted themselves, not to the themes which might have been suggested by the country's rapid industrial expansion, but to the life of the frontier, or of quiet rural sections, or of genteel streets in long established cities. The decade since the World War has shown a somewhat analogous, though less clearly defined, development. Such writers as Dreiser, Lewis and Anderson, by winning a large audience, may have given the impression that their kind of writing dominated the period; but the literary historian of the future is likely to find the decline in influence of these writers more significant than their popularity, and to note as the most characteristic and important development of the period the rise of such forces as the new sectionalism, Southern agrarianism, Humanism, and neo-Thomism. The impulse to record industrial America, to reveal its evils and work for its improvement, the impulse that moved through the novels of Robert Herrick, has in great measure spent itself; and the desiderata of large numbers of contemporary poets, novelists and critics are formal excellence, individual perfection and metaphysical enlightenment.

Most of the younger writers today find their themes in those areas of life, past or present, that are untouched by industrialism. John Dos Passos is an exception. And yet we cannot understand him without realizing that he too has felt, and felt strongly, the desire to retreat from the existing chaos and find refuge in the kind of life in which security reigns. When Martin Howe dreams of monastic calm in *One Man's Initiation*, when John Andrews plans a romantic tone poem about the Queen of Sheba in *Three Soldiers*, when Fanshaw Macdougan longs for Renaissance Italy in *Streets of Night*, they express an impulse with which their creator is not unfamiliar. When Dos Passos speaks in his own person, as in *Rosinante to the Road Again* and *Orient Express*, he shows how much he prefers *lo flamenco* to the qualities cultivated in industrial centers, and how much nobler he finds the life of Eastern deserts than that of Western cities. His very longing, in those post-war years, to visit Spain and Asia Minor is evidence enough of the strength in him of the emotions he shares with the writers who have turned their backs on 'the twilight madness of cities, the wheels, the grinding cogs, the sheets of print endlessly unrolling.'

But John Dos Passos has not turned his back. He has confronted every aspect, no matter how hideous, of contemporary life. Finding much that is hateful in that life, he has cast his lot with those who stay and fight, not with those who run away. His books show that as early as 1920, and probably earlier, he was contemplating the possibility of changing the social order. But something more than doctrinaire radicalism has kept his attention fastened on things as they are, some quality of mind, combining the ruthlessness of the scientist and the sensitiveness of the artist. *Rosinante to the Road Again* helps us to define the quality: here is a man hastening to Spain after the horror of the War; once there he seeks not to lose, but to find, himself; he studies the labor movement as well as peasant life, occupies himself with thoughtful books as well as beguiling adventures, discusses Spanish problems as well as Spanish wines. Compare this book with *Castilian Days*, and you will see that Dos Passos is not likely to be deceived as John Hay was; Dos Passos has the ability to see things for himself.

He returned to America, still trying to see for himself. The results are in his books, *Manhattan Transfer* and *The 42nd Parallel*, and in his two plays, *The Garbage Man* and *Airways, Inc.* In only one of these works, the second play, has he directly dealt with the factory system, and even in *Airways, Inc.* the strike is a secondary theme, subordinated to an account of commercialism triumphing over courage and hope. But as a picture of the kind of life industrialism has shaped, Dos Passos' books are unequaled. The many strands woven together in *Manhattan Transfer*—stories of actresses, journalists, bootleggers, lawyers, business men, politicians—combine in an overwhelming picture of megalopolitan civilization. In *The 42nd Parallel* the lives of a Wobbly, a stenographer, an advertising man and an interior decorator—characteristic products all of twentieth-century America—unroll before a curtain painted with sketches of persons and events of the nineteen-hundreds. In both books Dos Passos catches, as no other author has done, the peculiar quality of life in our era—the new forces and their effects on men's thoughts and actions.

To this resolute contemplation of American life, he has brought—and otherwise, of course, he would not be important—qualities not incommensurate with the task he has undertaken. He has, in the first place, the kind of poetic imagination that lies behind almost all first-rate prose fiction. I do not mean that Dos Passos is an important poet; on the contrary, I find only three or four poems in *A Pushcart at the Curb* that are even moderately distinguished; but he looks at people and things as a poet would look at them. This gift, as applied to the description of objects, is seen at perhaps its highest point in *Orient Express*, pages of which, without any of that straining for picturesque effect so common in travel books, thrust their scenes upon the reader's mind with a vividness that cannot be ignored. But his projection of character is quite as poetic, in the broad sense, as his description of places. What could be more richly, more persuasively imaginative than the presentation in *The 42nd Parallel* of the flow of Janey's mind during the canoe trip? Even in *Streets of Night*, which is surely Dos Passos' poorest book, the description of Wendell's progress from bar to bar, ending with his suicide on the bridge, has that kind of unchallengeable authenticity that is the sign of a true creator.

In the second place, Dos Passos is a radical. This is important, not because his social views color his novels—though they do—but because his communistic theories give him a definite and advantageous attitude toward the material he works with—since the communist, unlike the liberal, wholeheartedly accepts industry and all its natural consequences, rejecting only those features of our order that derive from the private ownership of property. John

Hay, as we have seen, could not understand the workers, nor is it likely that any of the concrete facts of industrialism, aside from the flow of dividends, were ever real to him. Robert Herrick saw many of the evils of capitalism, but his fundamental impulses were opposed not merely to capitalistic control of industry, but to industrialism itself. Neither attitude is possible for Dos Passos. All his temperamental longing for a world of peace and beauty and security has been canalized in his determination to build such a world in fact and upon the ruins of the existing order. On the one hand, he can accept industry because he has affirmed his faith in the possibility of controlling it with reference to human values; on the other hand, he can, in a different sense, accept the chaos of modern life because he has an ideal by which he can measure it and according to which he proposes to change it.

In the third place, Dos Passos is an experimentalist. John Hay was so limited by contemporary canons of novel writing that he divided his energies in *The Breadwinners* between a conventional love story and the vigorous new theme of industrial conflict. Robert Herrick tried in his earlier work to make the well built novel serve to portray the complexities of industrialized America; later he abandoned the effort, but the loose structure of *Waste* represented a break with older forms rather than an effort to create new ones. Dos Passos has from the very first sought for a form that would make it possible for him to have his say. Just as most of his poems are unconventional in structure, and as his two plays are drastically experimental, so his novels may be regarded as stages in an attempt to create a new kind of prose fiction. In *Three Soldiers* he hit upon the method of multiple themes and episodic narrative, the only method, if we are to judge from the failure of *Streets of Night*, that can serve his purpose, and the basis of all his subsequent experiments. *Manhattan Transfer* and *The 42nd Parallel* disclose extraordinarily ingenious and skillful variations of this method. Though it is rather difficult, as one reads the book for the first time, to recognize the pattern of *Manhattan Transfer*, anyone who cares to list the different episodes can easily detect their rhythm. A different and more easily defined rhythm makes itself felt in the longer episodes of *The 42nd Parallel*. It would be absurd to assert that there are no forms suited to material of this kind other than those Dos Passos has created; indeed, it is impossible at this point to be sure that they are the right methods for him, to say nothing of other writers; but he is surely sound in his belief that for such purposes as his the structure of the novel must be changed, and the originality he has already shown is at least encouraging.

Not even Dos Passos' most fervent admirer is likely to argue that he has yet written the kind of novel of industrial America for which we have waited seventy years. A good many episodes in *Manhattan Transfer* and *The 42nd Parallel* are left on the journalistic level, untouched by any poetic insight, unrelated to any centralizing vision. Sometimes, especially in *Manhattan Transfer*, the author's single-mindedness is betrayed by the intrusion of personal dilemmas; sometimes the characteristic futilitarianism of the age creeps slimily across the pages. Always there is the feelings that complete mastery is just eluding Dos Passos' fingers, that he just falls short of the insight that would make us say, 'Here is America; we have seen all the things this man describes, and yet we have not seen them; we have known all the elements of this America, but this America we have not known.'

Such reservations must be made, but there is no need of dwelling upon them. Already Dos Passos' accomplishments are more important than his failures, and his promise is perhaps more important than his achievement. For he seems to be pointing a way; he seems to be finding a path where conservatives such as Hay and liberals such as Herrick found none. His acceptance of industrialism, it now seems safe to say, is the advantageous approach; his experimentalism is the right technical attitude; his poetic imagination is an essential attribute. Of course the statement of such a formula is perfectly easy, but to have written the books that not only suggest the formula but also give it concreteness and validity is enough to place Dos Passos high among contemporary writers.

And perhaps we need to be reminded that, whatever happens to our social order, whether industry continues under private ownership or is taken over by a communist regime, the necessity for humanizing the machine will remain. Not all the problems of maladjustment can be solved by a change in the basis of control, nor can the elimination of injustice guarantee the development of a rich culture. There will still be tasks for the creative imagination, tasks that Dos Passos helps us to face with a firmer resolution and a steadier hope.

24. Mary Ross, review, *New York Herald Tribune Books*

13 March 1932, 5

To hear each of the instruments play separately its part of the score of a symphony could give but a faint idea of the richness and variety of the composition itself when strings, flutes, oboes, clarinets, horns, trumpets and drums are carrying each their part in a whole that is more than their sum. One or another may rule or recede; may pause or seem to fly against the current along which the theme is riding. Out of distinct entities the orchestra achieves a whole which is also distinct, but complex, as the differing qualities and pitches of tone melt together, modifying each other, in their common pattern.

It is in a pattern like this, but infinitely more complex, that *1919* is laid, like Mr. Dos Passos' preceding novel, *The 42nd Parallel.* Its elements are not tones of music, but the complex of emotions bound up in separate personalities, swayed by what surrounds them and in turn weaving their own fates, pouring out words and actions and feelings of whose meanings and motives they themselves are only partly aware.

1919 is a word-symphony of the war years. Working through words, the author cannot give simultaneously, as can the orchestra, the various qualities that are intermingled in a common rhythm, flowing continuously. Hence first one then another comes to the printed page. It may not be stretching the simile too far to say that his orchestration uses four instruments: The Camera Eye, subjection, lyric, bringing back at intervals the memories of a young man at Harvard, in Spain, France, Italy; Newsreel, the blare of newspaper headlines, snatches of popular songs, excerpts from the mouthings of statesmen, recalling the jerky rhythms, the errant undertones, of the war mob; a series of brief, edged biographies of men who were significant of those years; 'Meester Veelson,' Randolph Bourne, Joe Hill of the I.W.W. and Jack Reed, Paxton Hibben, 'The Happy Warrior' (Theodore Roosevelt); and interspersed with these, chapters in the stories of five young people—a girl from Texas, the daughter of a Chicago minister, a New York 'radical,' a sailor, a young poet with the Ambulance.

A novel could have been made of the stories of any one of the five, or of two or three as their ways accidentally cross, just as whole books have been written on lives of some of the men who emerge with most extraordinary clarity and force in Mr. Dos Passos' biographies of a half dozen pages or less. But though each individual has to the author the validity, the wholeness, which any part of a creative work must have to an artist, it is not merely a series of separate people in whom he is interested, but the movement and interaction of persons, of classes, and of circumstance whose conflicts and harmonies give the quality of a certain time in a certain part of our globe.

It is almost impossible to write about *1919* without making it sound confused, though this is the very last quality that could be imputed to a book with its really amazing economy and precision of word. Yet it is only fair to the author and to the reader who may not have seen *The 42d Parallel* (with which *1919* is continuous in time, though the two books are not dependent) to point out a plan so different from that of the conventional novel. The typography varies in accordance with shifts to the four different strands of the book. Once one has a feeling of the plan according to which it is constructed, these shifts are as natural as the point in the symphony at which the clarinets come through, or the violins take up the theme, or the drums are the beat that stirs one's pulses.

With Joe Williams, the sailor, one starts 'on the beach' at Buenos Ayres, then the steaming heat of the Port of Spain, the gray cold of Liverpool, back to Hampton Roads and the empty frustration of a war marriage, on to Bordeaux—a shuttle of ships, lodging houses, girls. Richard Ellsworth Savage, the poet, started life with the benefits of a gentility overcast by the story of a father of whom one did not speak until he was safely dead; his education included summer sessions as a bell-hop in a New Jersey hotel, winters at Harvard, a medley of drinks and poetry; the Ambulance abroad. In the story of Eveline Hutchins lies the life of a minister's family in Chicago, a girl's groping toward 'art' in Chicago, Santa Fe and

New York; the whirligig of the American Red Cross in France. 'Daughter' came from Texas, spoiled child in a household of men; at home in a car, on a horse; lost in Eastern boarding schools, in Italy, where she knew Dick. Benny Compton peered at Flatbush through thick spectacles. The old people were Jews, but he wasn't a Jew because he had been born in Brooklyn and they owned their own home. He made the high school debating team. He learned about the class struggle. Almost blind because they had broken his glasses, Benny ran the gantlet with the Wobblies in Everett, Wash. It was his twenty-third birthday, he remembered with a start, when he set out with a deputy sheriff from the dark doorway of the Federal Building in New York, handcuffed, bound for Atlanta.

Such, superficially, is the map over which *1919* is spread through these stories of five young people, into which from time to time, like the orchestral theme or the chorus of a Greek tragedy, break the interludes of Newsreel, to show the goosestep of a world at war, the Camera Eye, the unrolling of one person's moving film of experience, and the stories of actual men who made and were made by those times. This attempt to give the material which enters into the book, however, can barely suggest its range and depth, for of course its concern is not with outward circumstance and place, but the lives of these separate people and the patterns in which they are interwoven.

A conventional viewpoint is as remote from the book as a conventional form. Mr. Dos Passos ignores the barricades that we try to build up to protect ourselves and others—the substance of his story is the movement of life, its sounds, sights, smells; the feelings which stir us individually or in crowds, whether or not they are those to which we give lip service. Mr. Dos Passos's writing is always distinguished by a remarkable sensuous perception, but more than that, he has a directness, independence and poignancy of thought and emotion that seems to me unexcelled in current fiction. For this very reason *1919* will disturb or offend some of its readers. Their recoil will be in itself a mark of its force. No novel of this season or of many seasons past has set itself a more original or ambitious aim; none with which I am familiar seems to me to have surpassed it in power, range and beauty.

25. John Chamberlain, 'News Novel', *New York Times Book Review*

13 March 1932, 2

Chamberlain (b. 1903) was assistant editor of the *New York Times Book Review* from 1928 to 1933. He also reviewed books (one a day for a period of three years) for *Saturday Review*, *Harper's*, and *Scribner's Magazine*. His book on the failure of the Progressives to effect needed reforms, *Farewell to Reform*, was published in the same year as this review.

In *1919*, John Dos Passos continues his explorations in the modern American and Americanized world which began with *The Forty-second Parallel* and which will continue, one assumes, until the series is rounded off in either a trilogy or a tetralogy. The initial panel in the series commenced with an America that was growing up after the Spanish-American War; it ended, inconclusively, with Charlie Anderson, a kid from North Dakota, setting out for Paris at the outset of our own participation in the World War. *1919* goes on from where *The Forty-second Parallel* leaves off. We meet old characters (J. Ward Moorehouse, the public relations counsel, and Joe Williams, the sailor) from the first book, and some new ones are introduced. Meanwhile, history spins on its crazy way; the war is fought; the peace is negotiated; A. Mitchell Palmer starts his Red-hunting campaign, which is resisted by Walter Lippmann and others; Wilson collapses; the Unknown Soldier is buried at Arlington, with President Harding making a speech. Some lives are explored by Mr. Dos Passos with finality; some are left poised on the edge of the unknown and waiting for the third panel of this *comédie humaine*. The trick of interspersing the separate stories of various characters with 'newsreel' features (which recall to mind Mark Sullivan's books), with a 'camera eye' department designed to give Dos Passos's own point of vantage in the time and space under consideration, and with driving, often splenetic Whitman-esque biographies of significant Americans, such as Randolph Bourne, John Reed, Woodrow Wilson and Theodore Roosevelt, is resorted to once more, as it was in *The Forty-second Parallel*. This trick of evoking mood by interspersed data is, again, successful; it saves Mr. Dos Passos from being 'discursive' in the middle of tense narrative and yet it enables him to retain the values of discursiveness. Precedent for this sort of thing may be found in Hemingway's *In our Time*—a book of short stories that is made homogeneous by alternating each story with a bit of autobiographical observation that accentuates the relationship of Hemingway to his material.

Like *The Forty-second Parallel*, *1919* is primarily a 'news' novel. It is, of course, a satire on expansionist, 'on the make,' raffish and vulgar America—the America which is such a fertile field for Florida booms and brokers' loans that double overnight. As such, it is close to books of social history like Frederick Allen's *Only Yesterday*. But it is more than a mere satire; it is also true characterization—more so than *The Forty-second Parallel*. It is able to stick as close to the headlines of the newspapers as it does because its characters, after the manner of so many Americans, live in and by the news. Dick Savage, the Harvard man; Eveline Hutchins, the Chicago girl; Ben Compton, the radical; even Joe Williams, the sailor, all are 'conditioned' by the daily papers to an extent that novelists of the past would be at a loss to understand. Even the personal problems of these people are shaped by the news and the men who make the news; private life, in *1919*, is merely what can be snatched by way of love and amusement while one is knocking about the world between jobs or missions. The daily paper, and what it brings over the orange juice and coffee in the morning, takes the place, in Mr. Dos Passos, of creeds and codes and the gods of one's forefathers. Mr. Dos Passos is dealing with relativists in a relative world and expediency is king with every one save Benny Compton.

Because Mr. Dos Passos has realized that a shot fired in China, a kidnapped baby, a reconstruction finance corporation, a tennis tournament, a rumor that Baltimore and Ohio bonds are a good buy, and so on, can cause more perturbation or elation or depression in the minds of more people than traditional problems of virtue and vice, his novel is more true to life on a tightly meshed planet than most of us like to admit. We of megalopolis, of suburbs, must regulate our lives in relation to balances of trade. The universal solvents of our grandfathers' world were, in settled areas, the community and the church, and the values engendered thereof; the solvents of our own urban life are the stock market quotation pages, the rumors of wars, the bulletins of the booms and the depressions. To take an example of the point we wish to make, even those whose purchasing power has increased since 1929 have been conditioned by the news of the last two years to gloom and nervousness; we have become, almost literally, all eyes and ears. Everyone knows as much; but our novelists have been slow to realize it.

Mr. Dos Passos is, however, an exception; one may safely call him the most adventurous, the most widely experienced, the man with the broadest sympathies (we do not say the deepest), among our novelists since Sinclair Lewis bade goodbye to Martin Arrowsmith. Others of Dos Passos's literary generation— Thornton Wilder, Elizabeth Roberts, Glenway Wescott—have limited theatres of action; they stick to the world of Terence and Mme. de Sévigné, of the Pigeon River region of Kentucky, of a Wisconsin that looks to pioneer days and pioneer virtues. Hemingway, who is Dos Passos's closest competitor in exploring the modern jungle, has been almost solely orientated in personal problems raised by the war; he is, as Malcolm Cowley has said, 'not yet demobilised.' Scott Fitzgerald, in *The Great Gatsby*, has utilized strictly contemporary material for a modern comedy of disenchantment; and a number of Southern writers have become fascinated by an agrarian decay that has been hastened by the onrush of industrialism. But no one has ranged as widely in post-Dreiserian and post-Howellsian America as Mr. Dos Passos.

Because of their living in and by the headlines, Mr. Dos Passos's characters are, sometimes, very flat and transparent. Mr. Moorehouse, for instance; this dollar-a-year man, who takes a government job in Paris and is seen moving about at the Peace Conference, is a four-flusher. Every newspaper reporter knows it, yet he has a mighty reputation. Mr. Moorehouse lies to himself because he has a living to make. Dick Savage, the Harvard poet, becomes an opportunist, and is responsible for the death of Daughter, the girl from Texas, who is on the Near East Relief committee, because opportunism is the condition of his existence in a world torn by wars, both military and economic. He simply has to live. Eveline Hutchins, from Chicago and a minister's family, gets involved in a number of cheap and casual love affairs because she is not living in a society in which 'status' is predominant. Daughter, the Texan, throws herself away because unharnessed energy, such as hers, must sputter out on thin air. And Joe Williams, who might have been content in a different society under his own vine and fig tree, is thrown about the world on tramp ships because that is the fate of willing souls without much brain-power in the contemporary world. We know of no better portrait in literature of the poor, dumb, driven devil than this Joe Williams.

Two of Mr. Dos Passos's characters are sounded out with much tenderness, sympathy and comprehension. They are Joe Williams and Eveline Hutchins; no characterisations in *The Forty-second Parallel* can equal them. One character, Dick Savage, is less successful precisely because he has no character to get hold of. Daughter goes through the book like a rocket; she falls before we really can get a grip on her. Ben Compton is merely started on his route at the end of *1919*; he will undoubtedly figure largely in the third panel, along with Charlie Anderson of *The Forty-second Parallel*.

All of the characters, however, have a public reason for existing in Mr. Dos Passos's book. They are used as symbols, as commentary on the war and the peace, as well as exemplars of the comédie américaine. Through them we see, at one remove, how Clemenceau and Lloyd George turned the flank of Woodrow Wilson; we see the turmoil and the stridency of the nations at war and at peace. We go back to the newspapers of the war decade, not by visiting a library or a newspaper morgue, but by making the acquaintance of certain typical onlookers of the decade. These people's lives, with the exception of Benny Compton's, are a sort of ambulatory journalism; they reflect no deep meaning; even their tragedies pass away as a new crop of headlines calls the world to new news.

The prose instrument which Mr. Dos Passos has fashioned for himself in *1919* is vastly superior to that of *Three Soldiers*, his early war novel. Although it abounds in clichés, vulgarisms, curses, illiterate ellipses and shorthands of speech, the language of *1919* is really a literary language; Mr. Dos Passos has quintessentialized and distilled, compressed and foreshortened, until he is able to give the overtones of common chatter without resorting to a dreary literalism.

26. Matthew Josephson, 'A Marxist Epic', *Saturday Review*

19 March 1932, vol. viii, 600

Josephson (1899–1978) was one of the American literary 'expatriates' in Paris during the 1920s. He first achieved prominence with the publication of *Zola and His Time*. He went on to write *Portrait of the Artist as American* (1930), *The Robber Barons* (1934), and biographies of Rousseau and Stendhal. Josephson apologized to Dos Passos for the 'hatchet job' Henry Seidel Canby, editor at *Saturday Review*, had performed on his review of *1919*. Canby had cut the central part of the review in which Josephson had sided with Dos Passos's angry revolt against the bourgeoisie (Carr, *Dos Passos: A Life*, 297).

John Dos Passos has distinguished himself among contemporary novelists for ambition, resolution, and fecundity. Reading *1919* as a companion-piece to *The 42nd Parallel*, as the second volume of a tetralogy—or is it to be perhaps an American 'Comédie Humaine'?—one is enabled to glimpse much more of the hull of a huge literary cargo vessel, in the process of building, and to guess at the form of its upper decks and bridges. One tends to liken this series of historical novels, based upon the recent World War period, to Balzac's long work rather than to Zola's twenty-volume epic of *The Rougon-Macquarts* or to Thomas Mann's *Buddenbrooks*, because both of the latter were confined to a single family, although Zola's, to be sure, was a family of a thousand members spreading into every corner of nineteenth century Europe. Proust, on the other hand, devoted himself solely to the upper class of French society.

The size of the author's framework, his social-historical objective, must be borne in mind if one would not be confused by the quick, episodic shifting of scenes and characters. The hero of *1919* is not a single person, but a great crowd, and more specifically a group of types out of the crowd. From one to another of these types the eye of the novelist moves back and forth: now he records the fictive biography of a 'wobbly' in the American Northwest, now of a hypocrite, Harvard intellectual, now of a common, drifting sailor, or of a big publicity agent, or a middle-class Chicago flapper. These chronicles are systematically interlarded with a section of 'newsreel,' which is composed of a picturesque summation of newspaper headlines of the period; also with brief 'biographies' of period characters, as likely to be of underground revolutionary fame, like John Reed or Wesley Everest, as of wider public note, like J.P. Morgan or 'Meester Veelson.' The style of the historical digression, a loose, dithyrambic, occasionally brilliant (through imagery) free verse, offers a marked contrast to that of the main narrative, soberly colloquial, behavioristic, almost monosyllabic. Besides lending some artistic relief, the digressions also serve as a sort of vivid backdrop against which the characters pass in procession. Yet the general reader should not be greatly disturbed by the impressionistic and experimental interruptions; for each chapter of narrative is often a finished episode in itself, or a character portrait in action. Sometimes, as in the long opening chapter upon the sailor, Joe Williams, they form complete and absorbing novelettes in themselves.

If we feared, in reading *The 42nd Parallel*, that we were watching too many disconnected characters and scenes falling apart, this fear subsides before the increased effectiveness of *1919*. We sense the 'collective' character of the various world-historical developments which, driving the characters of the Dos Passos epic before them, move toward the climax of the war's end.

The whole work is further unified by the author's consistent view of the history he deals with: this, it is perhaps embarrassing to relate, is nothing less than Marx's materialist conception of history as determined by the means of production. Indeed, the consistency of Dos Passos is his shining distinction. Ever since the World War, it seems to me, Dos Passos has stubbornly refused to believe either in the benevolence of American capitalism or in the wonders of American prosperity. Rather, he has been numbered among those who longed to see the present order exchanged for that of a socialist and proletarian state. And although such principles may seem vexing to many citizens who are perfectly aware that this is a free country, in which everyone is free to find a job and save money, it is necessary to touch upon them in passing so that the particular, grim color of Dos Passos's novel may be better understood.

It is a matter of little surprise, then, that the account of Dos Passos's troop of American characters in no way resembles a Horatio Alger fable. Here in *1919* there are only driven beasts, eating, drinking, fornicating, sliding always toward the line of least resistance. This qualification goes for the types who represent learning or heavy industry, as for the sailors, 'wobblies,' and up-to-date stenographers. Many gently bred readers may possibly be forced to shut their eyes and stop their noses at certain pages, since the novelist writes with so much deliberate 'bad taste.' On the other hand, Earl Carroll and a few movietones selected at random have left this reviewer wondering what there is that the American public may still be shocked by. The fecal is left—and Dos Passos does use this occasionally, like a naughty boy, to rouse us or horrify us out of our indifference.

In any case, Dos Passos, energetic and impassioned novelist, is leading the way—while groping at times—toward a proletarian literature; that is, a literature of revolution, something which certain of our critics have been calling for. His novels strike one as being far richer than those of the pedestrian Upton Sinclair (whom, however, he has resembled enough in point of view upon America to have won a considerable European success). He is more imaginative than Dreiser, more intelligent than Sinclair Lewis, and exceeds both these able *tendenz* novelists in natural culture. Dos Passos is little more than thirty-five; has written a dozen volumes of prose fiction and drama, and is improving in power. He has his pronounced limitations, over which, one hopes, his courage and will may prevail.

One may well quarrel with his style, for one thing. In the direct narrative of *1919* there is, plainly enough, a systematic avoidance of all rhetorical elegance, adherence only to bare, factual chronicle of outward movements, which admits of no 'inwardness' in the characters. In this behavioristic manner certain of our modern neo-realists believe they approach their subject more closely than ever before, and without the intervention of sentiment. Yet it cannot be denied that such a method gives at times a monotonous and unlovely texture to the literary monolith which Dos Passos is building, however respectable his motives may be. Besides, he contradicts these motives in his digressive interludes which are done, as I have pointed out, in a picturesque and impressionistic free verse. On the whole, Dos Passos' innovations of language (ugly neologisms) and of style (a heedless colloquialism introduced into the text, a pell-mell syntax), seem neither appetizing nor important. Tolstoy wrote epic novels designed for universal reading without holding himself to a nearly monosyllabic vocabulary; Zola, save for the instance of one early novel, wrote a tolerably pure French; and both of them have been read by millions of proletarians.

One still has the feeling, finally, that Dos Passos portrays types rather than characters, though he does seem to work out the destiny of each type within the logical limits of heredity and background. One could wish that he had Hemingway's shrewd eye for character and the special accidents thereof, with which a bullfighter is pictured as so thoroughly a bullfighter. Yet if Dos Passos had such an eye, perhaps he would not have so remarkable a bird's-eye view for the collective and panoramic drama which he evokes in *1919*.

27. Compton Mackenzie, 'Film or Book?', *Daily Mail*

14 June 1932, 4

The most recent novel by Mackenzie (1883–1972), the popular English novelist, had been *Our Street* (1931). He was at work on *Water on the Brain* (1933). Edmund Wilson felt critics were not paying enough attention to Mackenzie's work.

To deny the strength and richness of *Nineteen Nineteen*, by John Dos Passos, would be as absurd as to deny the existence of the United States of America. It would be equally absurd to deny the effectiveness of the technique used to ram home the author's criticism of life.

Yet one lays down *Nineteen Nineteen* after reading it in much the same mood as one emerges from a good film. One remembers how good this incident was or that description, but the final effect is of confusion and emptiness. Mr. Dos Passos might retort that life itself is formless to-day, but is it any more formless to-day than it always was?

The publishers think that *Nineteen Nineteen* may come to be regarded as a great book. My own opinion is that the first reading will remain the most impressive. I am much more inclined to regard *Nineteen Nineteen* as a great book at this moment than I shall be inclined to regard it ten years hence, when I fancy it will have the effect of an old newspaper.

Interspersed with the various narratives of imaginary life-stories are little biographies of actual people. With one of those people I came into contact myself during the war, and Mr. Dos Passos gives such a completely false picture of this particular person that he has shaken my confidence in him as an interpreter of human character.

Whatever may be the artistic merits of *Nineteen Nineteen* it is a novel which should be read by those who wish to consider themselves abreast of modernity in the same spirit as people read the daily paper to consider themselves abreast of the news.

28. L.A.G. Strong, review, *Spectator*

25 June 1932, vol. clxviii, 910

Strong (1896–1958) was an English poet, novelist, and critic who wrote more than thirty novels and collections of stories, poems, and criticism. Also reviewed were J.C. Hardwick's *A Professional Christian*, Naomi Royde-Smith's *Madam Julia's Tale*, Guy Gilpatric's *Half Seas Over*, and T.R. Feveral's *Jocund Day*.

The author of *The Forty-Second Parallel* has more than earned his right to use any form he chooses, and we must accept the manner of his new book as an integral part of what he has to say. *Nineteen-Nineteen* consists of six or seven brief fictional biographies, so presented as to overlap, interspersed with short sections called 'Newsreel' and others called 'The Camera's Eye.' The biographies are written in traditional, straightforward English: the 'Newsreels' purport to be cuttings: the 'Camera's Eye' sections are for the most part written in imitation Joyce.

There would be a case for the critic who represented that the author had tried to make the best of both worlds, writing the main part of his book in straightforward, intelligible American, and then, realizing that seven biographies did not make a novel, pasting up the joins with matter which would keep him in with the modernists. The critic would be wrong, for the man who could write *The Forty-Second Parallel* must be sincere, and sufficiently expert to know what he is doing. We must therefore take Mr. Dos Passos' book for what it is, and, dismissing all preconceptions, try to understand what exactly he has set out to do.

The biographies illustrate different types, all rather pessimistically. Joe Williams, a sailor, is twice torpedoed, has innumerable sordid adventures, and marries his Del, principally because she reminds him of his sister. Del keeps their relationship to that level, until she has learned to reciprocate, from others: and finally, poor bewildered oaf, Joe gets his quietus from a bottle. Dick Savage, a typical undergraduate, lays the small foundations of a literary career, then goes to France in the volunteer ambulance service. From there he is sent to Italy, is indiscreet, and is shipped home. He returns to France with a commission, is once more sent to Italy, and loves Ann Elizabeth neither wisely nor well. Eveline Hutchins also went to France:

When they'd climbed into a thirdclass compartment they sat silent bolt upright facing each other, their knees touching, looking out of the window without seeing the suburbs of Paris, not saying anything. At last Eveline said with a tight throat, 'I want to have the little brat, Paul.' Paul nodded. Then she couldn't see his face anymore. The train had gone into a tunnel.

'Daughter' went to France too. Linking his characters by this device, Mr. Dos Passos contrives to give us a cross-section of American life as it was affected by the War. The interpolated 'Newsreels' and 'Camera's Eyes' are part of his pattern, though personally I believe he could have got his effect more convincingly in another way. The reason for all this palaver about the form of the book is simply that there are a number of English readers who would be deeply interested in it, if they could once get over the initial difficulties the form presents. *Nineteen-Nineteen* is not for weak stomachs, but, with this warning, I strongly recommend it.

29. K. Selvinsky and P. Pavlenko, 'Russia to John Dos Passos', *International Literature*

October, 1932, vol. ii–iii, 109

Selvinsky and Pavlenco were editors of the journal *Literature of the World Revolution*, published in the Soviet Union.

Dear Comrade,

Your two correspondents are Soviet writers who live in Moscow, on the other side of the planet, and are both attentive readers of your writings. As you probably know, many of your books have been translated in Russian, from *Three Soldiers* to *Manhattan* and *42nd Parallel*; *1919* is in the press. Your works have played quite a part in our literary controversies. And this is quite comprehensible. The boldness and originality of certain of your artistic methods and your powerful devices for representation make necessary an analysis of their ideological significance, of the principles they involve. Why is this? All of us here in the lands of the Soviets feel that we are pioneers and bricklayers of the new communist culture. For the creative work of most of us there is one problem of paramount importance: what is the method of dialectical materialism in literature which would enable us to obtain the profoundest artistic perception of reality possible? We aim at verifying all aspects of literary productions—their themes, the choice of heroes, the methods of depicting these heroes and of drawing comparisons—from the viewpoint of their class significance. The influence of capitalism still survives in human consciousness and literary creativeness and we are all soldiers in the fight against these survivals. This struggle determines, today, our interests as writers.

We want from this standpoint to tell you about your *42nd Parallel*, while the impression it made on us is still fresh in our minds (it was recently published here). This book made a great impression on us. You relate the history of your heroes, famous Americans, with a skill truly wonderful. You have discovered a striking and exact method of recording phenomena in their ebb and flow. But in your efforts to be as objective as possible you tend to become mentally divorced from life. In striving to 'catch the moment', you fall under the influence of James Joyce's *Ulysses*. The stenographic reports of daily happenings in your *42nd Parallel* involuntarily call to mind the empirical method of James Joyce, which attempts to make an inventory of the world like a sheriff or law agent in carrying out his duties. This is not our approach, but a bourgeois one. Our task is not merely to see the world. We don't want to be like ants, crawling from one speck of earth to another. Our task is to understand the true structure of the world in order to change it. The fact that an artist's vision is conditioned by a definite viewpoint is no indication of prejudice. This was very well understood by Goethe whose centenary is now being celebrated by the whole cultured world.

We are interested in all these artistic problems not for their own sake. For us they are closely bound up with the class struggle for reconstructing the world in which we want to fight with the weapon of our creative work. Your sketch on Harlan is a case in point. Here, also, as an artist, you are honest and objective. But you shed light on one enormous phase of contemporary life which the bourgeoisie hopes to conceal. The struggle continues. The terrible pictures you draw of Kentucky are for all the world like the incidents described by Bill Heywood in his well-known auto-biography. Whole decades lie between these two stages of American history. But exploitation and the terroristic methods employed by the capitalists against the proletariat not only have not undergone radical changes but have become still fiercer. The struggle intensifies. Everything is full of this struggle. And the artist's creations, his inner world, cannot be something apart.

In all lands today, the capitalists have mastered a new tactic. Its essence is in camouflage. Loud speeches about prosperity while millions are unemployed. Diplomatic high masses at Geneva and the rattle of machine-guns in Shanghai. The blow struck by Japanese imperialism in the Far East gives rise to exceptional concern. The fact that peaceful Chinese are shot down and their lands seized with impunity—a state of war without its official declaration—is an eloquent example of imperialism's new tactic. These happenings are also one of the reasons for our writing this letter. It is difficult to separate creative writing from politics. The one is but the continuation of the other. The events in the Far East have no less right to the attention of the civilized world than the celebrations at Weimar, whither the bourgeois press hopes to turn all eyes (this it does with the express purpose of drawing attention from other matters). The lullabies of the press, the mumbling of the League of Nations, and Japan's policy of plunder—these are not isolated affairs but links in a single chain of imperialist machinations. The imperialists may quarrel among themselves. But they see a common enemy in the revolutionary proletariat and the Soviet Union, the land of the victorious proletariat. The fact that we are successfully building socialism is sufficient to make the capitalists seek every possible means to destroy us. We must not forget this. The bourgeois press loves to accuse us of being unduly suspicious. But the facts, unfortunately, have another tale to tell. We are surrounded on all sides by provocation.

That is why all who hold dear the cause of socialism, which the Soviet proletarians are building, must be active in exposing and fighting the policies of the capitalists. We regard you as our friend, that is, the friend of our cause. And it is our desire that you, like Romain Rolland, come out in the press against the new tactic of imperialism, which is planning a new world war from the East, which is planning to invade the Soviet Union.

We should greatly appreciate a reply to our letter and hope to keep up our literary discussion with you.

With fraternal greetings

K. Selvinsky
P. Pavlenko

30. Michael Gold, 'The Education of John Dos Passos', *The English Journal*

February 1933, vol. xxii, 95–7

What follows is the conclusion to Gold's summary of Dos Passos's political education. Gold hoped Dos Passos would develop Whitman's faith in the 'American masses' on which his 'future revolutionary growth' depended.

In 1930 John Dos Passos published his *42nd Parallel*, first novel of a trilogy which is to document American life for the two momentous decades, 1910–1930. The second volume, *1919*, appeared last year. These two books mark a turning point in the career of John Dos Passos, besides having won recognition as new landmarks in the history of American literature.

They extend the experiment begun in *Manhattan Transfer*. There he tried to portray all of the life of a great city; now he has tried to digest a continent.

The architecture of these novels is masterly, and has provoked discussion among the critics—I am not exaggerating—of all Europe, America, and Asia. The novel has always been the most fluid of all fiction forms, but Dos Passos has enlarged its range. James Joyce wrote in *Ulysses* the ultimate novel of the tortured consciousness of the bourgeois individual. Dos Passos has written one of the first collective novels. I envy his achievement rather than that of Joyce's, for Dos Passos leads to the future. The collective emotion is the new and inevitable hope of the world. In every land the young writers have been effected by the Communist movement which is building the new collective society, where men will be brothers, instead of bitter, futile, competitive individuals. And these young writers, trying to speak in art what they have felt in life, must find new forms. Dos Passos has hewed out at least one path for them.

There are really a dozen novels in these two books, fitted together in a continuity and context that makes each narrative a comment on the other. Dos Passos ranges through all the strata of the social order. He is the geologist and historian of American society. The characters whose lives are followed through war and peace are a stenographer, a publicity man, an I.W.W. migratory worker, an interior decorator, a sailor, a minister's daughter, a Harvard graduate, an impulsive Texan, a Jewish radical from New York.

Some of their stories interlock; in the last volume of the trilogy all the loose ends will probably be tied. What we have now is a cross-section of American humanity which, as much as any history, gives the authentic inside facts of the past twenty years.

To add historic poignancy to these individual lives, and to relate them to their background, there is a Greek chorus of newspaper headlines and Americana. This adds to the strangeness of the novels, yet, after careful reading, one finds them an organic part of the massive effect at which Dos Passos was aiming.

So, too, are the score or more of cameo biographies of significant Americans which Dos Passos has interpolated on his narrative. Bryan, Debs, John Reed, Bill Haywood, Burbank, La Follette, Edison—these terse bitter passionate portraits add an extraordinary flavor of historic truth to the novels, and contain, besides, germs of the future revolutionary growth of John Dos Passos.

It is a chaos again, but Nietzsche said 'one must have chaos to give birth to a dancing star.' In the complexity and confusion of these novels the drive is felt toward a new communist world; and, if the aesthetes and gin-soaked Harvard futilitarians are present, it is that they may serve as contrast to the obscure, almost unmarked hero of this epic canvas—the rising Proletaire.

Granville Hicks, English professor at Rensselaer Polytechnic, and a leader among the younger men who are reviving the art of criticism and making it a formidable arm in the war between the old and new cultures, must be permitted the last word on these novels:

What *Three Soldiers* barely hinted, what *Manhattan Transfer* merely suggested we might dare to hope, these two books make it reasonable to assert; we now have an American writer capable of giving us the America we know....

We can say now that the Harvard aesthete in Dos Passos is almost dead. The spiritual malady of tourism no longer drains his powers. He has entered the real world. He has definitely broken with capitalism, and knows it is but a walking corpse. He wars upon it, and records its degeneration. But he has not yet found the faith of Walt Whitman in the American masses. He cannot believe that they have within them the creative forces for a new world. This is still his dilemma; a hangover of his aristocratic past; yet this man grows like corn in the Iowa sun; his education proceeds; the future will find his vast talents, his gift of epic poetry, his observation, his daring experimentalism, and personal courage enlisted completely in the service of the co-operative society. He does not retreat; he goes forward. Dos Passos belongs to the marvelous future.

31. Clifford Bower-Shore, review, *Bookman* (London)

December 1933, vol. lxxxv, 198–9

At the time of this review, Bower-Shore had just completed a short book on Lytton Strachey. I have omitted the first three paragraphs of the review, which summarized Dos Passos's career.

Dos Passos seeks to discover the power that nullifies and thwarts the hopes of the people. He recognises the futility of the planning of lives, and acknowledges the incalculable power which is dominative and wantonly destroys the carefully laid schemes of humanity. Fully aware that everyone works, consciously or unconsciously, towards a definite, and in many cases an identical goal, Dos Passos questions their failure to attain that objective. His preoccupation with this theme was responsible for *The 42nd Parallel*, an odd yet perversely brilliant book consisting of several distinct narratives, all of which converge on the entry of America into the Great War. In this work Dos Passos exploits a new form of fictional technique. From his experiments it is clearly apparent that Dos Passos aims to portray life as a whole, at the same time presenting a series of individual experiences. His method of interpolating the main narratives with what he terms 'Newsreels'—which summarise in the form of newspaper headings and paragraphs, typical happenings in America and abroad from the nineties to the outbreak of war—and 'Camera Eyes'—intimate flashes of thought and life of a boy (the author himself) during the transition from childhood to maturity—is not entirely successful, a fact of which Dos Passos is well aware, for he has intimated that it is only a temporary expedient. He hopes later to achieve the unification essential to the success of such a literary experiment. *The 42nd Parallel*, in keeping with all Dos Passos's work, is an ultra-realistic narrative, frequently squalid and often incoherent, but illuminative in its revelation of American life. Here is J. Ward Moorhouse, business magnate, insufferable prig, and asinine follower of the creed that adopts prosperity as the synonym of righteousness—perhaps the greatest, certainly the most caustic of all Dos Passos's character creations.

Nineteen-Nineteen, Dos Passos's latest novel, carries on the theme of *The 42nd Parallel*, and interlards its various narratives with newspaper extracts and acid commentaries on the passing world. The period covered is from the entry of America into the Great War to the close of 1919. It is a raw and bitter book, but it scintillates with a savage brilliance. The narratives starkly reveal the degenerative effect of war on the ordinary merchant seaman, the doughboy, the pacifist, the neurotic, sex-starved woman, the young girl eager to go to France for war work and the revolutionary. Their reactions are laid naked by callous dissecting skill. This is no portrayal of the war of the trenches, of physical wounds and bloodshed. It is an acute reflection of the struggle of the mind, and a story of the chaotic influences of war, that malignant, parasitic growth from which flows licence, greed and a macabre, careless fun. *Nineteen-Nineteen* is a chronicle of humbug and cruelty, violence and subtle horror. But beneath the rugged surface there is latent beauty, and a quiet sympathy and pity. The brief biographical sketches of Morgan, Roosevelt, Meester Veelson and Wesley Everest are trenchant and powerful, the latter being a perfect cameo of horror—but it is not wise to shirk reality. Dos Passos is a man of abnormal energy and ultra-sensibility. Devoid of such faculties, it would have been impossible for him to have written such a great and terrible book as *Nineteen-Nineteen*.

The vigour and fecundity of Dos Passos's imagination is

astonishing. He is a master and never the slave of words. His style is staccato. As an interpreter of modern life, the chaotic medley of his prose is akin to the irregular beat of life itself. Dos Passos has the power of intensifying the commonplace, rendering it impressive by repetition of detail. It is the *mind*—the conception—which is of salient importance to Dos Passos. With ironical observation he presents the infinite variety of American life and character in a revealing nudity. The characters he selects at random are typical of the thousands enslaved to the stifling grind of modern civilised life. They are at once graphically and delicately differentiated. Charged with a certain sparseness and grim innuendo, his work reveals the crudeness of the American. Through the microscope of genius one sees the squirming mass of human organisms which spread across a continent to make America. But Dos Passos not only portrays America and the American. His choice of the individual type stands as a representative symbol of universal character. The opulence of Dos Passos's social and moral criticism is equalled only by the brilliance and clarity of his introspective survey of that sham existence many people term life, wherein he reveals the world of clash between the superficial amenities of a smug civilisation and the inherent primitive instincts of human nature.

Like Dickens, Dos Passos recreates the farce and tragedy of his time. Always he appraises the forces that make life a stage for the setting of comedy and drama and tragedy: love and passion, jealousy and ambition, hate and despair. His all-embracing consciousness is revealed with penetrative venom, but despite his strength he does not wield the cumbersome bludgeon of invective. His irony is neat, his wit light. Although often sombre, his work is devoid of morbidity, and he overcomes minor defects of style by dynamic force of theme. He is no heavy moraliser, and his prose is free from that tortured and tautologous phraseology which detracts from the work of Dreiser.

Dos Passos is no facile and genial demagogue. He is in fact a trifle *gauche*. But he is sincere and vital. He has the power of seeing things suddenly; his conclusions are not the residue of any definable or discernible process. Immune from sentiment, but seeking the termini of the keenest emotions, Dos Passos is prone to attacks of manly sensitiveness. Eager, impatient, questioning, he has an unfailing insight into the motives and actions of his characters. A strict realist, a fearless adherent to trught, he has little time for the superficial abstractions of the shallow and romantic novelist. His brusqueness occasionally nauseates the sensitive palate, but he is never too brutally objective, nor is he unduly egotistical.

There is a certain insistence on sex in Dos Passos's work. But this only reveals that he is vitally concerned with the emotions of life. Sex is the most important instinct of life. The impulse is spontaneous and cannot lie—and is therefore a state of naked sincerity. It is essential that matters of the flesh be treated with a vital warmth and not with the snobbish coldness of the intellect. Dos Passos details love—or lust—episodes with an unflinching physical force.

Undoubtedly John Dos Passos has lived. His work throbs in every line with an all-dominating intensity of feeling for life. He has been triumphantly sensitive. He has felt insults and splendidly avenged them. Looking at life, he finds it mysterious and terrible. But he is also impressed by the wonder of it—and the occasional beauty. He is mildly obsessed by the apparent helplessness of human beings to thwart their predestined end, their futile struggles against inevitability. Endowed with that masculine creative fertility and brooding intuitive power—a powerful combination essential to the making of a great novelist—Dos Passos's view is not one of extraordinary detachment or serenity, but one of hearty and ordinary dislike. Rigorously detailing human experience as he does, Dos Passos must dilute the sombre with the expression of light, and his hearty, pungent hilarity is thrown into bolder relief by the contrasting tones of bitter experience. His grisly humour is reminiscent of Carlyle, for it is more in the style than the matter.

The bulk of Dos Passos' work betrays a marked leaning towards the political 'left,' but it never degenerates to class propaganda. Writing of the present day when ethics are severely subordinated to economics, when to seek the material is apparently the only thing that counts, and when life's worth is appraised merely by a financial standard of values, Dos Passos is an inveterate enemy of Mammon in high places and a vehement defender of the under-dog.

THE BIG MONEY

August 1936

---

32. Bernard De Voto, 'John Dos Passos: Anatomist of Our Time,' *Saturday Review*

August 1936, 3–4, 12–13

De Voto (1897–1955), the American critic and historian, was editor of *Saturday Review* from 1936 to 1938 (succeeding Henry Seidel Canby) and wrote the 'Easy Chair' column for *Harper's Magazine* from 1935 until his death. Author of a trilogy of histories covering the westward expansion across the frontier (including *Across the Wide Missouri* (1947)), he is best known for his studies of Mark Twain, such as *Mark Twain's America*, which stressed Twain's frontier background. In this review De Voto examines Dos Passos's development as a writer and questions the accuracy of his social history. He also notes Dos Passos's failure to invent memorable characters.

John Dos Passos has developed more consistently than any other American novelist of his time. With the exception of *Streets of Night*, which fell far below *Three Soldiers* and is surely one of the worst novels of the generation, every book he has written has been distinctly better than its predecessors. *The Big Money* is better than *1919*, which came out four years ago and was then easily his best novel. Whether it is the end of a trilogy, or whether it will be succeeded by a volume carrying the anatomy of our times still closer to today's headlines, cannot be made out—the method of discontinuity does not permit endings but only terminations, and there is no reason why the surviving Richard Savage, Margo Dowling, and Mary French should not move on into the depression years. But at any rate the enterprise, the most ambitious one that American fiction has embarked on since Frank Norris's unfinished trilogy of the wheat, has gone far enough to justify a few conclusions.

The habit of criticism, following the lead of Mr. Cowley's essay,[1] has been to divide Mr. Dos Passos's career into two parts, the unconverted years when he wrote his first three novels, and the years following the journey to Damascus when, tenderly loving those whom he had previously resented as vulgarians, he turned from an unmanly and individual estheticism to the social sternness of which *The Big Money* is the latest issue. The division is useful but deals only with accessory qualities of his work. For the faults of *The Big Money* are the faults of *Three Soldiers*, and its virtues are those of *Three Soldiers* and *Manhattan Transfer*. In the trilogy we have the mature expression of a mind that has worked toward an interpretation of American life. But the qualities of that mind were established in 1921, when *Three Soldiers* appeared, and the interpretation has developed in the channels then laid down without breaking through them.

Three Soldiers was a very courageous book, the more so in that America, having suffered least from the war, most strongly tabooed discussion of it. Barbusse and Latzko, who wrote while the war was actually going on, had preceded Mr. Dos Passos, but he was a good many years in advance of the reaction that gave us *The Revolt of Sergeant Grischa*, *All Quiet on the Western Front*, and a succession of novels akin to them. It had conspicuous faults and obvious merits. Of the latter, the most striking was the author's burning vision of his characters as mere atoms of personality buffeted by the tremendous forces in which they were caught. Most of its demerits were due to insufficient apprenticeship. The dialects, for instance, were almost indecently bad. Except for Chris, who spoke a combination of Georgia cracker and Minnesota squarehead, everyone, including Private Mandlebaum, expressed himself in a vaudeville Irish brogue as vile as any that has been called poetic in the plays of Eugene O'Neill.

But there were aspects of *Three Soldiers* which, if not defects, signalized biases or limitations of the author's mind which he has never since transcended. The novel, in so far as it was a representation of the A.E.F. and not a biography of three wind-tossed atoms—and it sometimes had to be such a representation—failed almost grotesquely to convey any feeling of experience. The choice of two deserters and a venereal victim loaded the dice to begin with. But what was much worse, the book nowhere suggested any of the fascination, the delight, or the consummation that made army service a fulfilment for many hundreds of thousands—and are, it may be, the most terrible attribute of war. There was none of the gusto, the male fellowship, the day by day satisfaction, the adventurousness, the honed senses, the awareness of common living splendidly stepped up which made the war a climactic experience—as anyone may verify by listening to two veterans over their beer. There was no pleasure in this most terrible, most deadly of pleasures—even the boys on pass going down to get drunk and find a mamselle seemed to be doing so drearily, lethargically, in a conviction of logical necessity rather than anticipation. There was not, even, any humor—the book contains no wisecracks, no jokes, none of the camaraderie of men at ease with one another. The result was, certainly, a memorable record of horror and brutality, but it left out many things that exist on the record, things that, rounding out the picture, might well have increased its horror. It narrowed the war to its impact on one mind, it was one man's initiation as Mr. Dos Passos put it in another title. It thus lost its representative purpose in a marked individualism—and came close to trivializing its subject by suggesting that the tragedy of war chiefly consisted of its preventing a sensitive man from composing a tone poem.

Time passed; Mr Dos Passos published his second and bad novel; he read Joyce, and in 1925 *Manhattan Transfer* appeared. Here, too, he saw his characters as mere filings in great fields of force but he had considerably matured his conception of those fields. His apprenticeship was over; he was now not only an expert technician but an experimenter as well. He had arrived at the novel of masses, which he had tried but failed to reach in *Three Soldiers*. It was the form which all his succeeding novels have taken: little groups of associates whose lives are carried forward discontinuously, whose planes only partly and infrequently intersect those of the other groups, who exist like the brush work of an impressionist painter less for themselves than for the canvas as a whole. He had worked out a swift narrative method, behavioristic and marvellously condensed, which gave the book a higher specific gravity than anything he had written before. It was an instrument excellently fitted to achieve the effects his new objectives called for.

He had also begun a revolt against the conventions of typography which, as he has gone on with it, has become increasingly annoying. It is at once pedantic, inconsistent, and absurd. He trips over his own principles, he is sometimes an enemy and sometimes an ally of the comma, he fiercely rejects the hyphen but crooks the pregnant hinges of the knee to the apostrophe. What is more to the point, he distracts the reader's attention from the matter at hand, to facilitate which is the sole purpose of typography, and so endangers the effect he sets out to produce. And he has begotten dozens of imitators who think that you can become a significant novelist by writing 'towhair,' 'legalaid,' 'toothick,' 'antisepticlooking,' and 'carvedivory.'... Whereas 'uneeda' and 'drivurself' are bourgeois Philistinism and, it may be, the rot of democracy.

Manhattan Transfer is a surface novel. A brilliant evocation of the metropolis, full of color and sound and movement, its patterns shift expertly between chaos and implied design. With every device that can serve versatility it assails the reader's imagination, hurrying him on with the breathlessness and rhythm of the crowds it symbolizes. But, though the surface is hard and jeweled, the book lacks depth. Mr. Cowley says that its lack of significance proceeds from the failure to establish a scale of social values, that like *Three Soldiers* it comes down to a basic assertion that life is is painful for sensitive people. But its true weakness is much simpler: the characters are not sufficiently alive to engage one's sympathies.

Mr. Dos Passos was interested in depicting mass man, the mass experience obliterating the individual. The war carried the theme in *Three Soldiers*, the metropolis in *Manhattan Transfer*. In the trilogy it is identified with the mighty currents of American life during the pre-war years, the war, and boom. He set an ambitious goal: to convey the movement of continental United States during more than a quarter of a century. In the maturity of his powers he has splendidly succeeded. In scope and in multiplicity no comparable achievement exists in our fiction. *The Big Money*, for instance, gives us not only New York but Detroit, Miami, and Hollywood as well; not only a Minnesota rural community but a Colorado mining town; not only brokers, promoters, publicity men, engineers, movie directors, inventors, senators, and salesmen, but labor leaders, social workers, literary socialists, communist organizers, and a counter-revolutionary; not only the insipid daughters of millionaires, hostesses of salons, wealthy widows, and suburban wives, but cabaret entertainers and a movie queen. This scale is maintained throughout the trilogy, and it is supported by a truly amazing fecundity of incident, and by a rushing narrative that is one of the finest technical accomplishments of our time. Mr. Dos Passos does indeed cover the continent from ocean to ocean, from farm to factory, from mine to mill, from proletariat to the master class. And he has mastered his details. He knows the provinces and geographies of America, the rituals and etiquettes, the creeds and superstitions, the avenues of tradition, the lines of force, the flowing shape of things. He has got a greater variety of them into fiction than any other novelist of his time.

1919 was a better novel than *The 42nd Parallel*, and *The Big Money* is better still, more in the round, more nearly three-dimensional, more mature and finished. It carries J. Ward Moorehouse, the Ivy Lee image, up to collapse and invalidism; and Richard Savage, his faintly poetic, faintly homosexual understudy, up to a partnership in his firm. Eveline Hutchins works through a series of adulteries to suicide. Ben Compton gets out of Atlanta and is excommunicated from the Party, in whose councils Don Stevens has risen so high that he makes a secret trip to Moscow. G.H. Barrow makes a good thing out of the trades unions. But the main burden of the book is carried by Mary French, a Vassar girl from Colorado who sleeps and weeps her way into the Party and finally into dedication to its purposes; by Margo Dowling, whose career takes her from a vaudeville act to Hollywood by way of a Cuban marriage and the most extensive whoring anyone has yet done in the series; and especially by Charley Anderson, who makes his first appearance since the end of *The 42nd Parallel*. Charley, whom we had seen as a farmer, garage mechanic, and hobo, has meanwhile been, it now appears, a member of the LaFayette Escadrille and something of an inventor. He patents improvements in airplane design, falls in with promoters and makes several killings on the stock market, boozes his way through his first partnership, through his marriage, and through a number of affairs, ending with Margo Dowling, and finally, bankrupt and burnt out, drives his car in front of an express train while drunk.

Accompanying all this are the rockets and pinwheels of Mr. Dos Passos's fantasia on the boom years, with the fateful shadow of collapse moving close. There are also a number of genre pieces, such as Margolies, the movie director, who gives the author a field day of caricature: he is done to a turn and he will not be forgotten. And there are—innovations. When Charley Anderson, getting drunk, passes himself off as Charles Edward Holden, the writer, he precipitates the first joke in more than a thousand pages of fiction. Irony Mr. Dos Passos has plentifully provided before, suave or corrosive at need, and a fine sardonic quality runs through most of his work, but this is the first bit of fun. It seems lonely in all that expanse of mechanized behavior. But there is another novelty: in Mary French's Daddy, in Charley Anderson's partner Joe Askew, and in the treatment of the death of Charley's mother one comes upon something recognizable as human emotion. It has not been perceptible in any of the death, violence, or torture that has gone before. Looking back over the trilogy, one can remember only one small incident when any of the characters seemed to be feeling anything at all, the passage in 1919 where the reluctant Sister, during a mountain rain-storm, was putting off Richard Savage to another time. She seemed to be feeling a genuine emotion at the time, which is more than she did when, pregnant and drunk, she started on the airplane ride that killed her. That incident in the rain stuck out as sharply as a metaphysician would in a novel by Ernest Hemingway.

With that realization we come to Mr. Dos Passos's principal deficiency as a novelist. How far it is also a deficiency of the fiction of mass man is indeterminable. It may be that the rigorous behaviorism of his method is what deprives his characters of intellectual life. It may be that you cannot show the interests and passions of the mind, its reveries, its analyses, its preoccupations, its satisfactions and anxieties, when you limit yourself to exhibiting only motor and verbal behavior. Certainly, no character in the trilogy thinks at all, none of them follows an idea for none has an idea to follow, and no intellectual value affects any of them in the least. But if that complete atrophy of the cerebrum must be charged to technical rigorousness, surely something other than technique is responsible for the atrophy of the emotions. A technique of fiction is only a means of presenting human beings—and human beings feel. But the automatons of Mr. Dos Passos do not feel.

They have no emotions of any kind. It is not only that the more complex pleasures and pains pass them by, so that they are not stimulated by anything esthetic or depressed by anything spiritual—but that all pleasures and pains pass them by. They sleep with each other every page or two and they drink enough liquor to make this the most eloquent temperance tract since *The Beautiful and Damned*. But they seem to enjoy neither the flesh nor the devil; they invoke both in a nerveless and even bodiless lethargy that looks like an abstract concept being mathematically worked out. They feel no lust and no love, nor any other of the common experiences of mankind. From page 1 of *The 42nd Parallel* to page 561 of *The Big Money* there is neither anger nor hate, neither loyalty nor admiration. neither affection nor fellowship, neither jealousy nor envy. Violent stresses are laid on the characters, their ambitions are frustrated, their bodies are mangled, savage cruelties and repulsive deaths are inflicted on them—but though they grimace they do not suffer. Oppress them and they do not cry out, cut them and they do not bleed.

But that is to say that one essential of fiction is slighted, that the atoms blown about the universe by Mr. Dos Passos's intergalactic winds remain atoms, remain symbols, and do not come alive. And so the reader does not much care what happens to them— interesting, spectacular, kaleidoscopic, pyrotechnic, expertly con- trived, a fine movie, but you remain untouched. Compared to Mr. Dos Passos, Mr. Sinclair Lewis, for instance, is an unsophisticated technician—but his people have nervous systems. More life resides in even the minor characters of a Lewis novel than ever gets between the covers of this trilogy. You remember what Fran Dodsworth was doing in 1929—what was Eleanor Stoddard doing a year later? J. Ward Moorehouse is a stylized statement of a conception—George Babbitt is a living man. Or, for an exact parallel, consult the Benda mask of E.R. Bingham in *The Big Money* and reflect on the hideousness, but the living hideousness, of Dr. Almus Pickerbaugh.... Not Mr. Lewis alone need be invoked. In the six novels of Mr. Dos Passos there is no one with blood and flesh comparable to Catherine Barkley, or Maidy Forrester, or Jean Marie Latour, or Jay Gatsby, or Dr. Bull, or Clyde Griffiths, or Studs Lonigan, or Oliver Gant. Whatever power and brilliance his art may have, it is only imperfectly an art of giving life to fictitious characters.

Now it may be that there are reciprocal forces in fiction—that if you want mass man, the movement of classes and groups and geographies, you must reconcile yourself to doing without individuals. And certainly it is the essence of Mr. Dos Passos's intention to reduce personality to a mere pulsation of behavior under the impersonal and implacable drive of circumstance. But it may be also that in opening to fiction the area which Mr. Wolfe calls the manswarm you risk depriving it of its preëminent value—the exploration of individual human nature that has been the unifying theme in all the diverse kinds of fiction. And it may be that the intricate and dazzling technique that has produced this trilogy rationalizes a personal inadequacy and veils an inability to come to grips with experience. Why otherwise would the short biographies of real people interspersed through the narrative of imaginary ones have so much more feeling and so much more vitality? And certainly, when the individual disappears from fiction the most powerful means of enlisting the reader has gone also, and in achieving a map-survey of America through a quarter-century, you may forfeit your touch with the Americans.

And that map-survey—how accurate is it? Granted its brilliant effects, its breathlessness, intensity, and force, how closely does it follow experience? Well, not very. It is a mature interpretation of our times, integrated throughout, interknit, and consistent, symphonically marshalling its themes to an indictment, a judgement, and even an obsequy. And yet... however cruel life in the United States may have been these thirty years it has not been so dreary as all that. The Americans have not had this stolidity, they have not so nervelessly gone down before so dull a destiny. Mr. Dos Passos sees them as noisy, drunken, and lecherous from a kind of tropism. But, really, they are rowdy because they enjoy rowdiness, they drink because liquor makes them feel good, they fornicate because they find fornication fun. They do not go on debauches from a sense of obligation, and they enormously enjoy the business, the bargaining, the sports, the contention, the boisterousness, the daily routine that he depicts as no more than cellular irritability. They sing a lot. They laugh a lot. They enjoy themselves. Millionaires and hoboes, strikers and scabs, they are incurable hedonists. They have gusto. You need only look out of your window, turn on your radio, or listen in the street. ... What kind of interpretation is this that leaves out gusto and delight, to say no more of anger and pain? What kind of interpretation, especially, of the expanding years? Those years had plenty of hangovers in them, but the way to a hangover has not led through solemnity. No, when you give us the Americans as a mere mass of contractile tissue quivering in a fog, you have turned inward from the street. You are in an atelier, and a damned odd one.

Literature is the richer for any interpretation so sincere and eloquent as this one, and its brilliance, its novelty, and the intensity of its conviction go far to compensate its distortion and the anemia of its characters. Nevertheless both weaknesses must tell against it in any final judgment, and that distortion is ominous in the one remaining aspect of Mr. Dos Passos that is inescapable in any discussion of his work. His sympathies are proletarian, but the proletarian critics have had difficulty with him, sometimes accepting him as orthodox, sometimes rejecting him as a social fascist. *The Big Money* will not ratify his orthodoxy. Talk about the 'rot of democracy' is disturbing, the presentation of two Party workers as saps will not be comforting, the frustration and defeat of them all run counter to the mythology of proletarian fiction, and though the treatment of the craven capitalists conforms more to precedent it is a counsel of folly. For the Movement, the whole importance of Charley Anderson is that, in general, he does not end as a drunken letch—but that he stays sober, perfects his director-ates, and more securely rivets his system on the dispossessed. The whole importance of the United States Senate is that it is not composed of homosexuals and cheap grafters—the Movement would have much easier going if it were. The whole importance of J. Ward Moorehouse is not that he is a fatuous fool—but that he is a highly intelligent man formidably skilled in the business of evil. And though throughout the trilogy, the proletarians, such as have not betrayed their class, have got the dirty end of the stick, they have also been presented with something of a theoretical argument, originating in formula, the aroma of a syllogism lingering round them, the warm and living reality ignored.

That is what it comes to, from whichever angle you approach the six novels. Experimentation, technical versatility, imagistic brilliance, the perfection of an advanced theoretical system of composition, and an advanced theoretical system of analysis and argument, all these exist almost to surfeit. But the thing lacks something in warmth, in a knowledge of life that is experienced rather than theorized about. A vast amount of fascinating sub-stance, but in the midst of it an artist who remains intensely individualistic and incurably solipsistic, and builds his structure out of logic rather than blood and breath.

NOTE

1 Malcolm Cowley, *New Republic*, lxx 27 (April 1932), 303.

33. Horace Gregory, 'Dos Passos Completes His Modern Trilogy', *New York Herald Tribune Books*

9 August 1936, 1

Gregory (1898–1982) contributed poetry to *Vanity Fair* and *The Nation* during the early 1920's, taught poetry and classical literature at Sarah Lawrence College in New York City for many years, did translations of Ovid and Catullus, made frequent contributions to literary periodicals, and wrote books on Amy Lowell and D.H. Lawrence.

It was perhaps inevitable that the Dos Passos trilogy, the work of some half dozen years, should at last betray concern for the problem of truth. I quote the forty-ninth installment of 'The Camera Eye' which appears in *The Big Money*:

pencil scrawls in my notebook the scraps of recollection the broken half-phrases the effort to intersect word with word to dovetail clause with clause to rebuild out of mangled memories unshakably (Oh Pontius Pilate) the truth

I suspect that the truth toward which Mr. Dos Passos reaches is of protean structure and not the least considerable of its influences has been the wise and saturnine instruction of Thorstein Veblen's *Theory of the Leisure Class*. Meanwhile we have the cumulative force of three novels, each complete in itself which in time read as one entire work.

It has been characteristic of Mr. Dos Passos never to stand still, never to take for granted those truths and realities accepted by other novelists. That is why *The Big Money*, with its rapidly moving scenes of action in New York, Washington, Detroit, Hollywood and Miami seems to reflect an energy which has its source in a fresh point of view. He has chosen the places where big money seems to pour in an unending stream, among politicians, movie magnates, the automotive industries, and real estate speculators. The people in *The Big Money* are ex-war aces, movie stars, promoters from Wall Street, social workers, reformers, Communist leaders and United States Senators—and all are influenced by the kind of living that demands the quick reward, the millions that are made today and lost tomorrow. *The Big Money* proves again that the popularity of Mr. Dos Passos's novels in Europe is well deserved for here, as in his earlier work, he has caught the reckless speed at which the big money is made, lost, wasted in America; he, more than any other living American writer, has exposed to public satire those peculiar contradictions of our poverty in the midst of plenty. And in each of the narratives which carry the theme of this novel to its conclusion the reader shares the sensations of speed and concentrated action. Only the most unresponsive reader would fail to appreciate the humor which is the force behind the keen stroke of Mr. Dos Passos's irony.

To those who have read *The 42d Parallel* and *1919* Mr. Dos Passos's devices of 'the camera eye' and 'newsreel' are familiar properties of a technic which has been skillfully borrowed from the motion picture. 'The camera eye' as he employs it is usually a subjective, soft-focus close-up and the 'newsreel' time sequence throughout the progress of thirty-five years, from 1900 to 1935, and contained within these thousand four hundred odd pages. But what was not clear in the earlier sections of the trilogy and which now emerges in *The Big Money* is the fact that the entire work may be described as an experiment in *montage* as applied to modern prose. We may assume that the work is a scenario of contemporary American life, and to appreciate its eloquence the trilogy should be read in three successive sittings quite as one might witness three successive performances of a single motion picture. I would almost insist that the three novels be read as fast as one can *see*, for here we are to be concerned with the stream of action in social history; no single character dominates the picture, no single force drives toward a conclusion; it is rather the cumulative forces, characters, episodes that are gathered together under the shifting lens of the camera: images of action are superimposed and from the long rolls of film Mr. Dos Passos (to complete the analogy) like another Griffith, Pabst or Eisenstein, has made a selection of cell units in news, subjective observation, biography and fictional narrative.

It is significant, I believe, that the trilogy opens on board a train going west to Chicago and closes in *The Big Money* with a flash of a large passenger plane in transcontinental flight far overhead speeding westward from the Atlantic seaboard to the Golden Gate. The first observation is made from the point of view of a small boy who was to share the poverty of his family in a Chicago slum; the last is seen through the eyes of a young man, jobless, distinctly one of the unemployed, hitch-hiking his way to anywhere, still following the forty-second parallel cross country to the Pacific Coast. Between the two we have news of events at home and abroad. Short biographies of American heroes, and the life history of more than a dozen characters of which the most important are Mac, J. Ward Morehouse, Richard Ellsworth Savage, Anne Elizabeth ('Daughter') Eveline Hutchins, Joe Williams, Ben Compton, Mary French, Margo Dowling and Charley Anderson.

We are introduced to Morehouse in *The 42d Parallel*: the shadow of his success story lengthens in *1919* (ex-advertising man, public relations counsel, dollar-a-year man, adviser to Woodrow Wilson at the Peace Conference in Paris) and the figure dwindles to a neurotic tangle of nerves and dyspepsia, half-dead from over-work in *The Big Money*. The blue-eyed charm is gone; the rosy platitudes now roll into heavy, sententious, oily phrases; his assistant, Richard Ellsworth Savage, now does most of his work, high pressure work, with periodic release in violent drinking.

Savage (we remember), once the handsome Harvard poet of *1919*, was an ambulance driver during the war (he resented the war, but at its close was made secure by appointment under Morehouse). We are led to assume that he will inherit the Morehouse rewards, the well oiled platitudes, the loss of energy.

Morehouse and Savage are good type specimens of the American success story on the upper middle class level, but I believe the careers of Joe Williams (*1919*) and Charley Anderson (*The 42nd Parallel* and *The Big Money*) are equally if not more significant. In these two lives we have the ironic recital of a fable in contemporary

American ethics: both boys start at the bottom of the social scale. Joe is a sailor, rises to second mate rating, then slips back to able seaman, and never dares to play for large stakes—perhaps his greatest crime is stealing a pair of women's silk stockings—and he is killed in a drunken brawl. Anderson, garage mechanic, enlists for war service, emerges from it an aviator, drifts home to the Middle West, drifts back to New York and enters airplane manufacturing. He then plays for larger stakes, dabbles in Wall Street speculation (the slow corruption of his character is vividly revealed in the succeeding episodes); he betrays his friends and climbs high into the infinities of paper profits; like Williams he is destined to complete his career in violent death, and it is important to remember that Anderson, like Williams, dies without a cent left to his name. Neither Williams nor Anderson escapes the threat of danger always near: from the very start their lives were insecure, and when at last they realize (however dimly, however subconsciously), that danger which surrounds them, they step forward to meet it, fulfilling their social destiny. Like the heroes in Stephen Crane's *War Is Kind*, 'These men were born to drill and die'; and it is one of Mr. Dos Passos's great merits that there are no tears wasted over their remains and we soon learn from him that such violence which seems so casual, so accidental, is actually a form of half-willed suicide.

I find Mr. Dos Passos's women less clearly defined than his men; they seem to follow the course of sex adventure with too much repetition, and in that sense they all seem too much alike. I would say that his detailed study of Eveline Hutchins (*1919*, *The Big Money*) is a shade too logical. We recognize her as the archetype of war heroine who wears short skirts, who posseses the restlessness as well as the kind of half-ironic despair which made her choose colorless, weak Paul Johnson as a father for a baby; but her disintegration throughout the narrative of *The Big Money* is all too obvious. Anne Elizabeth (*1919*) with her embarrassing aggressiveness, her helplessness and her death in dramatic suicide, is far more interesting; I suspect that she is an ironic portrait of the 'new woman,' one of those millions sacrificed to the 'new freedom' who were the girls who talked too loud, who believed too literally in the hope of a single standard and lost; it is her honesty which gives her a touch of awkward dignity. In *The Big Money* it is Margo Dowling who is most interesting as a typical American phenomenon; she is the shrewd little chorus-girl-dress-model who rises to the rewards of our bi-annual American sweethearts in Hollywood; she is the face behind that smooth close-up reflected from a million silver screens. Mr. Dos Passos's subtlety in recording her conversation saves him from the mere repetition of Anita Loos's earlier success in *Gentlemen Prefer Blondes*. It is Mr. Dos Passos's refusal to caricature Hollywood that makes his portrait of Margo and her associates convincing; they are both comic and terrifying and they are given the semblance of reality through understatement.

Granting that the origins of Mr. Dos Passos's technic may be found in the art of the motion picture, it is not surprising that some of the best passages in *The Big Money* should deal with Hollywood directly; and it is significant that Mr. Dos Passos's final commentary on the American success story should leave Wall Street and Hollywood with the few victories to be gained in the making of big money. There can be no doubt about *that* conclusion, that segment of the picture is perfectly clear. But it is also clear that the conclusion is a concrete statement of the ironic generalities contained in Veblen's *Theory of the Leisure Class*, and we must not confuse Mr. Dos Passos's objectives with those of the strictly Marxian critics. Mr. Dos Passos's trilogy is as important to them as Veblen's own work, no more, no less; but they must supply the means by which his work may be applied to fit Marxian theory.

By this route we return at last to Mr. Dos Passos's concern for truth which for the most part remains a split objective: on one side lies esthetic truth; on the other, the truth of social observation. The present work is an attempt to create a synthesis out of untractable material within a new technic (which has already resulted in a number of flattering imitations by younger novelists). In one sense the present trilogy has been a record of Mr. Dos Passos's own learning process, a record of unhasty knowledge in the use of the 'newsreel' and biography devices. Contrast the inadequate biographies of *The 42nd Parallel* with the brilliant sketches of Henry Ford, Frederick Winslow Taylor, Isadora Duncan, Frank Lloyd Wright and Thorstein Veblen in *The Big Money*. What was mere time notation in the earlier 'newsreels' is a well integrated instrument of commentary in 'newsreels' XLVII and LV. In these the potentialities of the device are excellently realized. But for a very few exceptions the problem of the 'camera eye' remains unsolved; in these Mr. Dos Passos always seems uncomfortably arty rather than artful—they seem to move contrary to that final truth, that final integration of method and content toward which Mr. Dos Passos is moving. There is still some doubt as to whether the Dos Passos method of recording social history (despite its accuracy in stating the truth of our present defeat in radical activity which is illustrated by the stories of Ben Compton and Mary French) can bring a satisfactory conclusion to the trilogy. There would be little to prevent a fourth volume being written to the refrain of the echo now heard in motion picture theaters: 'Time Marches On!' Yet while admitting these flaws in the structure of Mr. Dos Passos's trilogy it is also plain that the work is one of the most impressive contributions made to the literature of our time. The speed at which it travels is a cleansing force, dismissing the 'destructive elements' in our civilization as transitory and unreal. Mr. Dos Passos offers no consolations of prophecy. He continues to perceive the realities of the life around him and in that sense he remains one of the most important of our contemporary poets. *The Big Money* establishes his position as the most incisive and direct of American satirists. It has been his hope 'to rebuild...unshakably (Oh Pontius Pilate) the truth' and in that hope discover the truth that makes men free.

34. Malcolm Cowley, 'The End of a Trilogy', *New Republic*

12 August 1936, vol. lxxxviii, 23–4

Cowley (b. 1898) was associate editor of the *New Republic* from 1929 to 1944. He has also written several books on American literature, including *Exiles Return* (1934) and *A Second Flowering* (1956), which are historical and sociological in approach rather than formalist, focusing on the writer, his audience, and his milieu.

Most of the characters in *The Big Money* had been introduced to us in the two earlier novels of the series. Charley Anderson, for example, the wild Swedish boy from the Red River Valley, had first appeared at the end of *The 42nd Parallel*, where we saw him drifting over the country from job to job and girl friend to girl friend, then sailing for France as the automobile mechanic of an ambulance section. Now he comes sailing back as a bemedaled aviator, hero and ace. He helps to start an airplane manufacturing company (like Eddie Rickenbacker); he marries a banker's daughter, plunges in the stock market, drinks, loses his grip and gets killed in an automobile accident. Dick Savage, the Harvard esthete of doubtful sex, had appeared in *1919* as an ambulance driver. Now he is an advertising man, first lieutenant of the famous J. Ward Moorehouse in his campaign to popularize patent medicines as an expression of the American spirit, as self-reliance in medication. Eveline Hutchins, who played a small part in both the earlier novels, is now an unhappy middle-aged nymphomaniac. Don Stevens, the radical newspaper man, has become a Communist, a member of the Central Executive Committee after the dissenters have been expelled (and among them poor Ben Compton, who served ten years in Atlanta for fighting the draft). New people also appear: for example, Margo Dowling, a shanty-Irish girl who gets to be a movie actress by sleeping with the right people. Almost all the characters are now tied together by love or business, politics or pure hatred. And except for Mary French, a Colorado girl who half-kills herself working as the secretary of one radical relief organization after another—except for Mary French and poor honest Joe Askew, they have let themselves be caught in the race for easy money and tangible power; they have lost their personal values; they are like empty ships with their seams leaking, ready to go down in the first storm.

Read by itself, as most people will read it, *The Big Money* is the best of Dos Passos' novels, the sharpest and swiftest, the most unified in mood and story. Nobody has to refer to the earlier books in order to understand what is happening in this one. But after turning back to *The 42nd Parallel* and *1919*, one feels a new admiration for Dos Passos as an architect of plots and an interweaver of destinies. One learns much more about his problems and the original methods by which he has tried to solve them.

His central problem, of course, was that of writing a collective novel (defined simply as a novel without an individual hero, a novel of which the real protagonist is a social group). In this case the social group is almost the largest possible: it is the United States from the Spanish War to the crash of 1929, a whole nation during thirty years of its history. But a novelist is not a historian dealing with political tendencies or a sociologist reckoning statistical averages. If he undertakes to depict the national life, he has to do so in terms of individual lives, without slighting either one or the other. This double focus, on the social group and on the individual, explains the technical devices that Dos Passos has used in the course of his trilogy.

It is clear enough that each of these devices has been invented with the purpose of gaining a definite effect, of supplying a quality absent from the narrative passages that form the body of the book. Take the Newsreels as an example of these technical inventions. The narratives have dealt, necessarily, with short-sighted people pursuing their personal aims—and therefore the author intersperses them with passages consisting of newspaper headlines and snatches from popular songs, his purpose being to suggest the general or collective atmosphere of a given period. Or take the brief biographies of prominent Americans. The narrative sections have dealt with people like Charley Anderson and Dick Savage, fairly typical Americans, figures that might have been chosen from a crowd—and therefore the author also gives us life-sketches of Americans who were representative rather than typical, the leaders or rebels of their age.

The third of Dos Passos' technical devices, the Camera Eye, is something of a puzzle and one that I was a long time in solving to my own satisfaction. Obviously the Camera Eye passages are autobiographical, and obviously they are intended to represent the author's stream of consciousness (a fact that explains the lack of capitalization and punctuation). At first it seemed to me that they were completely out of tone with the hard and behavioristic style of the main narrative. But this must have been exactly the reason why Dos Passos introduced them. The hard, simple, behavioristic treatment of the characters has been tending to oversimplify them, to make it seem that they were being approached from the outside—and the author tries to counterbalance this weakness by inserting passages that are written from the inside, passages full of color and warmth and hesitation and little intimate perceptions.

I have heard Dos Passos violently attacked on the ground that all these devices—Newsreels and biographies and the Camera Eye—were presented arbitrarily, without relation to the novel. This attack is partly justified as regards *The 42nd Parallel*, though even in that first novel there is a clearer interrelation than most critics have noted. For instance, the Camera Eye describes the boyhood of a well-to-do lawyer's son and thereby points an artistically desirable contrast with the boyhood of tough little Fainy McCreary. Or again, the biography of Big Bill Haywood is inserted at the moment in the story when Fainy is leaving to help the Wobblies win their strike at Goldfield. Many other examples could be given. But when we come to *1919*, connections of this sort are so frequent and obvious that even a careless reader could not miss them; and in *The Big Money* all the technical devices are used to enforce the same mood and the same leading ideas.

Just what are these ideas that Dos Passos is trying to present? ... The question sounds more portentous than it is in reality. If novels could be reduced each to a single thesis, there would be no reason for writing novels: a few convincing short essays would be all we needed. Obviously any novelist is trying to picture life as it is or was or as he would like it to be. But his ideas are important in so far as they help him to organize the picture (not to mention the important question of their effect on the reader).

In Dos Passos' case, the leading idea is the one implicit in his choice of subject and form: it is the idea that life is collective, that individuals are neither heroes nor villains, that their destiny is controlled by the drift of society as a whole. But in what direction does he believe that American society is drifting? This question is more difficult to answer, and the author doesn't give us much direct help. Still, a certain drift or progress or decline can be deduced from the novel as a whole. At the beginning of *The 42nd Parallel* there was a general feeling of hope and restlessness and let's-take-a-chance. A journeyman printer like Fainy McCreary could wander almost anywhere and find a job. A goatish but not unlikable fraud like old Doc Bingham could dream of building a fortune and, what is more, could build it. But at the end of *The Big Money*, all this has changed. Competitive capitalism has been transformed into monopoly capitalism; American society has become crystalized and stratified. 'Vag'—the nameless young man described in the last three pages of the novel—is waiting at the edge of a concrete highway, his feet aching in broken shoes, his belly tight with hunger. Over his head flies a silver transcontinental plane filled with highly paid executives on their way to the Pacific Coast. The upper class has taken to the air, the lower class to the road; there is no longer any bond between them; they are two nations. And we ourselves, if we choose the side of the defeated nation, are reduced to being foreigners in the land where we were born.

That, I suppose, is the author's thesis, if we reduce it to a bald statement. Dos Passos prefers to keep it in the background, suggesting it time and again. The tone of his last volume is less argumentative than emotional—and indeed, we are likely to re-member it as a furious and somber poem, written in a mood of revulsion even more powerful than that which T.S. Eliot expressed in *The Waste Land*. Dos Passos loves the old America; he loathes the frozen country that the capitalists have been creating—and when he describes it he makes it seem like an inferno in which Americans true to the older spirit are crushed and broken. But for the hired soldiers of the conquering nation—for J. Ward Moorehouse and Eleanor Stoddard and Dick Savage and all their kind—he reserves an even sharper torture: to be hollow and enameled, to chirp in thin squeaky voices like insects with the pulp of life sucked out of them and nothing but thin poison left in their veins. Rich, empty, frantic, they preside over an icy hell from which Dos Passos sees no hope of our ever escaping.

35. Alvah C. Bessie, review, *Brooklyn Daily Eagle*

23 August 1936, 10C

Bessie (1904–85) worked as an actor and stage manager for the experimental Provincetown Players during the early 1920s. He later held staff positions on the *New Yorker, New York Herald Tribune, Brooklyn Daily Eagle,* and *New Masses.* Bessie fought for the Loyalists in Spain during the Spanish

Civil War, and returned to America to launch a career as a Hollywood screenwriter, only to become one of the 'Hollywood Ten' sentenced to prison in 1950 for refusing to tell the House Committee on Un-American Activities if they had ever been members of the Communist Party. He was subsequently blacklisted.

With the publication of *The Big Money* the trilogy that John Dos Passos launched in 1930 with *The 42nd Parallel* and carried forward in 1932 with the publication of *1919* has come to a close, and it is possible to make a relative evaluation of this contribution to American fiction.

Six years of actual time, at least, have gone into the fashioning of this 1460-page commentary on the past three decades of American life, and an immense expenditure of labor. That this enterprise has not been unrewarding, both from the standpoint of American literary history as well as the purely personal satisfaction of multitudes of readers, should be evident from the most casual perusal of the work. But that it has, with its completion, added up to a work of lasting significance may, and probably will, be the subject of conscientious debate. For with all his many gifts—of sardonic comment, of painstaking and pertinent research, of brilliant narrative technique, of the elaboration of fictional incident—Dos Passos falls very definitely short of possessing those gifts which are the stigmata of the great novelist: pervasive and profound understanding of character, inevitable organizational ability and style. These qualities he possesses in some measure; he is a man of intelligence and artistic integrity: he has a ready grasp of the multitudinous minutiae of human conduct. And he can write in so enthralling a fashion that the reader will be unable to put down his book until he is utterly fatigued. These attributes, at a time when the majority of writers find it difficult even to sustain their talents for short flights, are not to be lightly dismissed, but they are not the attributes of a man who can give us a book that will outlast its time as something more than contemporary documentation.

But documentation is there, and in full measure. The reader previously unacquainted with the main news stories of the past thirty years (if such exists), with the temper and the tendencies of his time—in history, in politics, in literature, in moral attitudes—

will be offered a thorough-going history and a commentary on these aspects of his fellows' lives. He will see the panoply of recent American and foreign history—the turn of the century, the fruition of commercial competition, the growth of monopoly, the labor struggles, the World War, the post-war release—all will be spread before him in colors that cannot fail to catch the eye. And these items of his background have been integrated, to a not entirely successful degree, with the purely narrative sections of the long novel. They provide it with heightened meaning and significance.

This, in the Dos Passos case, involves a purely technical approach: he has interrupted his narratives with these expository devices: The Camera Eye—short sections written from an entirely subjective point of view in impressionistic style, that catch and fix the emotional content of the time with which the narrative is immediately concerned; the Newsreel, which offers a page or so of contemporary headlines, excerpts from news reports, speeches, placards, popular songs and sayings, articles; and brief biographies, some more successful than others, of representative figures of the day. These last are frequently masterpieces of concision and expository comment, and they are generally suffused with an irony that rarely fails to sting. They fasten upon the pages of the reader's memory the prominent, the famous and notorious personalities of his day and they have their bearing upon the main course of the narrative.

But the main stream of the narrative is what we are most properly concerned with in this review. It is the substance of the three novels, their meat and the material by which they may be judged as achievements in the more important current of our literature. And while this narrative, that carries a dozen or so characters from point to point over a period of three decades is at all times engrossing, at all times provides a scintillating exposition of human behavior and its intricate inter-relationships, it lacks both depth of perception and cumulative power. For, with very few exceptions, the characters of *The 42nd Parallel*, do not carry over into *1919*, and the characters introduced in the second novel do not carry over into *The Big Money*. And when they do, they are treated (again with rare exceptions) in the most perfunctory fashion. They are mentioned, they appear for a brief moment and then disappear, and it is possible that this is one reason the three volumes, taken as a whole, lack the cohesive force of a work that carries a set of characters to their separate, logical and inevitable climax. Its power is diffused and scattered, and once Dos Passos has brought his people to their various conclusions, generally within the framework of a single book, he seems to have done with them, and, engrossed in the panorama of a new character's unfolding life, the earlier protagonists are readily forgotten. This is but one defect of his many virtues; yet it represents a fundamental flaw in a work that not only is a trilogy but should have been, essentially, of one piece.

The 42nd Parallel carries the separate narratives of Mac, of Janey, of J. Ward Moorehouse and of Eleanor Stoddard, to the outbreak of the World War. In one final chapter it also introduces Charley Anderson, who is destined to be the main protagonist of *The Big Money*, although he does not appear at all in *1919*. This second novel takes as its point of departure the return from France of the sailor, Joe Williams, and exploits the separate wartime narratives of Richard Ellsworth Savage, the assistant of J. Ward Moorehouse, the public-relations expert; Daughter, who dies in an airplane crash, Eveline Hutchins and Ben Compton. Eveline appears again in *The Big Money*, as do Dick Savage and Charley Anderson. There are also, in this third novel, the separate stories of Mary French, the social worker, and Margo Dowling, the movie star, and as in the previous volumes, these separate characters work out their relationships largely within the framework of one book, and their stories are informed with Dos Passos' uncanny ability to multiply incidents, to catch and reproduce the characteristic externalities of human personality. Yet they rarely move you and rarely do you become concerned with their eventual fate, for they seem to be people moving about for a brief time upon a brightly lighted stage, people you know are not real to begin with, and are only there to entertain you. They are representative, if you will, of our times, though in no rigidly stylized manner, and they fulfill the design the author has created for them and are readily forgotten, in the majority of cases. They are not created from the inside, but are the fictional images of men and women you may have known, but with whom you never could have been deeply involved. They act, they move, they experience hardship, exaltation and defeat, but they rarely think or convince you that they experience the emotion the author ascribes to them. And as a result of this fundamental failure to create his characters from the inside, Dos Passos as a novelist fails to assume the significance that even so unsatisfactory a writer as Jules Romains (whose methods and approach so closely resemble his own) may rightly claim as his due. And no cumulative increment of power is observable in the three novels, although they all have their moments of high effectiveness and emotional evocation.

But it is in the implications of these books that Dos Passos finds his primary significance as a contemporary writer. For they proceed from an attitude that is becoming increasingly prominent among creative artists of our time, and in their most unsatisfactory aspects they exemplify that attitude and the hold it has obtained upon the workers of our period. Especially is this true of *The Big Money*, which is a crystallization in fictional form of the growth and decay of our economy. In the lives of Charley Anderson, who rose from mechanic to stock-manipulator; of Margo Dowling, the orphaned child who by dint of sleeping with the right people (and with a goodly number of the wrong), lifted herself from humble beginnings to the dizzy pinnacles of Hollywood's golden hills; of Richard Ellsworth Savage, dipsomaniac publicity man who was destined to step into the shoes of the great J. Ward Moorehouse, and of Mary French, whose political education dated from her first contact with the newspaper world—in these lives the reader will find acute and penetrating analyses of the forces at work behind the scenes, the forces that have stolen our country from the vast majority of its people and used it for their own devices:

[Quotes from 'Camera Eye' (50), 462–3, of *The Big Money*.]

36. Unsigned review, *Times Literary Supplement*

24 October 1936, vol. xxxv, 859

With *The Big Money* Mr. Dos Passos completes his trilogy of which *The Forty-Second Parallel* and *Nineteen-Nineteen* were the first two volumes. The special technical devices of the first volumes are continued in the third—the turning from one narrative to another and back again, the brief 'newsreels' breaking in to document the popular preoccupations of the passing moment, the biographical portraits of representative real persons, the 'camera eye' ever and again projecting the author himself full into the front of the picture as though to prove his living participation. On the whole both the handling of the material and the actual writing seem better— firmer, brisker, more masterly—in this third volume than in either of the others, the improvement being general, if perhaps most noticeable, in the biographies, which are of Henry Ford, Thorstein Veblen, Isadora Duncan, Wilbur and Orville Wright, Samuel Insull, W.R. Hearst, the architect Frank Lloyd Wright, and F.W. Taylor, pioneer of 'scientific management' in industry.

The main fictional figures—no less of their times for being imagined rather than actual—are Charley Anderson, one-time motor mechanic, who returns from France a prominent aviator and goes into the aeroplane business, spending his money faster than he makes it till drink and women bring him to a final, fatal crash; Mary French, social worker and Socialist, mixing kisses with agitation; Margo Dowling, whose varied affairs are also incidental to her transition from vaudeville dancer to film star; and Richard Ellsworth Savage, once poet and then ambulance driver, now both imitative assistant to J. Ward Moorehouse, financial magnate, and very like Anderson in his pastimes.

All the narratives move forward rapidly and easily, each character being shown in his course and against his special background with a fine particularity. As a panorama of modern American life the vision has breadth and brilliance, immediacy and fullness. Conception, observation, arrangement, presentation are all professionally competent to the last degree. Three things alone detract from the achievement. One is the puppet-nature of the characters, causing them to seem automatons impelled by outer circumstance more than by any inner individuality. Another is a distinct narrowness in the individual response and action; the point is not that almost everyone lives mainly from bar to bed, but that one intoxication or loving is so greyly like all the rest. Mr. Dos Passos evidently intends to display a corrupt society, but even corruption has more psychological variety than this. There is also the matter of form. Granted that the 'newsreel' and other interpolations derive from the intention to evoke a fuller social and national background than the ordinary novel attempts, still this sectional presentation must be regarded as a failure, not a triumph, of synthesis. Nevertheless, *The Big Money* in itself, and the trilogy as a whole, must be recognized and acclaimed as an outstanding contribution to modern American fiction.

37. Goronwy Rees, review, *Spectator*

27 November 1936, vol. clvii, 960

Rees (1909–79) was an English novelist, educator, and journalist.

In the trilogy formed by *The 42nd Parallel, Nineteen-Nineteen* and *The Big Money* Mr. Dos Passos has tried to describe the growth of modern America. *The Big Money* is concerned with post-War America of the boom period; those who have read the first two volumes will notice that Mr. Dos Passos' hopes, founded on the socialist movement, have turned almost to despair. 'In America we are defeated,' he says. He still believes in the socialist movement and the values it embodies; he still admires the courage, stubbornness and integrity of the working-class; but he does not doubt the triumph of the Big Money. In this book his characters, with one exception, are among the victors and show what the victory means. The most typical and important of them is Charley Anderson, war-ace, aeroplane inventor, manufacturer and financier, whose hectic career of money, drink and bed ends in a car-smash in Florida; he has a female counterpart in Margot Dowling, who after an unfortunate marriage to a Cuban quean, and various amorous vicissitudes, becomes a screen star—the world's newest sweetheart. As in Mr. Dos Passos' other novels, these biographies are interspersed with News Reels composed of newspaper cuttings and extracts from popular songs, the Camera Eye which is an almost automatic record of immediate responses to the American scene, and sketches of actual persons typical of the period he describes; those especially of Carl Veblen and Valentino have a melancholy brilliance.

Mr. Dos Passos has an extraordinary knowledge of his subject. More perhaps than a novelist, he is a historian, a sociologist and a reporter. The descriptive passages of the Camera Eye are often reporting of the greatest service. He does not, however, succeed in dramatising all his knowledge. Mr. Dos Passos is indeed more interested in telling the truth, in explaining a historical process, in expressing certain moral values, than in creating works of art; his elaborate technique should not conceal this; and what he wishes to do he does with immense efficiency. I have seen him described, by those who dislike the truth, as industrious, patient, painstaking, as if these were the failings of mediocrity; what this really means is that Mr. Dos Passos, who has many very strong and sometimes naïve impulses, an admiration for size and power, a melodramatic sense of the struggle between capital and labour, an acute pleasure in the objective world and especially in landscape, a nostalgia for childhood which is repeated in a nostalgia for the vanished America of the frontier and small democracy, has disciplined these impulses by a technique which makes his writing sometimes monotonous and sometimes affected.

His methods have curious results. They divide the real and the fictional worlds; but the real characters are invested with far greater poetic force than the imagined ones. The real characters express directly the conditions under which they live; the fictional ones are submerged by them. The real characters are typical and heroic; the fictional characters are typical but puppets. Mr. Dos Passos' poetic gifts go into his descriptions of what is real; his patience and industry into what is imagined. In his work the real and the imaginative never perfectly coincide. This may be a fault, but in these books it is also a virtue. They escape that claustrophic quality which belongs almost necessarily to most novels, however good; they do not imprison us in the heads, emotions or lives of their characters. Mr Dos Passos always allows, or rather compels, us to look beyond his fictions into a wider and more varied world; in this his work has a real originality. That world is America and American democracy, the real heroes of his book, for which he has a feeling comparable to Whitman's. It is not Mr. Dos Passos' fault if he has at length to show us his heroes defeated, corrupted, betrayed and beaten up by the Big Money.

38. T.K. Whipple, 'Dos Passos and the U.S.A.', *Nation*

19 February 1938, vol. cxlvi, 210–12

In January of 1938 Harcourt Brace brought out a new one-volume edition of Dos Passos's *U.S.A.* trilogy, prompting fresh reviews and some retrospectives, of which this was among the first. Whipple (1890–1939) wrote several books of literary criticism.

The choice of the ambitious title *U.S.A.* for the volume which brings together Dos Passos's *The 42nd Parallel*, *Nineteen-Nineteen*, and *The Big Money* looks as if it might be intended to stake out a claim on the fabulous 'great American novel.' And Dos Passos's claim is not a weak one. A single book could hardly be more inclusive than his: in the stories of his main characters he covers most parts of the country during the first three decades of the twentieth century. His people have considerable social diversity, ranging from Mac, the I.W.W. typesetter, and Joe Williams, the feckless sailor, to Ben Compton, the radical leader, Eleanor Stoddard, the successful decorator, Margo Dowling, the movie star, and J. Ward Moorehouse, the big publicity man. The background of the panorama is filled out with 'newsreels' of newspaper headlines, popular songs, and the like, with the autobiographic 'camera eye' which gives snatches of Dos Passos's own experience, and with a series of biographical portraits of representative men—Debs, Edison, Wilson, Joe Hill, Ford, Veblen, Hearst, and twenty more. Probably no other American novel affords a picture so varied and so comprehensive.

Furthermore, the picture is rendered with extraordinary vividness and brilliance of detail, especially of sensory detail. Sights and sounds and above all smells abound until the reader is forced to wonder that so many people, of such different sorts, are all so constantly aware of what their eyes and ears and noses report to them: might not some of them, one asks, more often get absorbed in meditation or memory or planning or reverie? But it is no part of

Dos Passos's scheme to spend much time inside his characters' heads; he tells, for the most part, what an outsider would have seen or heard—gestures, actions, talk, as well as the surroundings. The result is a tribute to the keenness of the author's observation—not only of colors, noises, and odors but, even more important, of human behavior and of American speech. People as well as things are sharp and distinct.

Nor does the presentation lack point and significance. As the book goes on, the U.S.A. develops, with the precision of a vast and masterly photograph, into a picture of a business world in its final ripeness, ready to fall into decay. Though Dos Passos does not call himself a Marxist—and would seem in fact not to be one—his point of view is unmistakably radical. The class struggle is present as a minor theme; the major theme is the vitiation and degradation of character in such a civilization. Those who prostitute themselves and succeed are most completely corrupted; the less hard and less self-centered are baffled and beaten; those who might have made good workers are wasted; the radicals experience internal as well as external defeat. No one attains any real satisfaction. Disintegration and frustration are everywhere. The whole presentation leads to the summary: 'Life is a shambles.' Perhaps there are implications that it need not be; but no doubt is left that actually it is.

These generalities, when stated as generalities, have of course become the trite commonplaces of a whole school of literature. But actual people shown going through the process of victimization can never become trite or commonplace; the spectacle must always be pitiful and terrible. And no one, I should suppose, could look on Dos Passos's picture wholly untouched and unmoved. But still one might ask whether he has quite achieved the tragic effect which presumably he aimed at.

To complain that the picture is one-sided may appear captious and unreasonable, and in one sense of 'one-sided' it is. The whole truth about a hundred million people throughout thirty years cannot be told in fifteen hundred—or in fifteen million—pages. The novelist has to select what he considers representative and characteristic persons and events, and if Dos Passos has chosen to omit big business men, farmers, and factory workers, and to dwell chiefly on midway people in somewhat ambiguous positions— intellectuals, decorators, advertising men—perhaps that is his privilege. The question is whether this picture of his, which is surely extensive enough as novels go, is entirely satisfactory within the limitations which must be granted. How close does *U.S.A.* come to being a great American novel? That it comes within hailing distance is proved by the fact that it has already been so hailed; indeed, it comes close enough so that the burden of proof is on those who would deny the title. Yet to grant it offhand would be premature.

On one point at least everyone probably agrees: that the biographical portraits are magnificent, and are the best part of the book. But wherein are they superior? Is is not that these portraits have a greater depth and solidity than Dos Passos's fictional characterizations—a more complete humanity? If so, the implication must be that his creation of character is not complete. And indeed when Mac is put beside Big Bill Haywood, or Ben Compton beside Joe Hill and Jack Reed, or Margo Dowling beside Isadora Duncan, the contrast is unflattering to Dos Passos's powers as a novelist. There is more human reality in the 10 pages given to Henry Ford than in the 220 given to Charley Anderson. Nor is the explanation that the real people are exceptional, the fictitious ones ordinary, satisfactory: some of the fictitious ones are supposed to be leaders; and besides it is a novelist's business so to choose and treat his imagined characters as to reveal his themes in their utmost extension, not at their flattest. No; the contrast has nothing to do with the positions people occupy; it is a fundamental matter of the conception of human nature and the portrayal of it in literature.

In thinking of this contrast, one notices first that the real men have a far better time of it in the world, that they do find a good many genuine satisfactions, that even when they fail—when they are jailed like Debs or shot down like Joe Hill—they are not wholly defeated. Inside them is some motive power which keeps them going to the end. Some of them swim with the stream and some against it, but they all swim; they all put up a fight. They all have persistent ruling passions. Furthermore, they are all complex and many-sided, full of contradictions and tensions and conflicts. They have minds, consciousness, individuality, and personality.

Not that all these things are entirely lacking in the fictitious characters—Dos Passos is too good a novelist for that—but they do appear only in a much lower degree, played down, degraded, reduced to a minimum. As a result, the consciousness of these people is of a relatively low order. True, they are aware with an abnormal keenness of their sensations, but is not this sensory awareness the most elementary form of consciousness? On the other hand, these folk can hardly be said to think at all, and their feelings are rather sharp transitory reactions than long-continuing dominant emotions. Above all, they are devoid of will or purpose, helplessly impelled hither and yon by the circumstances of the moment. They have no strength of resistance. They are weak at the very core of personality, the power to choose. Now it may be that freedom of choice is an illusion, but if so it is an inescapable one, and even the most deterministic and behavioristic novelist cannot omit it or minimize it without denaturing human beings. When the mainspring of choice is weakened or left out, the conflicts and contradictions of character lose their virtue and significance, and personality almost disappears. Dos Passos often gives this effect: that in his people there is, so to speak, nobody much at home, or that he is holding out on us and that more must be happening than he is willing to let on. This deficiency shows itself most plainly in the personal relations of his characters—they are hardly persons enough to sustain real relations with one another, any more than billiard balls do—and in his treatment of crises, which he is apt to dispose of in some such way as: 'They had a row so that night he took the train....'

The final effect is one of banality—that human beings and human life are banal. Perhaps this is the effect Dos Passos aimed at, but that it is needless and even false is proved by the biographical portraits, in which neither the men nor their lives are ever banal. The same objection holds, therefore, to Dos Passos's whole social picture as to his treatment of individuals, that he has minimized something vital and something which ought to be made much of—namely, forces in conflict. Society is hardly just rotting away and drifting apart; the destructive forces are tremendously powerful and well organized, and so are the creative ones. Furthermore, they are inextricably intermingled in institutions and in individuals. If Dos Passos is forced, by sheer fact, to present them so when he writes of Ford and Steinmetz and Morgan, why should he make little of them in his fiction? Is it to illustrate a preconceived and misleading notion that life nowadays is a silly and futile 'shambles'?

One might hope, but in vain, to find the answer in the autobiographic 'camera eye.' To be sure, the author there appears as the extremest type of Dos Passos character, amazingly sensitive to impressions, and so amazingly devoid of anything else that most of the 'camera eye' is uninteresting in the extreme. The effect of this self-portrait is further heightened by the brief prologue which introduces *U.S.A.*: an account of a young man, plainly the author himself, who 'walks by himself searching through the crowd with greedy eyes, greedy ears taut to hear, by himself, alone,' longing to share everybody's life, finding his only link with other people in listening to their talk. If the obvious conclusion could be accepted that Dos Passos had been never a participant but always a mere onlooker hungry for participation, so that he had to depend only on observation from outside, it would explain much. But such is not the fact; he took part in the World War and in the Sacco-Vanzetti case and other activities. He has been no mere spectator of the world. Moreover, he must have had powerful and lasting purposes and emotions to have written his books, and it is hardly credible that he has done so little thinking as he makes out. His self-portrait must be heinously incomplete, if only because he is a real man. But it is possible that he may have chosen to suppress some things in himself and in his writing, and that he may have acquired a distrust of thought and feeling and will which has forced him back upon sensations as the only reliable part of experience. Some such process seems to have taken place in many writers contemporary with him, resulting in a kind of spiritual drought, and in a fear lest they betray themselves or be betrayed by life. Perhaps the disillusionment of the war had something to do with it, but more probably a partial view and experience of our present society are responsible.

According to any view, that society, in all conscience, is grim enough, but not banal, not undramatic. Dos Passos has reduced what ought to be a tale of full-bodied conflicts to an epic of disintegration and frustration. That reduction—*any* reduction—is open to objection, because it is an imperfect account of human beings and human society that does not present forces working in opposition. In that sense *U.S.A.* is one-sided, whereas life and good literature are two-sided or many-sided. In a word, what we want is a dialectic treatment of people and the world. Dos Passos does not call himself a Marxist; if he were more of one, he might have written a better novel. The biographical portraits are the best part of his book because they are the most nearly Marxist, showing the dynamic contradictions of our time in the only way they can be shown—namely, as they occur in the minds and lives of whole men. Nothing will do, in the end, but the whole man.

39. Michael Gold, 'The Keynote to Dos Passos' Works', *Daily Worker*

26 February 1938, 7

As a reporter Gold travelled all over America and contributed frequently to the *Daily Worker*, the official Communist newspaper in the U.S.A.

Arnold Gingrich, a smart young entrepreneur who publishes *Esquire* and other magazines, sent me recently the trilogy by John Dos Passos, with a note saying in effect: 'I think this the greatest book written in modern America, and would like to know whether you agree.'

I've read the book but haven't answered the letter. There are feelings involved—political feelings you can't explain satisfactorily to the publisher of a magazine that has gotten rich by re-telling the dirty stories of travelling salesmen. Such publishers always have the loftiest private morals about art (with a capital A).

But the problem of Dos Passos remains, and needs to be explained to oneself and to the workers—at least for the record.

First problem: Only a few years ago Dos Passos was the hope of our left-wing literature in America. I myself wrote enthusiastically about him in the official magazine of English teachers and in other places. Granville Hicks capped his book on American literature with the figure of Dos Passos. We were all doing it. Even some of the Soviet writers and critics were doing it.

Second problem: Dos Passos falls among Trotskyites, and goes sour on us. The climax arrives with his visit to fighting Spain. He returns, not hating the fascism that has committed this crime against the people, but hating Communism.

From now on he displays the familiar lunacy of Trotskyite

intellectuals: Stalin engineered the war in Spain. Stalin framed China to resist Japan. Stalin is trying to frame America, into a war against Japan. Stalin framed up the 'gentle old martyr' Trotsky, etc., etc.

Ernest Hemingway also went to Spain. He learned a different lesson. He and Dos Passos had been the most intimate friends since the World War. Now Hemingway, I understand, has completely broken off his old friendship with Dos Passos on the issue of Spain. Hemingway regards Franco as the enemy of Spain.

Third problem: How should one sit in 'esthetic' judgment on a book by a man who has gone through this evolution?

Well, I got the clue, I think, in reading through the trilogy. The most frequent word in it is 'merde,' a French euphemism I shall use for the four-letter word, s—t, that Dos Passos so boldly scatters through his pages (Oh, the courage of it!).

The merde was there formerly when we praised Dos Passos. But we praised him as a fellow-traveller, not as a Communist. We were anxious to win the fellow-travellers and ignored the merde and looked for every gleam of the proletarian hope.

There was such hope Dos Passos was moving up from the bourgeois merde. It was right that we recognised in him a powerful if bewildered talent, tried to help free that talent from the muck of bourgeois nihilism.

He was going somewhere; it was right to hope to the limit and to ignore the merde. Now Dos Passos is going nowhere. On rereading his trilogy, one cannot help seeing how important the merde is in his psychology, and how, after a brief, futile effort, he has sunk back into it, as into a native element.

Like the Frenchman Celine, Dos Passos hates Communists because organically he seems to hate the human race. It is strange to see how little real humaneness there is in his book. He takes a dull, sadistic joy in showing human beings at their filthiest, meanest, most degraded moments. They have no will power; they are amoeba, moved by chemistry. Everything about them is blah!

You cannot be a Communist on hate and disgust alone. Lenin 'deeply loved the people,' was his wife's final word upon him. There's not a spark of such dynamic love on the merde-writers like Dos Passos, Farrell, Dahlberg, et al. They reflect only the bourgeois decadence.

The transition to Trotskyism is easy for such folks. It is only a new form of hatred of the people and of life, and of whatever human hope there is.

Celine, the French merde-writer, came for a brief spell close to Communism, then departed. Now Celine is an avowed fascist. From merde he came, to merde he has returned.

What is the future of Dos Passos? You tell me, Mr. Gingrich!

40. Lionel Trilling, 'The America of John Dos Passos', *Partisan Review*

April 1938, vol. iv, 26–32

Trilling (1905–75), the American critic, taught at Columbia for more than forty years with visiting appointments at Harvard and Oxford. He is the author of many important works of literary criticism, including *The Liberal Imagination* (1950), *Beyond Culture* (1965), and *Sincerity and Authenticity* (1972).

U.S.A. is far more impressive than even its three impressive parts—*42nd Parallel, 1919, The Big Money*—might have led one to expect. It stands as the important American novel of the decade, on the whole more satisfying than anything else we have. It lacks any touch of eccentricity; it is startlingly normal; at the risk of seeming paradoxical one might say that it is exciting because of its quality of cliché: here are comprised the judgments about modern American life that many of us have been living on for years.

Yet too much must not be claimed for this book. To-day we are inclined to make literature too important, to estimate the writer's function at an impossibly high rate, to believe that he can encompass and resolve all the contradictions, and to demand that he should. We forget that, by reason of his human nature, he is likely to win the intense perception of a single truth at the cost of a relative blindness to other truths. We expect a single man to give us all the answers and produce the 'synthesis.' And then when the writer, hailed for giving us much, is discovered to have given us less than everything, we turn from him in a reaction of disappointment: he has given us nothing. A great deal has been claimed for Dos Passos and it is important, now that *U.S.A.* is completed, to mark off the boundaries of its enterprise and see what it does not do so that we may know what it does do.

One thing *U.S.A.* does not do is originate; it confirms but does not advance and it summarizes but does not suggest. There is no accent or tone of feeling that one is tempted to make one's own and carry further in one's own way. No writer, I think, will go to school to Dos Passos, and readers, however much they may admire him will not stand in the relation to him in which they stand, say, to Stendhal or Henry James or even E.M. Forster. Dos Passos' plan is greater than its result in feeling; his book *tells* more than it *is*. Yet what it tells, and tells with accuracy, subtlety and skill, is enormously important and no one else has yet told it half so well.

Nor is *U.S.A.* as all-embracing as its admirers claim. True, Dos Passos not only represents a great national scene but he embodies, as I have said, the cultural tradition of the intellectual Left. But he does not encompass—does not pretend to encompass in this book—all of either. Despite his title, he is consciously selective of his America and he is, as I shall try to show, consciously corrective of the cultural tradition from which he stems.

Briefly and crudely, this cultural tradition may be said to consist of the following beliefs, which are not so much formulations of theory or principles of action as they are emotional tendencies: that the collective aspects of life may be distinguished from the individual aspects; that the collective aspects are basically important and are good; that the individual aspects are, or should be, of small interest and that they contain a destructive principle; that the fate of the individual is determined by social forces; that the social forces now dominant are evil; that there is a conflict between the dominant social forces and other, better, rising forces; that it is certain or very likely that the rising forces will overcome the now dominant ones. *U.S.A.* conforms to some but not to all of these assumptions. The lack of any protagonists in the trilogy, the equal attention given to many people, have generally been taken to represent Dos Passos' recognition of the importance of the collective idea. The book's historical apparatus indicates the author's belief in social determination. And there can be no

slightest doubt of Dos Passos' attitude to the dominant forces of
our time: he hates them.

But Dos Passos modifies the tradition in three important
respects. Despite the collective elements of his trilogy, he puts a
peculiar importance upon the individual. Again, he avoids
propounding any sharp conflict between the dominant forces of
evil and the rising forces of good; more specifically, he does not
write of a class struggle, nor is he much concerned with the notion
of class in the political sense. Finally, he is not at all assured of the
eventual triumph of good; he pins no faith on any force or
party—indeed he is almost alone of the novelists of the Left (Silone
is the only other one that comes to mind) in saying that the creeds
and idealisms of the Left may bring corruption quite as well as the
greeds and cynicisms of the established order; he has refused to cry
'Allons! the road lies before us,' and, in short, his novel issues in
despair.—And it is this despair of Dos Passos' book which has
made his two ablest critics, Malcolm Cowley and T.K. Whipple,
seriously temper their admiration. Mr. Cowley says: 'They [the
novels comprising *U.S.A.*] give us an extraordinarily diversified
picture of contemporary life, but they fail to include at least one
side of it—the will to struggle ahead, the comradeship in struggle,
the consciousness of new men and new forces continually rising.'[1]
And Mr. Whipple: 'Dos Passos has reduced what ought to be a tale
of full-bodied conflicts to an epic of disintegration.'[2]

These critics are saying that Dos Passos has not truly observed
the political situation. Whether he has or not, whether his despair is
objectively justifiable, cannot, with the best political will in the
world, be settled on paper. We hope he has seen incorrectly; he
himself must hope so. But there is also an implicit meaning in the
objections which, if the writers themselves did not intend it, many
readers will derive, and if not from Mr. Whipple and Mr. Cowley
then from the book itself: that the emotion in which *U.S.A.* issues
is negative to the point of being politically harmful.

But to discover a political negativism in the despair of *U.S.A.* is
to subscribe to a naive conception of human emotion and of the
literary experience. It is to assert that the despair of a literary work
must inevitably engender despair in the reader. Actually, of course,
it need do nothing of the sort. To rework the old Aristotelian
insight, it may bring about a catharsis of an already existing
despair. But more important: the word 'despair' all by itself (or any

other such general word or phrase) can never characterize the emotion the artist is dealing with. There are many kinds of despair and what is really important is what goes along with the general emotion denoted by the word. Despair with its wits about it is very different from despair that is stupid; despair that is an abandonment of illusion is very different from despair which generates tender new cynicisms. The 'heartbreak' of *Heartbreak House*, for example, is the beginning of new courage and I can think of no more useful *political* job for the literary man today than, by the representation of despair, to cauterize the exposed soft tissue of too-easy hope.

Even more than the despair, what has disturbed the radical admirers of Dos Passos's work is his appearance of indifference to the idea of the class struggle. Mr. Whipple correctly points out that the characters of *U.S.A.* are all 'midway people in somewhat ambiguous positions.' Thus, there are no bankers or industrialists (except incidentally) but only J. Ward Morehouse, their servant; there are no factory workers (except, again, incidentally), no farmers, but only itinerant workers, individualistic mechanics, actresses, interior decorators.

This, surely, is a limitation in a book that has had claimed for it a complete national picture. But when we say limitation we may mean just that or we may mean falsification, and I do not think that Dos Passos has falsified. The idea of class is not simple but complex. Socially it is extremely difficult to determine. It cannot be determined, for instance, by asking individuals to what class they belong; nor is it easy to convince them that they belong to one class or another. We may, to be sure, demonstrate the idea of class at income-extremes or function-extremes, but when we leave these we must fall back upon the criterion of 'interest'—by which we must mean *real* interest ('real will' in the Rousseauian sense) and not what people say or think they want. Even the criterion of action will not determine completely the class to which people belong. Class, then, is a useful but often undetermined category of political and social thought. The political leader and the political theorist will make use of it in ways different from those of the novelist. For the former the important thing is people's perception that they are of one class or another and their resultant action. For the latter the interesting and suggestive things are likely to be the moral paradoxes that result from the conflict between real and apparent interest. And the 'midway people' of Dos Passos represent this moral-paradoxical aspect of class. They are a great fact in American life. It is they who show the symptoms of cultural change. Their movement from social group to social group—from class to class, if you will—makes for the uncertainty of their moral codes, their confusion, their indecision. Almost more than the people of fixed class, they are at the mercy of the social stream because their interests cannot be clear to them and give them direction. If Dos Passos has omitted the class struggle, as Mr. Whipple and Mr. Cowley complain, it is only the external class struggle he has left out; within his characters the class struggle is going on constantly.

This, perhaps, is another way of saying that Dos Passos is primarily concerned with morality, with personal morality. The national, collective, social elements of his trilogy should be seen not as a bid for completeness but rather as a great setting, brilliantly delineated, for his moral interest. In his novels, as in actual life, 'conditions' supply the opportunity for personal moral action. But if Dos Passos is a social historian, as he is so frequently said to be, he is that in order to be a more complete moralist. It is of the greatest significance that for him the barometer of social breakdown is not suffering through economic deprivation but always moral degeneration through moral choice.

This must be said in the face of Mr. Whipple's description of Dos Passos' people as 'devoid of will or purpose, helplessly impelled hither and yon by the circumstances of the moment. They have no strength of resistance. They are weak at the very core of personality, the power to choose.' These, it would seem, are scarcely the characters with which the moralist can best work. But here we must judge not only by the moral equipment of the characters (and it is not at all certain that Mr. Whipple's description is correct: choice of action is seldom made as the result of Socratic dialectic) but by the novelist's idea of morality—the nature of his judgments and his estimate of the power of circumstance.

Dos Passos' morality is concerned not so much with the utility of an action as with the quality of the person who performs it. *What* his people do is not so important as *how* they do it, or what they become by doing it. We despise J. Ward Morehouse not so much for his creation of the labor-relations board, his support of the war, his advertising of patent-medicines, though these are despicable enough; we despise him rather for the words he uses as he does these things, for his self-deception, the tone and style he generates.

We despise G.H. Barrow, the labor-faker, not because he betrays labor; we despise him because he is mealy-mouthed and talks about 'the art of living' when he means concupiscence. But we do not despise the palpable fraud, Doc Bingham, because, though he lies to everyone else, he does not lie to himself.

The moral assumption on which Dos Passos seems to work was expressed by John Dewey some thirty years ago; there are certain moral situations, Dewey says, where we cannot decide between the ends; we are forced to make our moral choice in terms of our preference for one kind of character or another: 'What sort of an agent, of a person shall he be? This is the question finally at stake in any genuinely moral situation: What shall the agent *be*? What sort of character shall he assume? On its face, the question is what he shall *do*, shall he act for this or that end. But the incompatibility of the ends forces the issue back into the questions of the kind of selfhood, of agency, involved in the respective ends.' One can imagine that this method of moral decision does not have meaning for all times and cultures. Although dilemmas exist in every age, we do not find Antigone settling her struggle between family and state by a reference to the kind of character she wants to be, nor Orestes settling his in that way; and so with the medieval dilemma of wife vs. friend, or the family oath of vengeance vs. the feudal oath of allegiance. But for our age with its intense self-consciousness and its uncertain moral codes, the reference to the quality of personality does have meaning, and the greater the social flux the more frequent will be the interest in qualities of character rather than in the rightness of the end.

The modern novel, with its devices for investigating the quality of character, is the aesthetic form almost specifically called forth to exercise this modern way of judgment. The novelist goes where the law cannot go; he tells the truth where the formulations of even the subtlest ethical theorist cannot. He turns the moral values inside out to question the worth of the deed by looking not at its actual outcome but at its tone and style. He is subversive of dominant morality and under his influence we learn to praise what dominant morality condemns; he reminds us that benevolence may be aggression, that the highest idealism may corrupt. Finally, he gives us the models of the examples by which, half-unconsciously, we make our own moral selves.

Dos Passos does not primarily concern himself with the burly sinners who inherit the earth. His people are those who sin against themselves and for him the wages of sin is death—of the spirit. The whole Dos Passos morality and the typical Dos Passos fate are expressed in Burns' quatrain:

> I waive the quantum o' the sin,
> The hazard of concealing;
> But, och! it hardens a' within
> And petrifies the feeling!

In the trilogy physical death sometimes follows upon this petrifaction of the feeling but only as its completion. Only two people die without petrifying, Joe Williams and Daughter, who kept in their inarticulate way a spark of innocence, generosity and protest. Idealism does not prevent the consequences of sinning against oneself and Mary French with her devotion to the working class and the Communist Party, with her courage and 'sacrifice' is quite as dead as Richard Savage who inherits Morehouse's mantle, and she is almost as much to blame.

It is this element of blame, of responsibility, that exempts Dos Passos from Malcolm Cowley's charge of being in some part committed to the morality of what Cowley calls the Art Novel—the story of the Poet and the World, the Poet always sensitive and right, the World always crass and wrong. An important element of Dos Passos' moral conception is that, although the World does sin against his characters, the characters themselves are very often as wrong as the World. There is no need to enter the theological purlieus to estimate how much responsibility Dos Passos puts upon them and whether this is the right amount. Clearly, however, he holds people like Savage, Fainy McCreary and Eveline Hutchins accountable in some important part for their own fates and their own ignobility.

The morality of Dos Passos, then, is a romantic morality. Perhaps this is calling it a bad name; people say they have got tired of a morality concerned with individuals 'saving' themselves and 'realizing' themselves. Conceivably only Dos Passos' aggressive contemporaneity has kept them from seeing how very similar is his morality to, say, Browning's—the moment to be snatched, the crucial choice to be made, and if it is made on the wrong (the safe) side, the loss of human quality, so that instead of a man we have a Success and instead of two lovers a Statue and a Bust in the public square. But too insistent a cry against the importance of the individual quality is a sick cry—as sick as the cry of 'Something to live for' as a motivation of political choice. Among members of a party the considerations of solidarity, discipline and expedience are claimed to replace all others and moral judgment is left to history; among liberals, the idea of social determination, on no good ground, appears tacitly to exclude the moral concern: witness the nearly complete conspiracy of silence or misinterpretation that greeted Silone's *Bread and Wine*, which said not a great deal more than that personal and moral—and eventually political—problems were not settled by membership in a revolutionary party. It is not at all certain that it is political wisdom to ignore what so much concerns the novelist. In the long run is not the political choice fundamentally a choice of personal quality?

NOTES

1 Malcolm Cowley, 'Afterthoughts on Dos Passos', *New Republic,* lxxxviii (9 September 1936), 34.
2 See No. 38.

41. Granville Hicks, 'The Moods and Tenses of John Dos Passos', *New Masses*

26 April 1938, vol. xxvii, 22–3

In this retrospective, Hicks reviews *U.S.A.* along with *Journeys Between Wars* (1938), a collection of Dos Passos's travel essays.

John Dos Passos' publishers are wisely doing their part to make the country conscious of him as a major literary figure, and they have accordingly issued two omnibus volumes of his work. *U.S.A.* is, of course, his famous trilogy: *The 42nd Parallel, 1919,* and *The Big*

Money. Journeys Between Wars is made up of his travel books: much of *Rosinante to the Road Again* (1922), almost the whole of *Orient Express* (1927), and most of those sections of *In All Countries* (1934) that deal with foreign lands. It also contains some sixty pages on Dos Passos' visit to Spain a year ago.

Comparison of the two books makes it quite clear that Dos Passos' deeper experiences go into his novels, leaving his more casual impressions to be recorded in the travel essays. *Journeys Between Wars* shows that he is at his best when he is describing the persons he meets or recording his own moods. The *padrone* in the Spanish restaurant, the Sayid on the Orient express, the Danish accountant on his way home from America—these are effectively drawn. And the journal of the camel ride from Bagdad to Dasmascus is as pleasant a personal record as can be found in modern literature. But there is not much—and I have now read most of these essays twice—that the mind holds onto. Other novelists—Gide, Lawrence, Huxley—have written travel books that belong with their major works, but not Dos Passos.

The explanation, which has some importance for the understanding of Dos Passos as a writer, seems to me fairly clear. He deals, consistently and no doubt deliberately, with impressions—the specific scene, the precise emotions, the exact conversation. The seeing eye—even 'the camera eye'—is admittedly the first virtue of the travel writer. But it is equally certain that the memorable travel writers have not been afraid to draw conclusions from what they saw. Don Passos is afraid: no milder word will do. What one feels in *Journeys Between Wars* is neither a casual holiday from the job of thinking nor a conscientious elimination of ideas for some literary purpose but a deep emotional unwillingness to face the intellectual implications of things seen and heard.

And the extraordinary thing is that this shrinking from conclusions is to be found even in the last section, the section dealing with Spain in 1937. Dos Passos tells of crossing the border from France, of a night on the road, of executions in Valencia, of a bombardment of Madrid, of a fiesta of the Fifteenth Brigade, of a trip through some villages, and of an interview with officials of the P.O.U.M. But there is not a word about the issues between the loyalists and the fascists, not a word about the differences between the loyalist government and the P.O.U.M. It seems incredible that any author, considering all that is involved in Spain today, could keep such silence. Do not suppose that Dos Passos is merely maintaining an artistic objectivity, holding back his own opinions so that the reader can arrive unhampered at the truth. He simply has refused to think his way through to clear convictions. He has sympathies—with the loyalists as against the fascists and apparently with the P.O.U.M. as against the government. But even the Spanish crisis cannot shake him into thought.

The only approximation to a conclusion comes as Dos Passos is leaving Spain, and, characteristically, it is in the form of a question: 'How can they win, I was thinking? How can the new world of confusion and crosspurposes and illusions and dazzled by the mirage of idealistic phrases win against the iron combination of men accustomed to run things who have only one idea binding them together, to hold on to what they've got?' This passage has been quoted by almost every conservative reviewer of the book, and quoted with undisguised satisfaction. 'We told you so,' one could hear them saying. 'There's no sense in trying to help Spain. It's all foolishness to hope for social justice anywhere. Let's make the best of things as they are.'

The truth is that it is impossible to avoid having opinions, and the only question is whether or not they are based on adequate information and clear thinking. If Dos Passos had faced the responsibility of the writer, and especially the radical writer, to use his intellect as well as his eyes, if he had been concerned, not with avoiding conclusions, but with arriving at sound ones, I think he would have come out of Spain with something more to say than these faltering words of despair. Afraid to think, he has yielded to a mood, and the reactionaries are delighted with his surrender. Both that surrender and his flirtation with the P.O.U.M. are results of an essential irresponsibility.

Dos Passos' irresponsibility takes two forms: unwillingness to think and unwillingness to act. Several years ago, I remember, at the time when he was perhaps closest to the Communist Party, he said something to the effect that he was merely a camp-follower. In *Journeys Between Wars* there is a revealing passage. (It is, of course, creditably characteristic of Dos Passos to reveal himself.) When he was leaving the Soviet Union in 1928, the director and the actors of the Sanitary Propaganda Theatre came to see him off. The director said, 'They want to know. They like you very much, but they want to ask you one question. They want you to show your face.

They want to know where you stand politically. Are you with us?'
Dos Passos continues: 'The iron twilight dims, the steam swirls
round us, we are muddled by the delicate crinkly steam of our
breath, the iron crown tightens on the head, throbbing with too
many men, too many women, too many youngsters seen, talked
to, asked questions of, too many hands shaken, too many foreign
languages badly understood. "But let me see.... But maybe I can
explain... But in so short a time... there's not time." The train
is moving. I have to run and jump for it.'

The passage, so palpably sincere and so pleasant, reminds us that,
even in a broader sense, Dos Passos has always been uncommonly
detached. Indeed, detachment is almost the keynote of *Journeys
Between Wars*. In the extracts from *Rosinante* Dos Passos is 'the
traveler'; in *Orient Express* he is 'the east-bound American'; in the
Russian section he is 'the American Peesatyel.' Perhaps it is no
wonder that in writing about Spain in 1937 he is still merely an
observer. It is no wonder that he has seldom tried to write about
the revolutionary movement from inside, and, when he has tried,
has failed. It is no wonder that he has never communicated the
sense of the reality of comradeship, as Malraux, for example,
communicates it in *Days of Wrath*.

Yet there was a time when Dos Passos seemed willing to try to
think clearly and to feel deeply. His second play, *Airways, Inc.*, was
bad dramatically, but in it Dos Passos at least made an attempt to be
clear. There was a sharp difference betwen that play and *The
Garbage Man*, and an even greater difference between *The 42nd
Parallel*, first novel of his triology, and *Manhattan Transfer*. In *The
42nd Parallel* Dos Passos seemed for the first time to have mastered
the American scene. The technical devices used in this novel and
1919 perplexed some readers, but Dos Passos himself appeared to be
relatively clear about what he was trying to do.

Airways, Inc. was published in 1928, *The 42nd Parallel* in 1930,
and *1919* in 1932. Here, then, are three or four years of comparative
clarity. And in those years Dos Passos was close to Communism.
At this time he actually believed in something like the Marxian
analysis of history, and it worked. He also felt a stronger
confidence in the working class. Communism did not make him a
novelist, but it made him a better novelist.

What I failed to realize at the time of the publication of *1919* was
the extent to which Dos Passos' interest in the Communist Party

was a matter of mood. He had not sufficiently overcome his fear of conclusions to make a serious study of Marxism, and he had only partly subdued his passion for aloofness. Little things could—and, as it happened, did—disturb him. He was on the right track, but not much was required to derail him.

In the four years since he left the track Dos Passos has gone a long and disastrous way. Last summer, as has been said, he came out of Spain with nothing but a question mark, and committed himself to a hysterical isolationism that might almost be called chauvinistic. Last December he and Theodore Dreiser held a conversation that was published in *Direction*. Dos Passos' confusion—equaled, I hasten to say, by Dreiser's—is unpleasant to contemplate for anyone who expects some semblance of intellectual dignity in a prominent novelist. He is still looking for an impartial observer of the Soviet Union, and thinks he has found one in Victor Serge. His new-found devotion to the United States continues to run high: 'America is probably the country where the average guy has got a better break.' 'You can't get anywhere,' he says, 'in talking to fanatic Communists.' He talks about revolution: 'A sensible government would take over industries and compensate the present owners, and then deflate the money afterwards.' And this is his contribution to economics: 'Every time there is a rise in wages, prices go up at the A. & P.'

After one has noted the banality, the naïveté, and the sheer stupidity of most of Dos Passos' remarks in his talk with Dreiser, one knows that politically he is as unreliable as a man can be and is capable of any kind of preposterous vagary. But I am interested in Dos Passos' politics only insofar as they influence his writing, as of course they do. When *1919* appeared, I believed that Dos Passos had established his position as the most talented of American novelists—a position he still holds. As early as 1934, however, I was distressed by his failure to shake off habits of mind that I had thought—quite erroneously, as it turns out—were dissolving under the influence of contact with the revolutionary movement. At that time, reviewing *In All Countries*, I said: 'Dos Passos, I believe, is superior to his bourgeois contemporaries because he is, however incompletely, a revolutionist, and shares, however imperfectly, in the vigor of the revolutionary movement, its sense of purpose, its awareness of the meaning of events, and its defiance of bourgeois pessimism and decay. He is also, it seems to me,

superior to any other revolutionary writer because of the sensitiveness and the related qualities that are to be found in this book and,
much more abundantly, in his novels. Some day, however, we
shall have a writer who surpasses Dos Passos, who has all that he
has and more. He will not be a camp-follower.'

Now that Dos Passos is not in any sense a revolutionist and does
not share at all in the vigor of the revolutionary movement, what
about the virtues that I attributed to his association with the
Communist Party? I am afraid the answer is in *The Big Money*,
most of which was written after 1934. One figure dominates *The
Big Money* to an extent that no one figure dominated either *The
42nd Parallel* or *1919*. It is Charley Anderson, the symbol of the
easy-money Twenties, the working stiff who gets to be a big shot.
('America is probably the country where the average guy has got a
better break.') His desperate money-making and drinking and
fornicating take place against a background of unhappy rich people
and their unhappy parasites. Further in the background are some
equally unhappy revolutionists, who are either futile or vicious.
('You can't get anywhere in talking to fanatic Communists'.)

It seems to me foolish to pretend that an author doesn't choose
his material. Dos Passos didn't have to lay his principal emphasis
on the hopeless mess that the capitalist system makes of a good
many lives. He didn't have to make his two Communists narrow
sectarians. He didn't have to make the strongest personal note in
the book a futilitarian elegy for Sacco and Vanzetti. There must
have been a good deal in the Twenties that he left out, for large
masses of people did learn something from the collapse of the
boom, and the Communist Party did get rid of factionalism, and
the workers did save Angelo Herndon and the Scottsboro Boys,
even though they failed to save Sacco and Vanzetti. *The Big Money*,
in other words, grows out of the same prejudices and misconcep-
tions, the same confusion and blindness, as the conversation with
Dreiser.

The difference is, of course, that there is a lot in *The Big Money*
besides these faulty notions. I have written elsewhere about Dos
Passos' gifts, and I need only say here that I admire them as
strongly as ever. I know of no contemporary American work of
fiction to set beside *U.S.A.* But I also know that, because of the
change in mood that came between *1919* and *The Big Money*,
U.S.A. is not so true, not so comprehensive, not so strong as it

might have been. And, though I have acquired caution enough not to predict Dos Passos' future direction, I know that, if he follows the path he is now on, his claims to greatness are already laid before us and later critics will only have to fill in the details of another story of genius half-fulfilled.

42. Jean-Paul Sartre, 'John Dos Passos and *1919*'

August 1938

Sartre (1905–80), the French existentialist philosopher, critic, and writer, published his autobiographical novel, *Nausea*, in the same year he wrote this essay. Most of his philosophical works, which emphasized the necessity and inescapability of free choice, were written during the 1940s, including *Being and Nothingness* (1943). In this essay Sartre attempts to explain why he believes Dos Passos is 'the greatest writer of our time'. The essay was first printed by Gallimard in *Situations I* (1947). Reprinted here is Annette Michelson's translation from Sartre's *Literary and Philosophical Essays* (London: Rider, 1955), 88–96.

A novel is a mirror. So everyone says. But what is meant by *reading* a novel? It means, I think, jumping into the mirror. You suddenly find yourself on the other side of the glass, among people and objects that have a familiar look. But they merely look familiar. We have never really seen them. The things of our world have, in turn, become outside reflections. You close the book, step over the edge of the mirror and return to this honest-to-goodness world, and you find furniture, gardens and people who have nothing to say to you. The mirror that closed behind you reflects them peacefully, and now you would swear that art is a reflection. There are clever people who go so far as to talk of distorting mirrors.

Dos Passos very consciously uses this absurd and insistent illusion to impel us to revolt. He had done everything possible to make his novel seem a mere reflection. He has even donned the garb of populism. The reason is that his art is not gratuitous; he wants to prove something. But observe what a curious aim he has. He wants to show us this world, our own—to *show* it only, without explanations or comment. There are no revelations about the machinations of the police, the imperialism of the oil kings or the Ku-Klux-Klan, no cruel pictures of poverty. We have already seen everything he wants to show us, and, so it seems at first glance, seen it exactly as he wants us to see it. We recognize immediately the sad abundance of these untragic lives. They are our own lives, these innumerable, planned, botched, immediately forgotten and constantly renewed adventures that slip by without leaving a trace, without involving anyone, until the time when one of them, no different from any of the others, suddenly, as if through some clumsy trickery, sickens a man for good and throws a mechanism out of gear.

Now, it is by depicting, as we ourselves might depict, these too familiar appearances with which we all put up that Dos Passos makes them unbearable. He arouses indignation in people who never get indignant, he frightens people who fear nothing. But hasn't there been some sleight-of-hand? I look about me and see people, cities, boats, the war. But they aren't the real thing; they are discreetly queer and sinister, as in a nightmare. My indignation against this world also seems dubious to me; it only faintly resembles the other indignation, the kind that a mere news item can arouse. I am on the other side of the mirror.

Dos Passos' hate, despair and lofty contempt are real. But that is precisely why his world is not real; it is a created object. I know of none—not even Faulkner's or Kafka's—in which the art is greater or better hidden. I know of none that is more precious, more touching or closer to us. This is because he takes his material from our world. And yet, there is no stranger or more distant world. Dos Passos has invented only one thing, an art of story-telling. But that is enough to create a universe.

We live in time, we calculate in time. The novel, like life, unfolds in the present. The perfect tense exists on the surface only; it must be interpreted as a present *with aesthetic distance,* as a stage device. In the novel the dice are not loaded, for fictional man is free. He develops before our eyes; our impatience, our ignorance, our expectancy are the same as the hero's. The tale, on the other hand, as Fernàndez has shown, develops in the past. But the tale explains. Chronological order, life's order, barely conceals the causal order, which is an order for the understanding. The event does not touch us; it stands half-way between fact and law. Dos Passos' time is his own creation; it is neither fictional nor narrative. It is rather, if you like, historical time. The perfect and imperfect tenses are not used simply to observe the rules; the reality of Joe's or of Eveline's adventures lies in the fact they are now part of the past. Everything is told as if by someone who is remembering.

'*The years Dick was little* he never heard anything about his Dad....' 'All Eveline thought about *that winter* was going to the Art Institute....' 'They waited two weeks in Vigo while the officials quarrelled about their status and they got pretty fed up with it.'

The fictional event is a nameless presence; there is nothing one can say about it, for it develops. We may be shown two men combing a city for their mistresses, but we are not told that they 'do not find them,' for this is not true. So long as there remains one street, one café, one house to explore, it is not yet true. In Dos Passos, the things that happen are named first, and then the dice are cast, as they are in our memories.

Glen and Joe only got ashore for a few hours and couldn't find Marcelline and Loulou.

The facts are clearly outlined; they are ready for *thinking about*. But Dos Passos never thinks them. Not for an instant does the order of causality betray itself in chronological order. There is no narrative, but rather the jerky unreeling of a rough and uneven memory, which sums up a period of several years in a few words only to dwell languidly over a minute fact. Like our real memories, it is a jumble of miniatures and frescoes. There is relief enough, but it is cunningly scattered at random. One step further would give us the famous idiot's monologue in *The Sound and the Fury*. But that would still involve intellectualizing, suggesting an explanation in terms of the irrational, suggesting a Freudian order beneath this disorder. Dos Passos stops just in time. As a result of this, past things retain a flavour of the present; they still remain, in their exile, what they once were, inexplicable tumults of colour, sound and passion. Each event is irreducible, a gleaming and solitary *thing* that does not flow from anything else, but suddenly arises to join other things. For Dos Passos, narrating means adding. This accounts for the slack air of his style. 'And...and...and...' The great disturbing phenomena—war, love, political movements, strikes—fade and crumble into an infinity of little odds and ends which can just about be set side by side. Here is the armistice:

In early November rumours of an armistice began to fly around and then suddenly one afternoon Major Wood ran into the office that Eleanor and Eveline shared and dragged them both away from their desks and kissed them both and shouted, 'At last it's come.' Before she knew it Eveline found herself kissing Major Moorehouse right on the mouth. The Red Cross office turned into a college dormitory the night of a football victory: it was the Armistice.

Everybody seemed suddenly to have bottles of cognac and to be singing, *There's a long trail awinding* or *La Madel-lon pour nous n'est pas sévère.*

These Americans see war the way Fabrizio saw the battle of Waterloo. And the intention, like the method, is clear upon reflection. But you must close the book and reflect.

Passions and gestures are also things. Proust analysed them, related them to former states and thereby made them inevitable. Dos Passos wants to retain only their factual nature. All he is allowed to say is, 'In that place and at that time Richard was that way, and at another time, he was different.' Love and decisions are great spheres that rotate on their own axes. The most we can grasp is a kind of *conformity* between the psychological state and the exterior situation, something resembling a colour harmony. We may also suspect that explanations are *possible*, but they seem as frivolous and futile as a spider-web on a heavy red flower. Yet, never do we have the feeling of fictional freedom: Dos Passos imposes upon us instead the unpleasant impression of an indeterminacy of detail. Acts, emotions and ideas suddenly settle within a character, make themselves at home and then disappear without his having much to say in the matter. You cannot say he submits to them. He experiences them. There seems to be no law governing their appearance.

Nevertheless, they once did exist. This lawless past is irremediable. Dos Passos has purposely chosen the perspective of history to tell a story. He wants to make us feel that the stakes are down. In

Man's Hope, Malraux says, more or less, that 'the tragic thing about death is that it transforms life into a destiny.' With the opening lines of his book, Dos Passos settles down into death. The lives he tells about are all closed in on themselves. They resemble those Bergsonian memories which, after the body's death, float about, lifeless and full of odours and lights and cries, through some forgotten limbo. We constantly have the feeling that these vague, human lives are destinies. Our own past is not at all like this. There is not one of our acts whose meaning and value we cannot still transform even now. But beneath the violent colours of these beautiful, motley objects that Dos Passos presents there is something petrified. Their significance is fixed. Close your eyes and try to remember your own life, try to remember it *that way*; you will stifle. It is this unrelieved stifling that Dos Passos wanted to express. In capitalist society, men do not have lives, they have only destinies. He never says this, but he makes it felt throughout. He expresses it discreetly, cautiously, until we feel like smashing our destinies. We have become rebels; he has achieved his purpose.

We are rebels *behind the looking-glass*. For that is not what the rebel of this world wants to change. He wants to transform Man's *present* condition, the one that develops day by day. Using the past tense to tell about the present means using a device, creating a strange and beautiful world, as frozen as one of those Mardi-Gras masks that become frightening on the faces of real, living men.

But whose memories are these that unfold through the novel? At first glance, they seem to be those of the heroes, of Joe, Dick, Fillette and Eveline. And, on occasion, they are. As a rule, whenever a character is sincere, whenever he is bursting with something, no matter how, or with what:

When he went off duty he'd walk home achingly tired through the strawberry-scented early Parisian morning, thinking of the faces and the eyes and the sweat-drenched hair and the clenched fingers clotted with blood and dirt...

But the narrator often ceases to coincide completely with the hero. The hero could not quite have said what he does say, but you feel a discreet complicity between them. The narrator relates from the outside what the hero would have wanted him to relate. By means of this complicity, Dos Passos, without warning us, has us make the transition he was after. We suddenly find ourselves inside

a horrible memory whose every recollection makes us uneasy, a
bewildering memory that is no longer that of either the characters
or the author. It seems like a chorus that remembers, a sententious
chorus that is accessory to the deed.

All the same he got along very well at school and the teachers liked him,
particularly Miss Teazle, the English teacher, because he had nice manners
and said little things that weren't fresh but that made them laugh. Miss
Teazle said he showed real feeling for English composition. One
Christmas he sent her a little rhyme he made up about the Christ Child and
the three Kings and she declared he had a gift.

The narration takes on a slightly stilted manner, and everything
that is reported about the hero assumes the solemn quality of a
public announcement: '...she declared he had a gift.' The sentence
is not accompanied by any comment, but acquires a sort of
collective resonance. It is a *declaration*. And indeed, whenever we
want to know his characters' thoughts, Dos Passos, with respectful
objectivity, generally gives us their declarations.

Fred...said the last night before they left he was going to tear loose. When
they got to the front he might get killed and then what? Dick said he liked
talking to the girls but that the whole business was too commercial and
turned his stomach. Ed Schuyler, who'd been nicknamed Frenchie and was
getting very continental in his ways, said that the street girls were too
naive.

I open *Paris-Soir* and read, '*From our special correspondent*; Charlie
Chaplin declares that he has put an end to Charlie.' Now I have it!
Dos Passos reports all his characters' utterances to us in the style of
a statement to the Press. Their words are thereby cut off from
thought, and become pure utterances, simple reactions that must be
registered as such, in the behaviourist style upon which Dos Passos
draws when it suits him to do so. But, at the same time, the
utterance takes on a social importance; it is inviolable, it becomes a
maxim. Little does it matter, thinks the satisfied chorus, what Dick
had in mind when he spoke that sentence. What matters is that it
has been uttered. Besides, it was not formed inside him, it came
from afar. Even before he uttered it, it existed as a pompous sound,
a taboo. All he has done is to lend it his power of affirmation. It is
as if there were a Platonic heaven of words and commonplaces to
which we all go to find words suitable to a given situation. There is
a heaven of gestures, too. Dos Passos makes a pretence of

presenting gestures as pure events, as mere exteriors, as free, animal movements. But this is only appearance. Actually, in relating them, he adopts the point of view of the chorus, of public opinion. There is no single one of Dick's or of Eleanor's gestures which is not a public demonstration, performed to a humming accompaniment of flattery.

At Chantilly they went through the château and fed the big carp in the moat. They ate their lunch in the woods, sitting on rubber cushions. J.W. kept everybody laughing explaining how he hated picnics, asking everybody what it was that got into even the most intelligent women that they were always trying to make people go on picnics. After lunch they drove out to Senlis to see the houses that the Uhlans had destroyed there in the battle of the Marne.

Doesn't it sound like a local newspaper's account of an exservicemen's banquet? All of a sudden, as the gesture dwindles until it is no more than a thin film, we see that it *counts*, that it is sacred in character and that, at the same time, it involves commitment. But for whom? For the object consciousness of 'everyman,' for what Heidegger calls 'das Mann.' But still, where does it spring from? Who is its representative as I read? *I* am. In order to understand the words, in order to make sense out of the paragraphs, I first have to adopt his point of view. I have to play the role of the obliging chorus. This consciousness exists only through me; without me there would be nothing but black spots on white paper. But even while I *am* this collective consciousness, I want to wrench away from it, to see it from the judge's point of view, that is, to get free of myself. This is the source of the shame and uneasiness with which Dos Passos knows how to fill the reader. I am a reluctant accomplice (though I am not even sure that I am reluctant), creating and rejecting social taboos. I am, deep in my heart, a revolutionary again, an unwilling one.

In return, how I hate Dos Passos' men! I am given a fleeting glimpse of their minds, just enough to see that they are living animals. Then, they begin to unwind their endless tissue of ritual statements and sacred gestures. For them, there is no break between inside and outside, between body and consciousness, but only between the stammerings of an individual's timid, intermittent, fumbling thinking and the messy world of collective representations. What a simple process this is, and how effective!

All one need do is use American journalistic technique in telling the story of a life, and like the Salzburg reed, a life crystallizes into the Social, and the problem of the transition to the typical—stumbling-block of the social novel—is thereby resolved. There is no further need to present a working man type, to compose (as Nizan does in *Antoine Bloyé*) an existence which represents the exact average of thousands of existences. Dos Passos, on the contrary, can give all his attention to rendering a single life's special character. Each of his characters is unique; what happens to him could happen to no one else. What does it matter, since Society has marked him more deeply than could any special circumstance, since *he is* Society? Thus, we get a glimpse of an order beyond the accidents of fate or the contingency of detail, an order more supple than Zola's physiological necessity or Proust's psychological mechanism, a soft and insinuating constraint which seems to release its victims, letting them go only to take possession of them again without their suspecting, in other words, a statistical determinism. These men, submerged in their own existences, live as they can. They struggle; what comes their way is not determined in advance. And yet, neither their efforts, their faults, nor their most extreme violence can interfere with the regularity of births, marriages and suicides. The pressure exerted by a gas on the walls of its container does not depend upon the individual histories of the molecules composing it.

We are still on the other side of the looking-glass. Yesterday you saw your best friend and expressed to him your passionate hatred of war. Now try to relate this conversation to yourself in the style of Dos Passos. 'And they ordered two beers and said that war was hateful. Paul declared he would rather do anything than fight and John said he agreed with him and both got excited and said they were glad they agreed. On his way home, Paul decided to see John more often.' You will start hating yourself immediately. It will not take you long, however, to decide that you *cannot* use this tone in talking about yourself. However insincere you may have been, you were at least living out your insincerity, playing it out on your own, continuously creating and extending its existence from one moment to the next. And even if you got caught up in collective representations, you had first to experience them as personal resignation. We are neither mechanical objects nor possessed souls, but something worse; we are free. We exist either entirely *within* or entirely *without*. Dos Passos' man is a hybrid creature, an interior-exterior being. We go on living with him and within him, with his vacillating, individual consciousness, when suddenly it wavers, weakens, and is diluted in the collective consciousness. We follow it up to that point and suddenly, before we notice, we are on the outside. The man behind the looking-glass is a strange, contemptible, fascinating creature. Dos Passos knows how to use this constant shifting to fine effect. I know of nothing more gripping than Joe's death.

Joe laid out a couple of frogs and was backing off towards the door, when he saw in the mirror that a big guy in a blouse was bringing down a bottle on his head held with both hands. He tried to swing around but he didn't have time. The bottle crashed his skull and he was out.

We are inside with him, until the shock of the bottle on his skull. Then immediately, we find ourselves outside with the chorus, part of the collective memory, '. . .and he was out.' Nothing gives you a clearer feeling of annihilation. And from then on, each page we turn, each page that tells of other minds and of a world going on without Joe, is like a spadeful of earth over our bodies. But it is a behind-the-looking-glass death: all we really get is the fine *appearance* of nothingness. True nothingness can neither be felt nor thought. Neither you nor I, nor anyone after us, will ever have anything to say about our real deaths.

Dos Passos' world—like those of Faulkner, Kafka and Stendhal—is impossible because it is contradictory. But therein lies its beauty. Beauty is a veiled contradiction. I regard Dos Passos as the greatest writer of our time.

43. Delmore Schwartz, 'John Dos Passos and the Whole Truth', *Southern Review*

October 1938, vol. iv, 351–67

Schwartz (1913–66), the American writer, was an editor of *Partisan Review* (1943–55) and later the *New Republic*. His first book, *In Dreams Begin Responsibilities and Other Stories*, was published in the same year as this review. Schwartz believed Dos Passos had told only part of America's story because naturalism leaves out human possibility and potential.

If we think for a moment of the newspaper as a representation of American life, we get some idea of the basis of John Dos Passos' enormous novel. It is not merely that one of the devices of this novel is the 'newsreel' and consists of an arrangement of quotations from newspapers of the past thirty years; nor that another device is the 'camera eye,' and still another consists of biographies of Americans who have for the most part been prominent in the newspaper. It is in its whole sense of American life and in its formal character—its omnibus, omnivorous span—that Dos Passos' novel seems to at least one reader to derive from the newspaper. The sense of the unknown lives behind the wedding announcements and the obituaries, the immense gap between private life and public events, and between the private experience of the individual and the public experience represented in the newspaper as being constituted by accident, violence, scandal, the speeches of politicians, and the deliberations of Congress—all this would seem to have a good deal to do with determining Dos Passos' vision and his intention. There were concerts, club meetings, and lectures in St. Petersburg on the night in October, 1917, when the Russian Revolution occurred—it is such a curious mixture of the private worlds and the public world that seems to obsess Dos Passos.

Another and related way of characterizing his novels is through the names he has given them: *Three Soldiers*, a 'picture' of the World War (which, curiously enough, delighted Amy Lowell), *Manhattan Transfer*, a 'picture' of New York City, *The 42nd Parallel*, and *1919*. And thus it is interesting to remark that the name of *U.S.A.* apparently was chosen for Dos Passos by the reviewer in *Time* who said, when a part of the book appeared as a separate novel, that 'Alone among U.S. writers, John Dos Passos has taken as his subject the whole U.S.A. and attempted to organize its chaotic high-pressure life into an understandable artistic pattern.' The source of the title suggests that Dos Passos' way of grasping experience has a good deal, although not everything, in common not only with the triumvirate of *Time*, *Life*, and *Fortune*, but also with the whole tendency to get documents, to record facts, and to swallow the whole rich chaos of modern life. The motion picture called *The River*, with its mixture of lyricism and economic discourse, the picture-and-text books, the Federal theater plays about housing and the AAA, and even the poetry, in some of its aspects, of Mr. Horace Gregory and Miss Muriel Rukeyser are like examples of a distinct method of attempting to take hold of experience in its breathless and disordered contemporaneity. How widespread the sense of life exemplified in Dos Passos is, and what its basis is, can be seen in these words of a preface to a book of short stories edited by a wholly different kind of writer:

[Quotes from *365 Days*, a chronicle of events during the year 1934, edited by Kay Boyle. Lawrence Vail, and Nina Conarain (New York: Harcourt Brace, 1936).]

The poetic fashioned by this kind of awareness can perhaps be stated in this way: there are facts and things and processes continually going on in the world and the writer intends nothing so much as to provide portraits, even photographs, of them through the conventions of fiction—and sometimes without those conventions. Of Dos Passos we can say—and regard this as the best praise for anyone's intention—that his intention has been to tell the truth about the world in which he has had to exist. But more than that, he has apparently gone from one end of the world to the other in the effort to find the truth and not to permit the *Zeitgeist* to evade him. So, at any rate, his travel book[1] indicates, providing an image of the author as the sensitive, unassuming, anonymous observer who is intent upon seeing all that is to be seen—even when, as in Russia in 1928 and in Barcelona in 1937, he is compelled to see so much that will be contrary to his expectation and dearest hope.

At the conclusion of the last book of *U.S.A.* and after having written some 1400 pages, Dos Passos wrote a brief chapter to head the whole book and called the chapter *U.S.A.*, and here defined his intention, at the conclusion of his efforts, when he would know it best.

[Quotes from *U.S.A.*, v–vi.]

And the only link, we are told, between the young man walking alone and the life he wished to know so fully was in the speech of the people. U.S.A. meant and was many things—a part of a continent, a group of holding companies, the soldiers who died for the U.S.A., the letters on an address, a stack of newspapers on file—'but mostly U.S.A. is the speech of the people.' And Dos Passos has told us this before, in the introduction written to *Three Soldiers*, in 1932, when that book was canonized by The Modern Library. Again what he says is worth quoting for its expression of the utter honesty and clarity of his intention.

You wake up one morning and find that what was to have been a *springboard into reality* [*my italics*] is a profession. Making a living by selling daydreams is all right, but few men feel it's much of a life for a man... What I'm trying to get out is the difference in kind between the work of James Joyce, say, and that of any current dispenser of daydreams.... What do you write for, then? To convince people of something? That's preaching, and a part of the business of everyone who deals with words.... but outside of preaching I think there is such a thing as straight writing... The mind of a generation is its speech. A writer makes aspects of that speech enduring... makes of them forms to set the mind of tomorrow's generation. That's history. A writer who writes straight is the architect of history... Those of us who have lived through [these times] have seen the years strip the bunting off the great illusions of our time. We must deal with the raw structure of history now, we must deal with it quick, before it stamps us out.

One may regret the slanging tone, as of Mr. Otis Ferguson (as if Dos Passos too were afraid that if he used abstract terms and an unconversational diction, he would be considered a sissy), and one may feel that an 'architect of history' is rather a fancy claim, but one cannot deny that Dos Passos knows very well what he wants to do in his novels.

Naturally such motives have infected his style and method in every aspect. In *U.S.A.*, Dos Passos uses four 'forms' or 'frames,' each of them deriving directly from his representative intention, his desire to get at the truth about his time with any available instrument. Each of these forms needs to be considered in itself.

There is the camera eye, an intermittent sequence of prose poems in an impressionist style: 'all week the fog clung to the sea and cliffs....gray flakes green sea gray houses white fog lap of the waves against the wharf scream of gulls circling and swooping,' or another brief example: 'all over Tours you can smell the linden in bloom it's hot my uniform sticks the O.D. chafes me under the chin.' Each impression is apparently autobiographical and dates from the childhood of the author to the 'twenties. The writing takes on the lyricism of a quasi-Joycean stream-of-consciousness and the emphasis is almost always upon the look and feel of things, mostly apart from any narrative context. At first glance the texture seems the crudity of an undergraduate determined to be modern, but upon examination this entirely disappears and one finds that all is based on faithful observation and is never pretentious, nor false. But these passages have no direct relation to the main story, although at times there is some link—just before a leading character goes to Havana, for example, the autobiographical impression is of a trip on a Spanish boat to Cuba.

Secondly, there are the newsreel passages which are inserted just as the camera eye panels are, between narratives. They consist of quotations from newspapers of a given time and period and also of its popular songs. Many amusing juxtapositions of headlines and stories are made by means of clever arrangements, and the lyrics are (where the present reader is able to judge) perfectly reminiscent. But the central intention of this form—to suggest the quality of various years and its public events—is not fulfilled for the most part. The newsreels are sometimes merely frivolous and trivial. One example may suffice to show this:

the first thing the volunteer firefighters did was to open the windows to let the smoke out. This created a draft and the fire with a good thirty-mile wind from the ocean did the rest

RECORD TURNOVER IN INSURANCE SHARES
AS TRADING PROGRESSES
Change all of your grey skies
Turn them into blue skies
And keep sweeping the cobwebs off the moon.
BROKERS LOANS HIT NEW HIGH
MARKETS OPTIMISTIC

learn new uses for concrete. How to develop profitable concrete business. How to judge materials. How to figure jobs. How to reinforce concrete. How to build forms, roads, sidewalks, floors, culverts, cellars.

The time, one would suppose, is 1927 or 1928. The stock market headlines indicate that time and are loosely relevant to the main narrative. The first passage is a news story, however, and the last is an advertisement. They are disjunct parts and they could with no difficulty be transposed to any other of the fifty-eight newsreels going back to the turn of the century.

A third form is the 'Biography.' Here we are provided with concise recitatives in a Whitmanesque diction which is used at times with power. Each biography concerns a great figure of the period, and there are twenty-six of them. Four leaders of the working class, Eugene V. Debs, Joe Hill, Bill Haywood, and Wesley Everest; seven capitalists, Andrew Carnegie, Henry Ford, William Randolph Hearst, J.P. Morgan, Samuel Insull, and Minor C. Keith; four politicians, Robert LaFollette (Sr.), Theodore Roosevelt, Woodrow Wilson, and William Jennings Bryan; four inventors, Luther Burbank, the Wright Brothers, Thomas Edison, and Charles Steinmetz; three journalists, John Reed, Randolph Bourne, and Paxton Hibben; an actor, Rudolph Valentino; a dancer, Isadora Duncan; an efficiency expert, Frederick W. Taylor; an architect, Frank Lloyd Wright; and one genuine intellectual, Thorstein Veblen. One remarks that naturally enough there are no musicians, musical life being what it is in America. But one regrets the omission of poets, unless John Reed be considered one—Harriet Monroe, Vachel Lindsay, Amy Lowell, and even Hart Crane suggest themselves. There is no characteristic Broadway actor, such as Al Jolson. Professional sport, particularly major league baseball, which in fact prepossesses at least two million American souls for six months a year, might also have been represented, at least in the newsreels; and for biographies, one thinks of Christy Matthewson, Connie Mack, Red Grange, and Gertrude Ederle. But on the whole the biographies are as representative as one could wish and are written with a fine power of generalization and concision—the gist abstracted from the life of a man and presented in four or five pages, concluding very well at times in the form of a simple contradiction, Henry Ford's nostalgic desire for the horse-and-buggy days, which his whole career, of course, worked to destroy, and Andrew Carnegie's bestowal of millions for world peace, the millions being acquired, of course, by the manufacture of steel used in munitions and battleships.

The major part of the novel, perhaps as much as 1200 pages, is, however, constituted by direct narratives of the lives of eleven leading characters and perhaps three times as many minor ones who are notable. In creating a mode in which to present the lives of these characters, Dos Passos has definitely extended the art of narration. It is difficult to describe what he has accomplished because it is so much a matter of the digestion of a great many details and the use of facts which rise from the historical sense—all caught into a smooth-running story which, taken in itself, cannot fail to hold the reader's attention. The narratives are always in the third person and yet have all the warm interior flow of a story presented through the medium of a stream-of-consciousness first-person. One remarkable achievement is the way in which the element of time is disposed. With no break or unevenness at all, the narrative passes quickly through several years of the character's life, presenting much that is essential briefly, and then contracts, without warning, without being noted, and focuses for several pages upon a single episode which is important. It is an ability which an apprentice writer can best appreciate and comes from the indispensable knowledge of how very much the writer can *omit*—Hemingway knows this very well also—and a knowledge of how each sentence can expand in the reader's mind to include a whole context of experience. Another feature to be noted is Dos Passos' immense command of details which seem to come from a thousand American places and to be invested with a kind of historical idiom at all times. There is, for example, the story of Eleanor Stoddard, which begins:

When she was small she hated everything. She hated her father, a stout red haired man smelling of whiskers and stale pipe tobacco. He worked in an office in the stockyards... Nights she used to dream she lived alone with her mother in a big clean white house in Oak Park in winter when there was snow on the ground and she'd been setting a white linen table cloth with bright white silver... When she was sixteen in highschool she and a girl named Isabelle swore together that if a boy ever touched them they'd kill themselves... The only other person Eleanor liked was Miss Oliphant, her English teacher... It was Miss Oliphant who induced Eleanor to take courses at the Art Institute. She had reproductions on her walls of pictures by Rossetti and Burne-Jones... She made Eleanor feel that Art was something ivory white and very pure and noble and distant and sad... She was reading through the complete works of George Eliot.

The whiskers and stale pipe smoke, the white house and the snow, the pictures of Rossetti and Burne-Jones, and the novels of George Eliot (as understood by such a person)—with such qualitative details a whole type of girlhood is summoned up and placed in time. The utterance, as if from the movement of the character's mind, is completely convincing and is achieved by a discreet use of speech diction and speech rhythms and words of direct feeling. Dos Passos has had to work for a long time to attain to this kind of mastery. In his earlier novels, the description was always thick, heavy, isolated, and the use of dialects at times approximated a vaudeville show. But these faults have been pursued to the point where they are magnificent virtues.

The thirteen leading characters who are presented through the medium of this kind of narrative are all members of the lower middle-class. The very rich and the working-class are not the subjects of direct attention, although they participate also in a variety of ways. It is true too that some of these characters are for all practical purposes reduced to the status of workers and most of them, on the other hand, desire to be rich, while three of them devote themselves to the cause of the working-class. But in the main, what we get is the typical life of the lower middle-class between 1900 and 1930. Typical indeed, for there is a constant 'averaging,' a constant effort to describe each character in terms which will reduce him to a type. The same motive seems to have dictated the kinds of character. There is an IWW typesetter, a Jewish radical leader, a movie star, an interior decorator, a publicity man, a stenographer, a Harvard aesthete, a sailor, an aviator, a social worker, a Red Cross nurse—all of them, I should add, might be characterized differently since they engage in other activities from time to time. Their chief values, which they do not examine or question in the least (except for the radicals), are 'love' and 'money.' The accuracy of this presentation can be verified by examining a fair sample of advertising in order to see on what the advertisers are basing their appeals. And the fate of almost all the characters is defeat, inhuman, untragic defeat—either defeat of a violent death without meaning or the more complete degradation of 'selling out'—selling one's friends, one's integrity, one's earnest ambition and hope, for nothing more than 'the big money.' By the conclusion of the book, every character with the exception of Ben Compton, the radical leader, has come to the point where self-respect is not remote, but a term as of a dead language. Compton has been thrown out of the Communist Party for being an 'oppositionist' (a note which would indicate a change of heart in Dos Passos, a loss of faith in the radical movement, which has occurred since the writing of U.S.A. was begun). The conclusion, to repeat, is that of utter loss, degradation, and hopelessness, the suicide of one character, the killing of another, the disgusting lives of the others, and the final contrast of a vagabond who has not eaten for some time waiting for a lift on the highway while a plane passes overhead, containing the rich, one of whom 'sickens and vomits into the carton container the steak and mushrooms he ate in New York.'

Whatever else we may say of American life as represented in these narratives, there is one statement which we must make first: it is so, it is true; we have seen this with our own eyes and many of us have lived in this way. This is a true picture of the lives of many Americans, and anyone who doubts the fact can learn for himself very quickly how accurate Dos Passos is. But there is, on the other hand, a great deal more to be said about the truth which the novel as a form is capable of presenting.

To begin the attempt at a thorough judgment, the formal inadequacy of *U.S.A.*, taken as a whole, is the direct experience of every reader. There is no need to summon up abstract canons, nor to make that very interesting approach which can be summed up in the question: what would Henry James say? No reader can go from page one to page 1449 without feeling that the newsreels, camera eyes, and biographies, however good they may be in themselves, are interruptions which thwart his interest and break the novel into many isolated parts.[a] Even in the central narratives, where, as in the greatest pure prose (that of Stendhal and Tolstoy, where the word is transparent as glass), the reader passes without an awareness of style to the intense, ragged actuality presented, even here the novel falls into separate parts, even though there is an occasional interweaving of lives. The unity, the *felt* unity, is only the loose grab-bag of time and place, 1919 and the U.S.A. The binding together of lives (and thus of the reader's interest and gaze) into the progress of a plot—an element present even in a work of the scope of *War and Peace*—is wholly lacking. This heaping together of fragments of valuable perception is a characteristic of the best poetry of our time and the connection is interesting. *The Waste Land*, Pound's *Cantos*, *The Bridge*, and *The Orators* of Auden are all examples. And as there is a separation or gap between the sensibility of the camera eye and the narrative form in *U.S.A.*, so in the history of modern poetry we can remark the converse phenomenon, how, since Coleridge wrote marginal summaries of the narrative to 'The Ancient Mariner,' the capacity for a narrative framework has gradually disappeared from poetry of the first order: modern poetic style can bear the utmost strain of sensibility, but it cannot tell a story. In the medium of poetry, however, a unity of tone and mood and theme can substitute, although imperfectly, for other kinds of unity. *U.S.A.* cannot be considered a poem, however, and even if it could, Dos Passos does not rise to the level of the poets in question. As a narrative, it becomes a suit of narratives in which panels without direct relation to the subject are inserted (one would suppose that Dos Passos in fact put the book together as a motion-picture director composes his film, by a procedure of cutting, arranging, and interposing parts). As a novel, it is not in any careful sense a novel, but rather an anthology of long stories and prose poems. And it is to be insisted that the unity and form in question are not the abstractions of the critic, but the generic traits of the actual experience of reading fiction.

But form is not, of course, applied to a novel as a press to a tennis racket. It is, on the contrary, the way in which the writer sees his subject, the very means of attempting to see. And thus it is obvious that the formal gaps in *U.S.A.* spring from Dos Passos' effort to see his world in conflicting ways. It has been observed that the stream-of-consciousness lyricism of the camera eye is an attempt to compensate for the flat naturalism of the narratives, and it is perhaps to this that Malcolm Cowley referred when he spoke of the remnants of 'the Art Novel' in *U.S.A.* And T.K. Whipple, in his review of the book in *The Nation*, raises more serious questions and makes a much more negative judgment. Whipple remarks, with much insight, that there is an important contrast between the lives of the fictitious persons and the great persons in the biographies— the actual persons have 'minds, consciousness, individuality, and personality' and especially the power to choose and to struggle, while these attributes are 'reduced to a minimum' in the fictitious persons. This is very true, but, on the other hand, Dos Passos is not, as Whipple thinks, wrong and inaccurate—many American lives are of that quality and character.[2]

And again, a like judgment, this time of *Manhattan Transfer* was made by the Hungarian Marxist critic, Georg Lukacs, in a remarkable article in *International Literature* (which Howard Baker has already cited in *The Southern Review*). Lukacs is engaged in showing that the best novels of the past have depended a great deal on their ability to give their characters 'intellectual physiognomies,' that is, have made the ideas and beliefs of their characters a very important element of the substance and method. Of Dos Passos, Lukacs says with precision:

he describes, for example, a discussion of capitalism and socialism. The place in which the discussion takes place is excellently, vigorously described. We see the steaming Italian restaurant with the spots of tomato sauce on the tablecloth, the tricolored remains of melted ice cream on a plate, and the like. The individual tones of the various speakers are well described. But what they say is perfect banality, the commonplace for and against that can be heard at any time and at any place.

But here again it ought to be replied, at least to begin with, that in actual life such conversations are for the most part banal. Dos Passos is nothing if not accurate.

Both Whipple and Lukacs are excellent witnesses, but neither of them names what seems to me to be the root of the inadequacy which they have variously observed. Whipple attributes the lack to a conception of the individual which is 'one-sided' and not 'dialectical,' nor 'the whole man.' Lukacs would say that what is lacking is a philosophy, most of all, that of dialectical materialism. A third standpoint would be that which attributed the inadequacy and formal lack to a technical misconception, Mr. Winters' 'the fallacy of imitative form,' the error of naturalism for which art is merely a mirror of the disorder and incompleteness of life itself.

It seems to me, however, that one must dig much deeper to get to the basic reason for this novel's character as a novel. The root of the inadequacy is, I think, an inadequate conception of what the truth, the whole truth about the U.S.A., for example, is. The term, truth, is used merely in its common-sensical meaning, of an accurate report of that which is. The truth about the whole of experience is precisely what is more than the truth about any actual standpoint. It is merely the truth about the life of an individual person, as it appeared to the person himself, that we get from Dos Passos. The truth about the whole of experience is more than the sum of many or all standpoints, of many blind and limited lives. The whole truth includes what might have been and what may be and what is not (as not being). It includes the whole scale of imaginative possibilities and the nameless assumptions and values by which a society lives. It is exactly because the whole truth is so complex and various that the imagination is a necessity. And this is the reason why fiction is full of the fictitious and the imaginative. It ought to be said, to forestall the reader, that however sophisticated we are about the nature of truth, this statement of its *extent* (its formal width, apart from insisting on any particular truth) is incontestable. It does not depend upon any view of life, as of Montgomery Belgion,[b] but is rather involved in all views and all viewing. It is, moreover, presupposed in the very nature of literature.

But furthermore the whole truth is involved in literature in what seems to me a still more basic way. One fundamental postulate of literature seems to me to be here in question. It too cannot be argued about because it is the assumption by means of which we are enabled to speak. One can merely point to examples—all literary judgment and analysis being, in the end, comparative—and as it happens, Dos Passos himself provides his own examples in this novel.

The unquestionable postulate—or presumption—of all literature is the individual of the fullest intelligence and sensibility—at least with respect to the circumstances of the work itself. Perhaps one can call this individual not the omniscient, but the multiscient individual. He is the one who in some one of many quite different fashions *transcends* the situation and the subject. Often the multiscient individual enters into the work only in the style of the author, and thus it is through the style that a mind of the fullest intelligence and sensibility is brought to bear on the subject. Another way of saying this is to observe that a story must have a hero and to say with Aristotle that the hero must be '*superior*' enough to make his fate significant—not as, for example, the death of a cow. Or again, one has to repeat with Aristotle that literature must concern itself not only with what men are, but with what they 'ought' to be: ought is not used in its ethical sense (as of the didactic) for there is no Greek word equivalent to the ethical *ought*; but it is in the sense of the representation of the full scale of human potentialities that 'what men ought to be' is meant. When literature concerns itself merely with what men are or have been, it is indistinguishable from history and journalism. But the multiscient individual takes other guises also: he is sometimes the ideas and beliefs by which a work is given its direction. Another method—the one which fulfills the need of transcending the subject best of all—is the use of the supernatural or the mythical, and this is perhaps the most characteristic convention of literature, occurring as it does not only in Shakespeare, when the ghosts or witches appear, and obviously in Dante and other descents into hell, but even in our time, in the hallucination scene of *Ulysses* and in such a play as *The Ascent of F6*, by Auden and Isherwood. The supernatural and the mythical tend to be the most obvious attributes of the imagination. In some form or other the subject is transcended by a superior standpoint, and the superior standpoint reduces itself to one thing, a human being of the greatest intelligence and sensibility, who views all that occurs and is involved in the action, and who is best able to grasp the whole truth of the subject.

What we want of literature is the truth, and the truth is the only intention of *U.S.A.* But, to repeat, the truth is not merely the way in which human beings behave and feel, nor is it wholly contained in their conscious experience. In Racine and in Henry James, to take extreme examples, many characters speak as no one has ever spoken, on land or sea. They speak so in order to contain many of the levels of truth present in any possible situation. The facts represented are always there, but a good many of them can never be consciously known by any actor involved up to his neck in the present moment, as the characters of *U.S.A.* usually are. Only through the focus of the imagination can the relevant facts be brought into the narrative. In Dos Passos, however, there is a beautiful imaginative sympathy which permits him to get under the skin of his characters, but there is no imagination, and no Don Quixote. Dos Passos testifies to all this by his use of newsreels, just as he seeks the full sensibility in the impressions of the camera eye and the heroic character in the biographies; but in his central narratives the standpoint is always narrowed to what the character himself knows as the quality of his existence, life as it appears to him. And this leveling drags with it and tends to make rather crude and sometimes commonplace the sensibility shown in the other panels. If Dos Passos were not so wholly successful in grasping this level of experience, then, undoubtedly, he would be less aware of the need to jump back to the other levels of truth, and his novel would not break into four 'eyes' of uncoördinated vision. Or to shift the metaphor, his novel attempts to achieve the whole truth by going rapidly in two opposite directions—the direction of the known experience of his characters, in all their blindness and limitation, and on the other hand, the direction of the transcendent knowledge of experience, the full truth about it. And thus the formal breakdown was scarcely avoidable.

The view of literature, of the truth, and of the individual assumed by Dos Passos may be attributed to two sources. First to the tradition of naturalism, a none too precise term, of which one need here observe only a few aspects. Naturalism has engaged the efforts of writers of the greatest gifts, such as Flaubert and Joyce, but each has managed to smuggle into the method of strict recording certain elements which are radically different. In Flaubert, it is a style of the greatest sensitivity; in Joyce, it is the style too, in a manifold way which seems at first mere virtuosity. Moreover, in these writers, as in the lesser examples of naturalism, one finds a most curious method of work, which alone is sufficient to indicate that the conception of the nature of literature and of the truth it can contain has altered very much. They deliberately observe experience; they seek out experience with a literary intention. Flaubert visited Carthage to get material for *Salammbo* and instructed Maupassant to sit in the park and write down all that he saw. Let us try, on the other hand, to conceive of Shakespeare, Cervantes, Dante, or Aeschylus engaging in such activities in order to write their works. They would say, one should suppose, that one writes from memory since one remembers what has deeply interested one, and one knows what has deeply interested one. And they would say that the imagination, with its compositional grasp, is the most important thing, the thing that one can get only from a work of art and nowhere else. The imagination which produces such figures as the Prince of Denmark and the Knight of the Doleful Countenance (apparently one of Dos Passos' favorite characters) is not derived from deliberate 'research.'

Moreover, we ought to remark that naturalism arose at the same time as the primacy of the physical sciences and industrialism; the intellectual and social relationship is this: the physical sciences and industrialism changed the conception of the nature of literature and truth in literature, and made writers of great genius attempt to compete with the scientist by adopting something of his special method. They thought, it would seem, that literature had changed or that its nature had been mistaken.

But naturalism and its external sources are merely effects of that society which has degraded the human being and his own conception of himself to the point where Dos Passos' presentation of him in his own terms is, in fact, perfectly true. One can only add that it is not the whole truth. The primary source of the formal breakdown of this novel is the U.S.A. It is only by distinguishing between the actual and the remotely potential that one can conceive of a different kind of life from that which Dos Passos accurately presents, on the part of most of the living. It is this mixture of the actual and the potential, however, which has made literature so precious to the human spirit.

One might, as a hypothesis, propose a brief theory of the relationship of the individual to the society as relevant to the contrast between Dos Passos' biographies and his narratives, and between the great imaginative figures of literature and the lives of most human beings as they are in any time and place. The elements, let us say, that constitute any person have their source in the society in which he lives and which produced him. The individual is always *in* the world and is inconceivable apart from it. But some individuals 'prehend' these given, unavoidable elements in a new way—and this new way, new composition, alters the character of society. This individual, to refer only to Dos Passos' biographies, is usually the inventor, the artist, the intellectual—Socrates, St. Francis, Lenin. Not only do his acts provide part of the basis of historical change, but, to return to the above consideration of the fundamental postulate of literature, he is the hero, he is the one whose fate as an individual is not merely an incident; and he is above all the type of the highest intelligence and sensibility. This view need not be mistaken for the romantic one of the poet against the world, nor for a stale individualism, nor for a class judgment: its validity here rests upon what, in actuality, literature has been (although certain of the other arts have obviously not). What happens to such an individual, as hero, or what he sees, believes and imagines, as author, is, in fact, one criterion by which all societies are judged. He is our utmost concern and the object of our genuine curiosity when we go to literature, for it is only in literature that we can be sure of finding him. The lives of most individuals are undoubtedly matters of much interest for the author, and the truth about those lives is important. But the whole truth of experience (if past literature is not wholly nonsense) is more than the quality of most lives. One is sure that Dos Passos knows this, since it is the reason for his four forms and his discontinuity. His novel is perhaps the greatest monument of naturalism because it betrays so fully the poverty and disintegration inherent in that method. Dos Passos is the gifted victim of his own extraordinary grasp of the truth. He is a victim of the truth and the whole truth.

NOTES

a In his essay on Dos Passos, Malcolm Cowley insists that there is a sufficient connection between the narratives and the other forms. There is, for example, a biography of Wilson when the fictional persons are concerned with the aftermath of the World War, a biography of Rudolph Valentino when one of the characters is a movie star. The connection is thus general, tangential, and wholly external, and occurs to the reader only as a passing afterthought, if at all. This kind of connection can be compared with the *internal* unity of any biography or narrative in the book, and then the difference between a unified whole and a loose collection will be clear in terms of the book itself.

b The most recent issue of *The Southern Review* contains an article by Belgion which proposes a notion of fiction directly contradictory to the above one. Mr. Belgion argues, and has argued for ten years, as if unable to persuade even himself, that literature is never a representation or the truth of actual life because (1) 'actual life is too various and vast to be brought as a whole within the compass of a novel,' and because (2) the writer is attempting to impose his own view of life upon the reader, is, in fact, 'the irresponsible propagandist' for his own view of life (in that he decides the consequences of his character's acts, for example), and hence, since, in the last analysis, the truth about life cannot be established by a rigorous logical demonstration, no novel can be said to be true to life.

In answer to the first point, one need merely observe that it is not a question of *either* all of life *or* none of it—merely the whole truth about a part of life will suffice—and moreover the part can stand for the whole, the symbol being of the very essence of literature. In answer to the second point, one need merely observe that the truth of much in any fiction does not rest upon ultimate metaphysical decisions, but is common to all mankind and verifiable by them, just as the sciences are thus independent of 'views' of life. One proof of this is the fact that we can and do admire works based on views directly opposed to our own.

1 *Journeys Between Wars* (1938).
2 See No. 40, n. 1, and No. 38.

ADVENTURES OF A YOUNG MAN

June 1939

44. John Chamberlain, review, *Saturday Review*

3 June 1939, vol. xx, 3–4, 14–15

Chamberlain was among those who signed a letter of protest against the Communist Party's disruption of a Socialist rally in New York City in February 1934. The letter appeared in the 6 March issue of the *New Masses*. Dos Passos had also signed, along with Edmund Wilson, Lionel Trilling, and twenty-one others. In this review essay Chamberlain places *Adventures of a Young Man* in the political context of Dos Passos's career as a writer.

When John Dos Passos was leaving Moscow in 1928 a group of young Soviet actors from the Sanitary Propaganda Theatre (they were factory workers by daytime) came to him to see him off. 'They want to say goodbye,' the theater director told Dos Passos; 'they like you very much, but they want to ask you one question. They want you to show your face. They want to know where you stand politically. Are you with us?'

One who knows Dos Passos can imagine him standing there in the cold northern twilight, the piston-rods of the engine already pumping slowly beside him....Scrupulously polite, given to deprecatory gestures, he starts up like a flushed partridge, his baldish head bobbing, his near-sighted eyes soft with pleased surprise. He wants to be kind, to make a gesture of solidarity, yet there is something in him goading him on, as always, to the absolute truth. 'But let me see,' he fumbles; 'but maybe I can explain....But in so short a time...there's no time.' No time to tell about the Bill of Rights and Thomas Jefferson and Liberty,

191

Equality, Fraternity and Voltaire and Fighting Bob La Follette; no time to go back over the nineteenth century fight between Marx and Bakunin over the corrupting nature of power and the inherent viciousness of the State. No time to quote his friend, e.e. cummings, the Amerikanski poet:

> but I mightn't think (and you mightn't, too)
> that a five-year plan's worth a gay-payoo.

No time, no time . . . the train is moving, and he has to jump for it. Back to the old habits of thirty years, back to the West and its 'carpets and easychairs and the hot and cold bathwater running and the cheerful accustomed world of shopwindows and women's hats and their ankles neat as trottinghorses' above the light hightapping heels. . . .' And away (though he does not say it) from the fear that he has seen in the eyes of those non-conforming Russians who expect a visit from the police in the dead of night. . . .

A decade has gone by since Dos Passos left Moscow and the country around it that reminded him so nostalgically of the rolling sections of Wisconsin and the birch-growths of cut-over lands in New England. Many things have kept Dos Passos busy in that decade: work for the oppressed Kentucky miners, and travels in France, Spain, Mexico, and all parts of the United States, reporting demonstrations, repressions, revolutions, and conventions. And, most important of all, there has been the writing of his trilogy, *U.S.A.* All of this moving about and 'writing objective' (*U.S.A* is a book that rigorously excludes any overt special pleading by the author) has served to keep Dos Passos from documenting his 'but maybe I can explain. . . .' His instinctive, all-pervasive sympathy for the underdog has caused the communists to hail him, at various times, as Number One Literary Fellow-Traveler, the grand-daddy of the modern proletarian novel. But even when Granville Hicks was praising him most fulsomely as the Proletarian Moses (praise that was later half-retracted), John Dos Passos was nursing his doubts of monolithic political systems and the One-Party State. All along Dos Passos has insisted that he is not a Marxist-Leninist-Stalinist; all along he has argued that writers should not bow to the exigencies of politics. ('Writers of the world, unite. You have nothing to lose but your brains,' he once said sarcastically.) To those who call him Red, he answers: 'You're wrong. I'm merely an old-fashioned believer in Liberty, Equality, Fraternity.' And now, in his *Adventures of a Young Man*, he has finally gotten around to the explanation he had no time to make back in that Moscow autumn of 1928.

By comparison with *The 42nd Parallel, Nineteen Nineteen*, and *The Big Money*, the three novels that go to make up the trilogy of *U.S.A., Adventures of a Young Man* is admittedly slight. But it is most important to the student of Dos Passos, for it clearly shows the trend of his mind. The protagonist of *Adventures of a Young Man*, Glenn Spotswood, is the idealistic son of a professor who lost his job at Columbia University during the World War for conscientious objection. Glenn has that 'ethical yearning' which Waldo Frank has described as typically American; he needs a Cause, and the only valid Cause of his particular period in time is that of the workers. The early 1930s were a time when objections to the harsher phases of the capitalist order were so obvious that they tended to obscure other considerations; hence Glenn, without much thinking of where political monolithism inevitably leads, became a member of the Communist Party, using the name of Comrade Sandy Crockett. Glenn is not a mere auctorial substitute for Dos Passos; he differs in numerous ways from his creator, for he is an active organizer and agitator, willing to have his head smashed by company police. But his intellectual autobiography converges with that of Dos Passos, for he finally comes to abhor the undemocratic features of what he once so glibly accepted as Marxist 'ideology.' Like Dos Passos, Glenn Spotswood wanders off the reservation; but unlike Dos Passos, who merely quarreled with his friend Ernest Hemingway over the shooting of anarchists and libertarians by Loyalist Madrid, Glenn Spotswood is 'liquidated' as a 'Trotskyist' in Spain. The lesson is disillusioning, even (as the communists claim) defeatist. But the point which Dos Passos makes elsewhere (see his 'Farewell to Europe,' which was printed in *Common Sense*)[1] is that it is only defeatist so far as the Old World is concerned; in the U.S.A. things move on a somewhat different tangent, and the choice may never be narrowed down to the barbarous one between monolithic communism and monolithic fascism.

In *Adventures of a Young Man* Dos Passos has turned full-circle, re-emphasizing in dramatic fashion all the libertarian values and feeling for the poor, dumb, driven common man that have controlled his thinking from the very beginning. Symbolically enough, John Roderigo Dos Passos was born in Chicago in 1896, both the place and the year being those of William Jennings Bryan's great cross-of-gold, crown-of-thorns speech. His father, who went to the Civil War as a drummer boy only to be invalided out of the Army of the Potomac at the age of fourteen, was a 'self-made literate,' as Dos Passos describes him, the son of a Portuguese immigrant who had settled in Philadelphia as a shoemaker. Possibly John Roderigo Dos Passos's amazingly intimate feeling for the Iberian and Latin American lands comes down from the grandfather. The son's relationships with his forebears, however, never comes clear in his books, although it is noteworthy that the father was a corporation lawyer and an anti-Bryan Democrat, two things which John Dos Passos distinctly is not. Probably the young Dos Passos's affections were chiefly centered on his mother, who came of old Virginia and Maryland stock and who bore her son at the age of forty-eight. As a boy John Roderigo was carted hither and yon all over the map, living in Mexico, England (where he went to private school), Belgium, Washington, D. C., and on a tidewater farm in the Northern Neck of Virginia. (Memories of these early years can be pieced together by the alert reader from the stream-of-consciousness Camera Eye sections of *The 42nd Parallel*, first panel in the *U.S.A.* trilogy.)

For a time Dos Passos hoped to enter Annapolis, largely because of a love for the sea which he got from reading the novels of Marryat and from living just inside the Virginia capes. But, after being graduated from Choate School, he compromised on Harvard, which he entered in 1912. His classmates included Robert Nathan and Robert Littell. The period, as Malcolm Cowley has described it, was that of the Harvard esthetes—of e.e. cummings and Gilbert Seldes, smart young men who went on from college to write for Schofield Thayer's *Dial*, which was considered 'decadent' by Professor C.T. ('Copey') Copeland, the Cambridge warden of Beautiful Letters.[2] Dos Passos, however, had a seemingly contradictory and entirely unesthetic hunger for raw experience, and after sailing for Spain in 1916 nominally to study architecture, he turned up in Paris as a member of the ambulance service. After the war was over there came the years of wandering as a newspaper correspondent and magazine freelance through Spain, Mexico, and the Near East. His Bible throughout his adolescent years had been Gibbon's *Decline and Fall of the Roman Empire*; it was from this, and not from Karl Marx, that Dos Passos presumably got his taste for history in great perspectives. The travel habit and the love for open water have persisted from Dos Passos's earlier days; year by year his normal routine is to mix expeditions to strange places with periods of quiet living on Cape Cod, where he writes in the mornings and swims and sails in the afternoons. Since he hates literary affectation and shop-talk, Dos Passos shuns others of his trade, preferring to spend his leisure dabbling with painting and sketching. His wife, Katy, writes for the magazines under the name of Katherine Smith.

Malcolm Cowley has called Dos Passos 'two novelists at war with each other.' One is 'an esthete traveling about the world in an ivory tower that is mounted on wheels and coupled to the last car of the Orient Express'. The other is a 'hardminded realist, a collectivist, a radical historian of the class struggle.' But Mr. Cowley shrewdly notes that the 'art novel,' or the novel about 'the poet against the world' (see Dos Passos's early *Streets of Night* for a prime example), is not really in antithesis to the 'radical history' of *The 42nd Parallel*, *Nineteen Nineteen*, and *The Big Money*. Both types of novel spring from the same central attitude towards a society in which the quest for money tends to crush other human aspirations. (As Edmund Wilson has pointed out in *Axel's Castle*, all the vital art forms of the past hundred years, whether Romanticist, Symbolist, or Realist, have derived from the writer's natural antipathy to the values of the bourgeoisie.) The 'art novel' and the novel as 'radical history' are, in psychoanalytic language, 'linked deviations.' When Dos Passos is writing about young Boston esthetes who wish they were 'leansouled people out of the Renaissance' (as in *Streets of Night*) or a musician (as in *Three Soldiers*) or a poet (see Jimmy Herf in *Manhattan Transfer*), he is lamenting the fact that artists are frequently run over by the juggernaut of what John Dewey has termed a 'money culture.' When he is writing about ordinary people (the Italian Fuselli of *Three Soldiers*, or sailor Joe Williams of *Nineteen Nineteen*), he is objecting that the same money culture robs the average human being of chances to loaf, to exercise, to work at jobs of his own choosing, to drink wine, to make love. Solicitous of both the acts of artistic creation and the acts of refreshment and renewal, it is the same Dos Passos no matter what type of novel he is writing. Personally, I think Dos Passos wastes some of his sympathies: after all, good poets manage to write even in spite of their times. Nevertheless, the fault of being over-sympathetic is a lovable fault—and if Dos Passos has assigned too little importance to the human will in his earlier books, he is, as we shall see, now making up for it in a character such as Paul Graves in *Adventures of a Young Man*.

The inner conflict of Dos Passos (if it can be called a conflict) is typical of his writing generation, for most of the 'Harvard esthetes' (or Yale or Princeton esthetes) of the war period had the same ambivalent desire to Escape From It All and to See It All. There was Eugene O'Neill, for example, whose tramp and sailor days were a mingled effort to Get Away from the humdrum and to experience the life of submerged and humdrum people. The pattern runs through the work of a whole group of young men who went to France along with Dos Passos to drive ambulances back in 1916 and 1917. In their constant fluctuation between the poles of Walter Pater and Emile Zola, the early novels of Dos Passos accurately reflect the same *Zeitgeist* that has pushed the 'exiles' of the 1920s from Dadaism to Revolution. This *Zeitgeist* breathes through Dos Passos's first crude attempt at fiction, *One Man's Initiation*, which was published in England in 1920. In this very adolescent book Martin Howe drives his ambulance through the bloody welter of war-time France, listens to radical criticism of the war—and spends his leisure moments admiring French cathedrals in the manner of the dilettantish Henry Adams. *Three Soldiers* (1921) continues the same mood, although it is orchestrated in terms of two supposedly hard-boiled babies, Fuselli, the Italian store clerk, and Chrisfield, the farm boy from the Middle West, and one softie, John Andrews, the sensitive musician who deserts after the Armistice. *Streets of Night* which was published in 1923, is the only pure 'art novel' that Dos Passos has written, and it is significant that it is his worst book—a sickly manifestation of the *fin de siècle* spirit that reached these shores two decades after it had sputtered out in London and Paris.

The obvious turning-point of Dos Passos's career as a novelist came in 1925 with *Manhattan Transfer*, a book that is both an 'art novel' and an attempt, the most successful to date, to paint a collective portrait of the huge sprawling organism of New York City. It is in his travel books, however, and not in the superficial changes in his novelistic technique, that the evolution of Dos Passos can best be followed. In his first travel book, *Rosinante to the*

Road Again, Dos Passos is chiefly interested in the sensuous aspects of Spain. The second travel book, *Orient Express*, is that of a man whose sympathies are constantly broadening. *In All Countries* (which includes the magnificent tributes to Sacco and Vanzetti) brings us abreast of the contemporary Dos Passos. Excerpts from the three travel books are combined with new material on Spain to make up *Journeys between Wars*, published last year.

The travel books are filled with testimony to Dos Passos's love for the 'little people.' Back in 1919 he was writing of Spanish Anarcho-Syndicalists who abhor governments and talk of developing the 'Machine' 'slowly for our benefit.' In his 'Russian Visa' chapters of *In All Countries*, written in 1928, Dos Passos is of two minds about communism; he likes what it has done for the young, yet fears, even then, the huge, concentrated State power of the Kremlin. 'Zapata's Ghost Walks' (see *In All Countries* or *Journeys between Wars*) is an infinitely tender memorial to a natural radical who loved, not power, but the landless Indians of the State of Morelos in Mexico. And the lyric biographies of Sacco and Vanzetti, which are unfortunately omitted from *Journeys between Wars*, continue the theme. Of Vanzetti, Dos Passos wrote in 1926: 'His anarchism... is less a matter of labels than of feeling, of gentle philosophic brooding. He shares the hope that has grown up in Latin countries of the Mediterranean basin that somehow men's predatory instincts, incarnate in the capitalist system, can be canalized into other channels, leaving free communities of artisans and farmers and fishermen and cattle breeders who would work for their livelihood with pleasure, because the work was itself enjoyable in the serene white light of a reasonable world.' For a time, Dos Passos hoped the Spanish revolution would go in the direction of the Anarcho-Syndicalist ideal. But in May, 1937, we find him writing: 'How can they win... how can the new world full of confusion and cross-purposes and illusion... win against the iron combination of men accustomed to run things who have only one idea binding them together, to hold on to what they've got?'[3]

Nevertheless, although Dos Passos has been disillusioned about Spain and Europe in general (including the Soviet Union), he clings to his hopes for a world in America similar to that portrayed in the biography of Vanzetti. The novels, from *Manhattan Transfer* to the trilogy of *U.S.A.*, have all been informed with a hatred of 'the iron combination of men accustomed to run things....' (So, too, with Dos Passos's plays, *The Garbage Man* and *Airways, Inc.*) When *Manhattan Transfer* was published (in 1925, before the Coolidge boom really hit its stride) it was hailed as 'James Joyce made interesting,' a *Ulysses* written for New York in vigorous, fast-moving Americanese.[4] Like Hemingway and Sherwood Anderson, Dos Passos was intent on expressing his country and his time in a distilled colloquialism, a literary language fashioned out of the common speech. Jimmy Herf, the newspaperman who leaves New York to go on the bum at the close of *Manhattan Transfer*, is a symbolic representation of Dos Passos himself, entranced by the complexity and color of American life but disgusted with the emphasis that is placed on money-getting, especially as practised on Manhattan Island. (How routine this criticism of America sounds in 1939!) When young U.S. critics were feeling their first flush of social consciousness back in 1930, it was the fashion to criticize Dos Passos-Herf as 'escapist' for not expressing his discontent by Joining a Party or signing a manifesto in favor of the Russian Experiment. But it is a little hard to see what alternative to 'escape' existed for an average newspaperman back in the middle twenties. Novels, after all, are supposed to approximate the movements of life, and in 1925 disillusioned reporters did not become conscious social rebels: they became skeptics and ironists, or they took to drink. There was not even a Newspaper Guild in those days to join.

The trilogy *U.S.A.* is an attempt to write a bifocal novel, with Society itself as the hero. Through one set of lenses Dos Passos looks closely at twenty or thirty individuals as they move through thirty years of American history; through another set of lenses he scrutinizes the broad social forces that limit and condition the lives of these individuals. The trick (and it is a trick) is worked by mingling the behavioristic studies of ordinary individuals with brief, Whitmanesque biographies of the American Great (Gene Debs, Luther Burbank, Big Bill Haywood, Edison, Carnegie, Steinmetz, Old Bob La Follette, 'Meester Veelson,' Randolph Bourne, and so on). Then there are the fragmentary Newsreel sections, consisting of bits skillfully excerpted from newspaper headlines and popular songs. The Camera-Eye paragraphs, which indicate the author's own position in the space and time he is writing about, are bewildering on first acquaintance, but as soon as

one has a few facts about Dos Passos's own past to go by, they fall
into place easily. Dos Passos has been criticized for the 'Artificial-
ity' of his devices, but it is difficult to see how he could have
written a *Vanity Fair* for a country three thousand miles wide, or a
'radical history' of his times, in any other way. In any event, the
Dos Passos technical innovations are no more 'artificial' than the
Victorian trick of spattering novels with independent essay
material.

Paul Elmer More once called *Manhattan Transfer* an 'explosion in
a sewer,' and to the superficial reader *U.S.A.* might suggest just
that.[5] Actually, however, *U.S.A.* is freighted with social,
economic, and moralistic meaning. There is, first of all, the general
criticism of our times for being shallow and rootless: the characters
of *U.S.A.* live not in relation to codes or values, but in relation to
the headlines. Family life is conspicuously absent from the trilogy;
human relationships are something to be snatched between
wanderings on various missions. In becoming all eyes and ears,
victims of the suggestibility of the radio, the newspaper, and the
moving picture, mankind has lost its heart.

The second lesson of *U.S.A.* is politico-economic. As Malcolm
Cowley has pointed out, the characters of *The 42nd Parallel* have
feelings of 'hope and restlessness and let's-take-a-chance.' But in
Nineteen Nineteen the U.S. is transformed into a monopoly-
capitalist nation, and the opportunities for the individual begin to
dry up. *The Big Money* ends with a prose-poem to 'Vag,' an
unidentified young man standing by the roadside while overhead
flies a plane on its way to the Pacific Coast. The 'haves' are
traveling *de luxe*; the 'have-nots' are compelled to hitchhike or to go
by jalopy. There is, as Mr. Cowley says, no longer any concourse
between them. (Or, rather, there wasn't until the New Deal
stepped in to destroy some of the meaning of the Dos Passos
trilogy by softening the conflicts which *U.S.A.* has been dramatiz-
ing.)

Intertwined with the politico-economic lesson of *U.S.A.* is a
lesson that is implicit in the contrast between the 'little people' of
the fictional sections and the subjects of the Whitmanesque
biographies: Veblen, Steinmetz, Edison, and the rest. Steinmetz
and Edison were purposeful people, while Dos Passos's fictional
characters are fatalistic and will-less. Both J. Donald Adams and
Burton Rascoe have suggested that the contrast points to a

deficiency in Dos Passos: *U.S.A.*, so these critics argue, concentrates on one phase of American life and seeks to substitute it by implication for the whole. There is doubtless some truth in what Rascoe and Adams say. Yet it is easy to read far-sighted calculation into Dos Passos's juxtaposition of the will-less common man and the dedicated Great. Isn't the author trying to tell us, without becoming didactic and destroying himself as a novelist, that the 'little man' is damned because something (call it 'Fate,' call it the 'System,' call it what you will) comes between him and opportunity to use the products of the brains of the Great?

Judging Dos Passos in terms of his intentions, there is only one flaw, as I see it, in *U.S.A.*, and that is in the symbolic weight attached to Charley Anderson, the inventor who loses the products of his ingenuity to predatory financiers. Charley, the drunkard, is made the personal goat of the 'price system' which the mordant Veblen has anatomized. Yet Charley clearly has only himself to blame. In making Charley do double duty as a symbol Dos Passos slips as an observer of American life, for technicians are, as a class, an abstemious, dedicated lot, given to concentration on the job at hand. I have met a number of them while doing corporation stories for *Fortune* Magazine, and none of them suggests Charley Anderson. But Dos Passos, in his latest novel, *Adventures of a Young Man*, suggests that he at last understands the job-enthralled human being; the character of the agricultural experimentalist, Paul Graves, subsidiary though it is, is an augury for the future. A much less negative Dos Passos is evidently in the making.

Adventures of a Young Man is a satire on the American radical movement, particularly as it has come under the sway of the communists. As satire, the book is going to set a good many teeth to gnashing in the Leagues-for-This-and-That. Yet it is a reasonably good story, and a true one: American radicals have been too prone in recent years to gloss over abuses of power by Their Side. U.S. 'proletarian' fiction has consisted recently of strike novels in which there is no Leftist self-criticism and only a minimum of moral conflict. The Greeks would not have known these novels for tragedy, for they are stories in which the protagonists have already made up their minds. The conflict in the average strike novel is wholly externalized, with the details of picketing, fighting, and sloganeering substituted for psychological turmoil. But in *Adventures of a Young Man* the soul of Glenn Spotswood, the communist organizer who is finally read out of the Party, is in itself the battlefield. A mighty fight rages throughout the book on this battlefield. And in reporting the private war of Glenn Spotswood, Dos Passos investigates all phases of the old dilemma: how to keep the political struggle for power from conquering or corrupting the humanity to which all reformers and revolutionists should aspire. Dos Passos doesn't know how to solve the dilemma: he is reduced to portraying the State as he portrayed it years ago, as something inherently vicious unless checked by 'limited' government. Back in 1920 he caused Martin Howe, the hero of his *One Man's Initiation*, to cry anathema on 'this cant of governments!' And when Glenn Spotswood sees what is happening in Spain, where the Loyalists become afflicted with spy-fever, Dos Passos cries out against the 'cant of governments' again.

Dos this mean that Dos Passos has abandoned the struggle for a better world? Communists (specifically, the communists of the Stalin persuasion) will say that Dos Passos is a renegade and a sell-out, a 'Trotskyist' like his hero, Glenn Spotswood. But in Glenn's boyhood friend, Paul Graves, we find a clue, I think, to the workings of Dos Passos's mind. Paul Graves is the undoctrinaire 'man of good will,' a humorous fellow who gets on with what he has to do and exploits nobody. Paul's job is the important one of discovering how to make soil yield a more intensive abundance. And in Paul's kind lies the hope of the world. Possibly Dos Passos perceives that; if so, *Adventures of a Young Man* is a 'Farewell and Hail' and not, as will be said in many circles, a 'Hail and Farewell.'

NOTES

1 Dos Passos, 'Farewell to Europe', *Common Sense*, vi (July 1937), 9–11.
2 See No. 32, n. 1, and *Exiles Return* (1934).
3 *Journey Between Wars* (1938), 393.
4 See No. 13.
5 See No. 16.

45. Alfred Kazin, 'American History in the Life of One Man', *New York Herald Tribune Books*

4 June 1939, 3

Arguably the heir to Edmund Wilson as America's foremost literary historian, Kazin (b. 1915) is the author of many articles, memoirs, reviews, and books, among them *On Native Grounds* (1942) and *An American Procession* (1984).

To most of our novelists, good and bad, America may be dull, magnificent, or just hateful; but it is never obvious. They find in it a culture staggering in its variety, often as exciting in its very disorganization as it is moving in its struggles. To John Dos Passos America is a proposition, and it reads that Americans are a race born to be damned, and everywhere in the same proportion. The life and death of any American is American history; suffering is everywhere the same response, and vanity the same illusion. In a Dos Passos novel people do not merely live under the shadow of doom; they are motivated by it. In the end everything cancels out to zero, all temptations are exposed, all hopes cheapened, all valor made ridiculous.

The various levels on which they live become the scaffolding of their damnation. Take an American anywhere, Dos Passos has said in his novels, and you have the necessary clue to our history. It is a seamless web; everywhere there is the same dreariness, the same plodding on to the good life, and the same defeat. Ever since *Three Soldiers*, that most poignant of American war novels, he has been chiefly interested in classifying the types of American disaster, in creating a biology of failure. In his trilogy, *U.S.A.*, that sense of doom was raised to the level of social history. The continent was sliced off, the crucial years of our development since the Spanish-American War painted into a back-drop of headlines, national gossip, popular songs; and the victims rolled out one by one.

Adventures of a Young Man is the first of a new series of novels, all of them to be contemporary portraits. In this it should be an extension of *U.S.A.*, which is not so much a 'collective novel' as a series of individual narratives between the same boards. The obvious difference, however, is that in these new volumes history is to be taken for granted. Dos Passos has moved up to that split-second, perennially post-mortem period in the Munich era where the headlines are so well known that to repeat them is to indulge in rhetoric.

The story of Glenn Spotswood, college graduate, sociologist, labor organizer, whom we follow from his boyhood to his death at twenty-nine in Spain, might have been included in *U.S.A.*, along with the story of Mary French. Glenn is one of Dos Passos's struggling little agonists, a hero trying to make his heroism pay. His father was a liberal professor and minister who lost his job during the war for doubting Woodrow Wilson's intentions; when his mother died, the father went to teach in the West, and Glenn was left on his own. Then an American boyhood and adolescence, working in summer camps on board and tuition money, washing dishes at Columbia for his A.B. cum laude, talks with Bronx Marxists, discussions with a friendly professor, and Glenn graduates to find himself a radical.

To Dos Passos radicals are the entrepreneurs of the present, committed to a vain search for certainty if they are honest, and rewarded with the fleshpots if they are politicians. It was not always thus. The brilliant biographies in *The Forty-Second Parallel* and *1919* of the great radical leaders and spokesmen of the past—Steinmetz, Debs, Big Bill Haywood, Randolph Bourne, John Reed, were shrines. But in *The Big Money* the most powerful scene was Mary French's dream on the eve of the Sacco-Vanzetti case, spelling out the catastrophe of liberal hopes and radical hopes in the twenties. The thirties have brought Dos Passos to a growing disaffection with the whole radical movement in America; and Glenn bears the weight of that disaffection.

Glenn is not so much a character as the honest radical to whom things happen. He is the Christian of the class struggle, but there is no redemption for him. Hillbillies from the Bronx nurse him on their bedroom dialectic, but they offend him. He makes love shyly in nineteenth-century terms to ladies streamlined with the Marxist armor and a twentieth-century conscience. Given a job in a small Texas bank, he joins the Mexicans shelling pecans, and is run out of town for aiding their union. He becomes a Communist, is sent down to organize the miners in the South, and is caught in the guerrilla warfare of local sheriffs and embattled unionists. The party line changes, the dual unions he has been trying to build up are canceled, and Glenn is locked up for his pains.

By the time he returns to New York, Glenn has become a heretic. The comrades turn upon him, he is expelled for subversive opinions, and he makes a shambles of a little radical sheet he has tried to run on his own. Blacklisted everywhere, he enlists to fight in Spain. There he gets into trouble for knowing the wrong people, is arrested by some of his former friends in New York, his diary is declared treasonable and he is sent out diabolically to his death. Farewell to Glenn, a naive little American boy who wanted a cooperative commonwealth and landed in a Spanish grave, unwept, unhonored and unloved. He has joined the long groaning list of the Dos Passos martyrs—the radicals who would not sell out, the poets who became advertising men, the engineers who drank themselves to death, the eternal victims of the American jungle.

Yet what is most significant in the novel is not Glenn's march to perdition, but the cold ferocity by which Dos Passos drags him from pillar to post. It is, in a sense, an intellectual melodrama in which all the positions are reversed, like that fable of Chesterton's in which all the policemen turn out to be anarchists and all the anarchists policemen. It has that distant tone which Dos Passos cultivated so brilliantly in *U.S.A.* as if everything rumbled back at the reader, and what one saw were gestures in shadow and what one heard the pulsations, rather than the words, of human speech. For Dos Passos irony itself has become the supreme style; the cold, methodical ferocity of his prose, with its light, bitter thrust, its extraordinary pliability and ease, becomes a cackling solemnity. The book really trembles with an internal disgust. Dos Passos has always disliked most of his characters, but here his characteristic repugnance and exasperation yield to pure hatred.

What troubles me in *Adventures of a Young Man* is not its submission to formula and its mechanical appearance, but the quality of its pessimism. As a novel it makes most American novels today look a little silly; but it adds nothing to Dos Passos's growth, and in a very real sense detracts from it. As a scrupulous and accomplished artist, he has his own defences to make against disillusion, and his own scores to settle with the intellectual fakers and bullies of our time. What I felt in this novel, however, was that he no longer had any choice to make. His books do not belong to the ranks of folksy satire, the enemies of Babbitt; they are peculiarly the novels of our machine age, and it has been given to him as to no other to explore firmly that region between what most of us want and where each of us fails that cuts through American lives. An artist can revolt against normal aspirations, but he cannot stifle his own. And in the funeral jazz of this novel I read just such a final and choking disillusionment. If *Adventures of a Young Man* is to be the type of his contemporary portraits, they may all be tombstones.

46. Malcolm Cowley, 'Disillusionment', *New Republic*

14 June 1939, vol. lcix, 163

In this review Cowley admits his judgment of the novel is coloured by his political sympathies. Dos Passos answered the questions Cowley raised in this review about his perceptions of the Spanish Civil War in the 19 July 1939 issue of the *New Republic*.

In the spring of 1937, John Dos Passos went to Spain with his friend Ernest Hemingway. He has described the trip vividly in the last few chapters of *Journeys Between Wars*. But in that book he gave only oblique hints of one episode, the key to much that followed. Dos Passos' Spanish translator, a young man whom almost everybody knew and liked, was arrested as a Fascist spy. People who ought to know tell me that the evidence against him was absolutely damning. Hemingway, who interceded for him with the highest officials of the Spanish government, became convinced of his guilt. Dos Passos continued to believe he was innocent, even after learning that he had been convicted and shot.

In those days Dos Passos was already full of doubts about the revolutionary movement. He didn't like the way the Communists had acted in the Harlan coal fields; he was skeptical about the Russian trials. But this Spanish episode was a final and definite turning point in his career. Hemingway tried to explain it to him, both privately (I imagine) and in an article published in *Esquire* but obviously written for Dos Passos alone. There are always traitors in a civil war, Hemingway said. Some of them are likable people in ordinary life, but a revolutionary government has to protect itself against them if it is going to survive. Malraux also answered him; at least it is likely that some passages of *Man's Hope* were written with Dos Passos in mind. But Dos Passos was moved neither by arguments nor by the strong personal feeling behind them. He had crossed a gulf so wide and deep that the voices of his friends were lost in it.

The sequel was that Hemingway wrote a play, *The Fifth Column*, in which the hero is an officer in the Spanish Republican counter-espisonage service. Dos Passos wrote a novel, *Adventures of a Young Man*.

His novel tells the story of an American middle-class radical of the post-war generation. When Glenn Spotswood is five years old, his mother asks him always to be a Christian gentleman, and essentially that is what he remains throughout his life, for all his adventures in free love and atheism. It is for reasons of conscience that he joins the Communist Party and helps to organize the Harlan County miners. It is for the same reasons that he leaves the party, after finding that its leaders are neglecting the real interests of the miners in order to make propaganda for a future revolution. He becomes a dogged, unhappy figure, head of a little group that is working quite alone for the unity of the working class. When the group dissolves, he joins the International Brigades in Spain. There he is suspected of being a Trotskyite and a saboteur and is thrown into military prison. He is killed by Franco's men after being released and sent on a mission so dangerous that no Communist is willing to undertake it.

Adventures of a Young Man is the weakest novel that Dos Passos has written since *One Man's Initiation*, published eighteen years ago. I make this statement with some diffidence, realizing that my judgment may have been affected by disagreement with his political ideas. On the other hand, if you subtract politics from his novel, there is not much left of it. Technically it is rather conventional, perhaps because Dos Passos was trying to answer some of the criticisms made against *U.S.A.* People had said that he used too many tricks of narration, like the Newsreels and the Camera Eye; now he tells a straight story. People had said that his characters were presented only from the outside; now he also tries to tell what happened in a man's head. People had said that his characters were passive, without any power of decision; now he deals with a moment of choice that determined his hero's life. The result is a book that reads more like other people's novels than anything Dos Passos has written. Everything depends on the hero; and Glenn Spotswood is simply not interesting or strong enough to carry the burden of the story.

Indeed he is presented in such a way as to make the title seem singularly inappropriate. These are not the adventures of a young man, as they seemed to the young man who was having the adventures. There is no youth in the writing, and hardly a trace of the pleasure a young man sometimes feels in simply being alive. From beginning to end of the story, the hero is being duped and used and cast aside, now by a sexually unsatisfied woman, now by a political party in need of converts. That isn't the fashion in which any young man would present his own career; it is the bitter judgment of middle age.

Yet the fault of this honestly and painfully disillusioned book is that it isn't disillusioned enough. Let us admit for the sake of argument that Dos Passos is right about the decay of American society as a whole. Let us also admit that he is right about the Communists. (He is factually wrong, I know, about some of the struggles in which Communists played a part, for example, the Harlan strike of 1932 and the Spanish Civil War, but morally justified in saying that a great many Communists are merely bureaucrats of the revolution, clinging to their own positions and careless about the liberty of others.) Why doesn't he go much further? Why doesn't he drop the illusions that he still seems to hold about the Communist Opposition and the Anarchists (I could tell him a story) and the happy scientists like Spotswood's friend Paul Graves? Once embarked on the path of cynicism, he has no logical stopping point until he finally admits that everybody's actions—yours and mine and his own—are based on habits, appetites and the desire for self-preservation. But even that is not the end of the journey. Having come down from the high mountains of idealism, having entered the common morass of human motives, he might see hillocks rising from the swamp. He might recognize the kindness of ordinary people for the astonishing thing it is. He might even celebrate the real (if impure and limited) heroism of an organizer risking his life in the Kentucky coalfields or a volunteer dying in Spain.

47. John Mair, review, *New Statesman*

24 June 1939, vol. xvii, 984

Mair, an English critic, has written a book on Shakespeare studies.

Superficially, *Adventures of a Young Man* is very similar to its author's previous novels. Young, toughish, idealistic Glenn, thrown out into the storm-water of capitalism; the pointless chance encounters with their significant undercurrents; the confused violence and treachery of the American class-war; and the vivid, tough-looking, staccato-sounding style are familiar enough to readers of *U.S.A.* There is, however, a very important development. In the earlier books the theme is the helplessness of the individual as such; the downtrodden and the downtreaders, the strikers, the bosses, the drunkards and all the rest are equally the puzzled instruments of vast social forces. The villain is the system itself. Here, there is a change; instead of an inferno we have a Pilgrim's Progress. Glenn is not whirled blindly through chaos, but seeks the truth as doggedly as Christian, and the enemies who beset him are as clear-cut and single-minded as figures in allegory. He is tricked by Captain Corruption and beaten by Boss Brutality, the will-o'-the-wisp tempts him into the marshes of Libido, and Giant Ideology imprisons him in the Castle of Inhumanity. His best friend melts into Mr. Enlightened Selfinterest, and Comrade Facing All-ways sits at the head of the Party plenum. Before long his burden of ideals has become much too heavy for him to bear, and the arrival of Apollyon must be almost a relief. Mr. Dos Passos does not make the identity of the Celestial City absolutely clear, but I suspect it to have been anarcho-syndicalist Barcelona.

Glenn's adventures are well adapted to point social morals, and his pilgrimage leads him through most of the ivory penthouses favoured by middle-class intellectuals. He works in a youth camp under a snobbish and grasping pantheist; he explores free love with the artists, hygienic love with the Freudians and earthy passion with a constant nymph of the coal mines; he is sickened by the rich liberal upholders of civil liberty, revolted by the ruthless stupidity of the Communists, and betrayed by the careless opportunism of his friends. He organises a strike amongst the simple, God-fearing miners of the Appalachian Mountains, is forced to betray them for the sake of the Party-Line, joins the International Column, and is judicially murdered as a Trotskyist traitor. In a way, Mr. Dos Passos is as puzzled as poor Glenn. His is the fastidious and Utopian radicalism that still survives among the more intelligent of the professional classes, and is neatly expressed in Mr. Mencken's dictum that 'every decent man is ashamed of the Government he lives under.' Mr. Dos Passos is in the unhappy position of hating the enemy for his intolerance, distrusting his friends for their incompetence and despising the neutrals for their neutrality. He knows that justice is no more use against a gun than reason is against a loud-speaker, but realises that to adopt the methods of the enemy is to become one with him. Glenn was killed before he found the answer; let us hope that the next book of Mr. Dos Passos's projected series will help to supply it.

48. Samuel Sillen, 'Misadventures of John Dos Passos', New Masses

4 July 1939, vol. xxxii, 21-2

Sillen (1911–73) was a marxist literary critic who became literary editor of *New Masses* in 1937. In 1947 he founded and edited *Mainstream*, a literary quarterly which merged with

New Masses in 1948. Sillen taught English literature at New York University, and wrote book reviews for *The New York Herald Tribune, The Nation, The New Republic,* and *New Masses.* Sillen's review is typical of those written from the Left, attacking Dos Passos's 'misanthropic vision' and comparing Dos Passos's latest novel unfavourably to Steinbeck's *The Grapes of Wrath* which was more 'hopeful'.

Last year it was Sinclair Lewis and *The Prodigal Parents.* This year it is John Dos Passos and *Adventures of a Young Man.* Both books are almost inconceivably rotten, and for very much the same reasons. Lewis and Dos Passos had gone around attacking 'artists in uniform'; and yet these books were bald political tracts written out of the narrowest sectarian impulse. They had made a great to-do about the integrity of the artist; and yet they built their stories with palpable lies. They had once written progressive books; now they were writing contemptible slanders, nasty, ill-tempered, and hysterical slanders against everything decent and hopeful in American life. Once upon a time they had been concerned about their craft; but now they were turning out sloppy writing, hollow characters, machine-made dialogue, editorial rubber stamps.

Dos Passos has written a crude piece of Trotskyist agit-prop. That's about as damaging a judgment as anyone could make about a writer. But nothing else seems quite accurate. Consider the following example.

On page 291 a muddleheaded myth of a hero named Glenn Spotswood decides to go to Spain. Why? Because he is disillusioned with the Communist Party—'The workers being defeated and murdered everywhere,' cries his latest girl friend, 'and they won't let us help.' Boo-hoo, the wicked Communists won't let anybody help the workers. So Glenn gets even by enlisting. The first question he is asked by the man in the mysterious tenement is 'Volunteer or mercenary?'—the distinct implication being that mercenary troops were hired in America to fight with the loyalists. Then Glenn is led into a room, and his guide calls out: 'Dr. Wiseman...here's another customer...right through the curtains, comrade.' Customer! Then we meet Dr. Wiseman, who is, according to Dos Passos and General Moseley, wearing 'a white Russian tunic'!

'Haha,' shouts Dr. Wiseman—and I am still quoting, so help me—'More cannon fodder.' Then Dr. Wiseman examines Glenn. The doctor says, with a 'rasping chuckle'—the villain—that he would really like to fight, but he has responsibilities: 'When you boys come back I'll give you free medical service.' He pronounces Glenn 'sound as a dollar... or ought I to say sound as a Soviet ruble?' And finally: 'They were still laughing when Glenn pocketed the two dollars, shook hands, and walked out onto the street again.'

When Glenn gets to Spain he meets Saul Chemnitz, who has a 'jewishlooking nose'—how Dos Passos hates the 'Jewish' Communists—Irving Silverstone, Gladys Funaroff, Dr. Wiseman. It turns out that the only good mechanics in Spain are Trotskyites. Frankie Perez of the POUM—at last, a man whom Dos Passos respects—tells Glenn that 'We fight Franco but also we fight Moscow.... We have to fight both sides to protect our revolution.' Fighting both sides! Dos Passos fails to tell his readers that the POUM was more successful in fighting against the side of the republic because that is what they were out to do with fascist help. At any rate, Glenn is thrown into jail by the horrible Reds, and he is released only because somebody has to carry water to the front. He is shot by the fascists. The gentle lamb is led to the slaughter by the blood-drinking loyalists.

But there is no point in going on with an account of this stuff. It fills almost every page, and it is as painful to describe as it is disgusting to read.

Harry Hansen, book reviewer of the New York *World-Telegram*, recently said that 'it will be interesting to see whether the congress [the Third American Writers Congress] will apply literary or political standards' to Dos Passos' novel. This is an utterly fantastic way to pose the question. For this novel vividly illustrates the organic relationship between form and content: The critics are almost unanimously agreed that *Adventures of a Young Man* is a shoddy literary job. Mr. Hansen himself says, for example, that 'what I miss in the book is evidence of the mental struggle in Glenn during various stages of his career'—a fairly serious defect in view of the fact that Glenn's development is presumably the theme of the book. Clifton Fadiman of the *New Yorker* had the feeling that by omitting the 'childhood experiences, youthful sex contacts, and all the rest of the regulation development-novel paraphernalia'—a good part of the book, in short—Dos Passos could have 'saved the reader's time.' And even John Chamberlain, who wrote a blurb pamphlet in support of Dos Passos' political line, was forced to admit that this is a 'slight' book compared to Dos Passos' trilogy.[1] In a separate box I have included other press comments.[2]

But why should Dos Passos, who has written some of the finest novels of our time, fall down so completely in this novel? His literary failure is very definitely related to his reactionary political orientation. His astonishing distortions of the real world are reflected in an equally astonishing literary crudeness. Glenn's decision to go to Spain—a crucial point in character development—is thoroughly unconvincing because it is motivated by Dos Passos' cynicism rather than by the mature social understanding of the boys who actually went to Spain. Anxious to attack the Soviet Union, Dos Passos creates a mechanical messenger boy who comes back to report that 'In Russia they've starved 'em deliberately.' Strongly editorialized conversations are constantly dragged in, and the spaces between sometimes read as if they were regarded by Dos Passos as necessary nuisances. He is in a terrific hurry to give the knockout blow. And the progression of this political story is determined not by the actual social changes taking place in America, but by the odd assortment of women with whom Glenn sleeps. At least Glenn vacillates, even if he does not grow; the other characters are entirely immobile.

Dos Passos has gone sour. It is not merely that he is bitterly and stupidly opposed to the Soviet Union. It is not merely that he misrepresents the battlers for freedom in Spain. He finds nothing that is good anywhere. Ultimately it is not the Soviet Union that he libels, but humanity everywhere. The man who wrote this book is a spiteful observer of life. He trusts nothing but his own contempt. He scorns the truly heroic. His misanthropic vision is incredibly mean in a world where a gigantic struggle is taking place between civilized values and barbarism.

The man, in short, has succumbed to the 'philosophy' of Trotskyism, which professionally breeds despair and confusion and division. In political terms it means spiking the republican government of Spain, plotting against the Soviet Union, working with reaction against the New Deal. In literature, it means the glorification of hate, the deliberate opposition of the individual to the masses of mankind, the butchering of sensibility. The gulf between *Adventures of a Young Man* and *The Grapes of Wrath* is the gulf between a retrograde and a progressive vision of life. Fortunately, the great majority of American writers, like the bulk of the American reading public, have chosen the latter. *Adventures of a Young Man* is a sufficient warning and example.

NOTES

1 See No. 44. An expanded version of Chamberlain's review was published by Harcourt Brace for promotion purposes.
2 All unfavourable and stacked up against the novel.

49. Edmund Wilson, letter to Dos Passos

16 July 1939

Wilson had declared himself a Communist during the mid-1930s, but soon after became disillusioned with events in Russia, especially Stalin's rise to power. He and Dos Passos had become good friends during the 1920s and remained so. Earlier in the year Wilson had written a letter to his friend expressing his reservations about the character development of Glenn Spotswood, the hero of *Adventures of a Young Man*. In June Dos Passos wrote back, defending his behaviouristic method of 'generating the insides of the characters by external description' (Ludington (ed.), *The Fourteenth Chronicle*, 522). What follows is Wilson's response, contained in a letter (Edmund Wilson, *Letters on Literature and Politics 1912–1972*, ed. Elena Wilson (New York: Farrar, Straus & Giroux, 1977, 319–20.))

Dear Dos: To begin with, I don't think your account of what you are doing in your books is accurate. You don't merely 'generate the insides of your characters by external description.' Actually, you do tell a good deal about what they think and feel. 'Behavioristic' only applies properly to the behavior of rats in mazes, etc.—that is, to animals whose minds we can't enter into, so that we can only take account of their actions. Maupassant, in the preface to *Pierre et Jean*, announced his intention of abolishing 'psychology' and using something like this method for human beings; but even he, as I remember, cheated; and in any case, how much or how little (in point of quantity) a writer chooses to tell you about his characters, or how directly or indirectly, is purely a technical matter. What has to be gotten over is what life was like for the characters (unless you're trying to give the effect of their being flies). You yourself in your books themselves make no pretense of not going inside your people whenever it suits you to do so. As for Defoe, he is so close to his people that you can't always tell whether he isn't merely ghostwriting them (since they tell their stories in the first person, he, too, gives you what they think and feel)—certainly, there isn't much criticism of them, in reference to moral standards, let alone social ideals, implied; whereas what you are doing is intensely critical and much closer to Stendhal-Flaubert-Tolstoy than to Defoe and the eighteenth-century novelists.

My idea about *Adventures of a Young Man* was that you hadn't conveyed—it doesn't matter by what means—the insides of Glen Spottwood. The sour picture of his experiences in New York is like *Manhattan Transfer* but off the track, it seemed to me, because the object of *M.T.* was to give a special kind of impression of New York, whereas in *Y.M.* you are concerned with the youthful years of an idealistic young man. You make all the ideas seem phony, all the women obvious bitches, etc.—you don't make the reader understand what people could ever have gotten out of those ideas and women—or even what they expected to get out of them. (In general, I've never understood why you give so grim a picture of life as it seems in the living—aside from the ultimate destinies of people. You yourself seem to enjoy life more than most people and are by way of being a brilliant talker; but you tend to make your characters talk clichés, and they always get a bad egg for breakfast. I sometimes think you consider this a duty of some kind.) And it seems to me that you have substituted for the hopes, loves, wounds, exhilarations, and depressions of Glen a great load of reporting of externals which have no organic connection with your subject. I never know what you are trying to do with such descriptions as those of the New Hampshire lake, of the New York streets, of Glen's arrival in Spain, etc. I feel that you ought to be showing these things in some particular way which would reveal his personality and state of mind or which would at least imply some criticism on your part of the whole situation. (You have sometimes done this admirably elsewhere—as when the Harvard boy in *U.S.A.* sees the façade of Notre-Dame in the twilight looking—I think—as if it were made of crumbly cigarette ashes.) Do you mean, for example, to suggest a contrast between the grandeur and beauty of the lake and the ignoble behavior of the man who runs the camp, to which the boys are subjected? I can't tell, because it seems to me that the descriptions are written exactly as you yourself might have written them in your notebook. And as for New York—though this may partly be due to my own rather moony tendencies—I believe that people get used to this kind of surroundings, so that they don't notice them but, as they are going from place to place, see their own thoughts instead. You don't spare Glen a single delicatessen store.

I must say, though, that the more I have thought about the book, the better it has seemed from the point of view of the idea itself, which, as one looks back on it, disengages itself and takes on life. But I don't think you quite wrote it. I take it, for example, that the critical moment is when Glen declares in court that he doesn't believe in lying, because he believes in the dignity of man; but most readers, I find in talking to people, don't notice this at all, because you haven't built it up. You haven't told them enough about Glen's soul (or whatever it is). He seems too much on the plane of banality of the other characters—the reader tends to think that you mean to make him banal, too. (About the best review I have seen, by the way, is one in—I think—the English *New Statesman*, which regards the book as a sort of *Pilgrim's Progress*.[1] Of course, the political issue has somewhat obscured it for people over here. They don't have the Trotsky-Stalin controversies in the same acute way in England.)

NOTE

1 See No. 47.

50. James T. Farrell, 'Dos Passos and his Critics', *American Mercury*

August 1939, vol. xlvii, 489–94

Farrell (1904–79), the prolific American novelist, is best
known for his trilogy of naturalistic novels about a hero from
Chicago named Studs Lonigan which he wrote during the
early 1930s. As an indictment of social and economic
inequalities in America, it bears comparing to Dos Passos's
U.S.A. Farrell had stated his political creed (an Americanized
version of Marxism) in *A Note on Literary Criticism* in 1936. In
this review he takes issue with critics of *Adventures of a Young
Man* who he felt had responded to Dos Passos's politics
instead of his art.

When John Dos Passos' latest novel, *The Adventures of a Young
Man*, appeared, a number of the critics went far out of their way to
have nothing to say, to make no commitments, to give no genuine
impression of the character and meaning of the book. Others
treated it in straight political terms, dismissing the book, in the
final analysis, because they would have none of its political
judgments. There were a few exceptions, notably John
Chamberlain[1] and Fred Dupee, who favored the novel, and Harry
Hansen who didn't but who criticized it on purely literary grounds.
The majority of the others showed a strange unanimity. Two
characteristics of their reviews must be noted: first, the novel was
attacked because of its subject matter and the type of characters it
attempted to portray; and second, irrelevant attempts were made to
psychologize the 'disillusionment' of John Dos Passos without
analyzing its content and nature, and without explaining why
'disillusionment' makes a novel bad although so many generally
recognized good books have been written in a mood of disillusionment.

The Adventures of a Young Man is a political novel. Glenn
Spotswood, its hero, is a young American who revolts against the
social injustices so rank in post-war America. He risks life and limb

in fighting for a better world. Moral idealism leads him into the Communist Party, for which he helps organize a mine strike in which police terror reigns and strikers are unjustly jailed. When Glenn is arrested he becomes a martyr-hero in the communist press. But in time he bruises his head and his conscience in conflict with the Party's totalitarian ways. For instance, he is interested in saving the jailed miners, while the Party is interested in enhancing its own prestige and making martyrs to exploit. Though his abilities are admitted, he is rejected as an organizer in Detroit because he will not make a blanket promise of loyalty to the Communist Party.

In episode after episode, his idealism collides with the cynical power politics—and the shifting 'party line'—of the comrades. He is ostracized from the movement to which he devoted himself. But he remains a revolutionary. He enlists to fight in Loyalist Spain. There, too, he does not lend himself to the Stalinist game, and is arrested, though he is fervently anti-fascist. In the end he is sent on a front-line mission which no communist will undertake, so that his death amounts to murder.

These are the major political features which have drawn objections from the critics. The novel also deals with Glenn's love affairs, his family background, his jobs, a summer he spends as a migratory worker, his efforts to work his way through college.

The fundamental meaning to be drawn from this novel is much similar to that in Ignazio Silone's *Bread and Wine*, although there are many differences between the two books.[2] Like Silone, Dos Passos is concerned with integrity, a theme which recurs in all his novels. Glenn Spotswood suffers and dies because he fights to retain his integrity. The book raises the same kind of a question Silone does—how is integrity to be maintained in revolutionary politics? Pessimism, disillusionment, the asking of questions such as this one are inevitable for radicals like Glenn in a period when defeats have exposed weaknesses, often producing the degeneration of revolutionary parties. The revolutionary party of Lenin has become the counter-revolutionary party of Stalin, Glenn begins to sense, and he is forced to ask how to defend his integrity against it. It is the worst kind of Philistinism to view the posing of such a question as mere sectarian radical politics. Some critics to the contrary, Dos Passos is not fighting battles of left-wing sectarianism; he is describing a dead end of a historic movement—the Communist Party.

It is nothing short of historical illiteracy when Ralph Thomson, reviewing the book in the New York *Times*, says that 'the long and short of what Mr. Dos Passos wants to show is that there are a lot of half-baked doctrinaires making mischief in the world,' and then adds the disingenuous reminder that of course some of them belong to 'the Stalinist wing of the Communist Party.' Another example is provided by the frivolous review by Clifton Fadiman in the *New Yorker*, in which he said: 'Whatever representative value the story has is marred by the introduction of a special theme—intra-communist politics.' Furthermore, reviewers like Thompson dismiss the novel because the characters are 'half-baked' when, as a matter of fact, they are no less baked than other characters in Dos Passos' previous novels which they have praised.

The fact is that there is much less difference in Dos Passos' manner between this book and his trilogy (*USA*) than some, for reasons of their own, have tried to make the public believe. The novel is still another biography of an American. To be sure, Dos Passos has eliminated his Camera Eye, Newsreels, and the separate sketches of the lives of historical figures. But these were never the essence of his writing. They were mechanically introduced into *USA*, rather than integrated into the context of the biographies which made up the major content of the work. They were calculated to reveal general aspects of the times, but that is not literary justification for their use. The aspects of the times that were important in the novels were those which impinged significantly on the consciousness of the characters. *USA* is a series of fictional biographies outlining the destinies of a number of Americans in a given period of time. *The Adventures of a Young Man* is a fictional biography of one American, over a given period of time, most of which overlaps that in *USA*. Dos Passos builds his fictional biographies out of documentation. The basis of his documentation for *The Adventures of a Young Man* is different in some of its content, but not in kind, from that underlying *USA*. Dos Passos is concerned with unfolding patterns of American life, the course of American destinies, showing by such an unfoldment the character of American society, and the manner in which this society either destroys integrity, or ruins those who struggle to maintain it.

Viewing Dos Passos in this light, we note how peculiarly silly was Louis Kronenberger's review in *The Nation*. He granted that the book is 'rich in observation.' But his chief objection was that it had a factual basis. He refused 'to allow that it proceeded out of a purely fictional impulse.' (What, Mr. Kronenberger, is a 'fictional impulse?') He complained that 'its crucial chapters rest on a factual rather than a fictional basis, yet create their effects as fiction.' In brief, Dos Passos was writing about something real, and the subject itself was 'inartistic.' If Mr. Kronenberger means this, he must then reject *USA*, because it is open to the same charges. But he does not do this. In fact, he speaks of *USA* favorably. But there is another commentary on Kronenberger. He wrote it himself. In October 1936, in an article in *Partisan Review* on 'Criticism in Transition' he defended 'social consciousness' in literature, and said that unless we get it, we might even lose our souls. He wrote:

Literature must go where life goes... it is more necessary to interest ourselves in an important subject treated without much merit than in an unimportant subject treated with considerable merit. *Culture herself* demands that we put the right social values ahead of the right literary values; and whenever we encounter people who want to keep art dustproof, who bewail the collapse of esthetic values, it is our duty to ascertain just how far their indignation is a screen for reactionary and unsocial thinking.

Strangely enough, he rejects this 'social consciousness' when it expresses itself, in Dos Passos' new novel, in a manner unwelcome to the fashionable Stalinists of the moment. Is Mr. Kronenberger really serious?

I think that the pertinent criticisms to be made of this new novel apply equally to its predecessors. Dos Passos' characters are typed, not individualized. Their reactions, perceptions, relationships with other characters are insufficiently individualized. In all of his books, Dos Passos has a tendency to catalog perceptions. When one of his characters goes to a new place, we practically always find that sights and smells are catalogued, and it begins to seem as if all of his characters have the same eyes, and the same nose. Besides, he tends to use vernacular without sufficiently differentiating the speech of one character from another. While his characters are typed, they are not literary conventionalizations in the sense, say, that the grandfather is in *The Grapes of Wrath*. His characters are *social* types. Although he writes with extraordinary skill, he does not create characters. This is a deficiency in his writing. But it does not destroy the truth that he tells us, the revelations he has to make about the life of our times.

The critics of this book sound like a well-trained dismal chorus keening because John Dos Passos is 'disillusioned.' There was Alfred Kazin in the New York *Herald Tribune*.[3] He asserted that Dos Passos reveals 'a growing disaffection with the whole radical movement in America.' (Read Communist Party!) It made him feel that Dos Passos 'no longer had any choice'; 'an artist cannot stifle his own aspirations.' But his dirge does not prove that Dos Passos is doing that. In fact, Kazin proves nothing. He has only lamentations to offer, no evaluations to make. If 'disillusionment' must disqualify a writer of fiction, we will have to throw out most of the great writers who have ever lived.

Another chirper in this chorus was Malcolm Cowley in the *New Republic*.[4] He defended human nature against the 'disillusionment' and excessive idealism of John Dos Passos. Cowley went outside the novel itself to suggest that the novelist wrote it because of a personal episode—because his translator was shot in Spain as a fascist. And Cowley reports that 'people who ought to know' told him that this translator *was* a fascist. But the hero of Dos Passos' book was not a fascist; he died at the hands of Stalinists as a fervent revolutionary enemy of fascism. There were many like him in Spain. This Cowley brushes aside. The trouble with Dos Passos, he adds, is that he is 'disillusioned' but not 'disillusioned enough,' and wants to know why Dos Passos is not disillusioned with other kinds of radicals. What Cowley is complaining about, in other words, is that Dos Passos defends the honor of honest anti-fascists like his hero against Stalinist slanders.

Cowley then says that once Dos Passos has reached this state of incompleted disillusionment, 'he has no logical stopping point until he finally admits that everybody's actions... are based on habits, appetites and the desire for self-preservation.' And he has some advice to offer. He wants Dos Passos to 'come down from the high mountains of idealism' and to enter 'the common morass of human motives.' If Dos Passos does this, he might, besides recognizing kindness in the world, 'even celebrate the real (if impure and limited) heroism of an organizer risking his life in the Kentucky coalfields or a volunteer dying in Spain.' This is the last sentence in his review and it contains his last contradiction. For Dos Passos' hero *is* an organizer who 'risks his life in the Kentucky coalfields,' and he *is* a volunteer in Spain who dies from fascist bullets. What does Cowley want then?

Further, by making a criterion of judgment out of 'disillusion-ment,' Cowley has established a basis for the rejection of all Nineteenth Century pessimistic literature, not to mention Joyce, Proust, and others. This includes books which he himself likes. Apparently what he means is not disillusionment in general. It is a specific kind of disillusionment, a disillusionment with the conduct of the Communist Party which Cowley consistently supports. His review is a political one calculated to discredit Dos Passos' novel. That is what he wants; and that is what he tries to do. And that, of course, is more or less what many of the other 'liberal' reviewers also tried to do.

The reception given *The Adventures of a Young Man* reads like a warning to writers not to stray off the reservations of the Stalinist-controlled League of American Writers to which more than one of the critics belong. What renders these critics suspect is their striking tone of unanimity. The reasons which they offered for disliking the novel cannot be accepted as valid literary ones. They were political reasons. These critics either opposed Dos Passos' revelations concerning Stalinism or else they said these were unimportant and did not constitute proper material for fiction. They even raised the author's 'disillusionment' with the Communist Party to the status of a general principle. Here we have the phenomenon of supposedly liberal critics turning themselves into advice-mongers and politico-literary legislators. We could respect them more had they disliked the book because of its binding.

NOTES

1 See No. 44.
2 Trilling also compares Dos Passos's work to Silone's in No. 40.
3 See No. 45.
4 See No. 46.

51. Wilbur Schramm, 'Careers at Crossroads', *Virginia Quarterly Review*

Autumn 1939, vol. xv, 629–30

Schramm (b. 1907) began his career as a reporter for Associated Press (1924–30). He eventually pioneered creative writing and mass communications programmes at the University of Iowa. Editor of *American Literature* in 1946, he has also written numerous books about the mass media. Also reviewed were Thomas Wolfe's *The Web and the Rock*, published posthumously, and John Steinbeck's *The Grapes of Wrath*. Schramm believed Steinbeck to be 'the most promising young novelist in America'.

John Dos Passos' new novel, *Adventures of a Young Man*, was opened eagerly because it might answer a riddle. Two years ago Dos Passos published an article called 'Farewell to Europe,' in which he paid his respects to Kremlin politics behind the Loyalist lines in Spain. Before that time he had been hailed heartily as Communist fellow-traveler and hope of the proletarian novel. Thereafter, he was hailed heartily as Trotskyite, Fascist, capitalist, or merely idiot—depending on how angry the commentator happened to be. But amidst all the critical storm, the trilogy *U.S.A.* stood as the most substantial monument of proletarian literature this country had produced. The riddle was, what did Trotskyite-Fascist-capitalist-Communist-proletarian novelist Dos Passos really think?

Adventures of a Young Man goes a long way toward answering the question. John Dos Passos is a friend of the underdog and a hater of 'money culture,' as he always has been. He is not a Stalinite—and probably never was—simply because he fears a heavy centralization of governmental power. This lesson is repeated over and over again in the new novel. It is the story of an American middle-class radical, who becomes a member of the Communist party through intellectual persuasion but is sincere enough to have his head bashed in by company thugs for what he thinks. The more he learns about the plight of the common man, the greater his sympathy; the more he learns about the inner politicking of the party, the greater his disillusionment. The leadership is separated from the masses, he decides. Finally he leaves the leadership, casts his lot with the masses, and goes to fight in Spain. He is soon liquidated— apparently on information furnished by the comrades back in New York.

If this new novel lacks the smashing impact of the U.S.A. trilogy it is possibly because Dos Passos has a new hero. In the trilogy his hero was society. The long procession of characters across the stage was used merely to illuminate the problems of the hero. But in *Adventures of a Young Man* the hero is an individual, and minute analysis of his development replaces the sweeping panorama of a money culture. Furthermore, it is more thrilling to point out on a grand scale what is wrong with society than to tangle oneself in the red tape consequent upon an attempt to repair society; the New Deal has proved that. But the book is better than it will be said to be by those who consider Dos Passos a fallen comrade. The characters are not great; the action is an occasionally monotonous round of women and meetings; the implication of the book is defeatist rather than magnificent affirmation; but there is about the book a convincing sincerity and penetration. It took courage to write this attack on the Left leadership and to burn so many bridges. It will take more courage to continue on the same path toward the orthodox novel, away from the News Reel and the Camera Eye, away from the hard-hitting dramas of society as a whole. The new book, it is announced, is the 'first of a series of contemporary portraits.'

52. Alfred Kazin, 'Dos Passos and the Lost Generation', from *On Native Grounds*

1942

Kazin sums up Dos Passos's achievement in *U.S.A.* in this excerpt from his study of modern American prose literature, *On Native Grounds* (New York: Harcourt Brace Jovanovich,

1942), 341–6, 352–9. It is interesting to compare this positive assessment of Dos Passos's work up through and including *U.S.A.* with Kazin's negative reactions to Dos Passos's later fiction (Nos. 45 and 54).

A chapter in the moral history of modern American writing does come to an end with Hemingway and the lost generation, and nowhere can this be more clearly seen than in the work of John Dos Passos, who rounds out the story of that generation and carries its values into the social novel of the thirties. For what is so significant about Dos Passos is that though he is a direct link between the postwar decade and the crisis novel of the depression period, the defeatism of the lost generation has been slowly and subtly transferred by him from persons to society itself. It is society that becomes the hero of his work, society that suffers the anguish and impending sense of damnation that the lost-generation individualists had suffered alone before. For him the lost generation becomes all the lost generations from the beginning of modern time in America—all who have known themselves to be lost in the fires of war or struggling up the icy slopes of modern capitalism. The tragic 'I' has become the tragic inclusive 'we' of modern society; the pace of sport, of the separate peace and the separate death, has become the pounding rhythm of the industrial machine. The central beliefs of his generation, though they have a different source in Dos Passos and a different expression, remain hauntingly the same. Working in politics and technology as Fitzgerald worked in the high world and Hemingway in war and sport, Dos Passos comes out with all his equations zero. They are almost too perfectly zero, and always uneasy and reluctantly defeatist. But the record of his novels from *One Man's Initiation* to *Adventures of a Young Man*, whatever the new faith revealed in his hymn to the American democratic tradition in *The Ground We Stand On*, is the last essential testimony of his generation, and in many respects the most embittered.

Dos Passos's zero is not the 'nada hail nada full of nada' of Hemingway's most famous period, the poetically felt nihilism and immersion in nothingness; nor is it the moody and ambiguous searching of Fitzgerald. The conviction of tragedy that rises out of his work is the steady protest of a sensitive democratic conscience against the tyranny and the ugliness of society, against the failure of a complete human development under industrial capitalism; it is the protest of a man who can participate formally in the struggles of society as Hemingway and Fitzgerald never do. To understand Dos Passos's social interests is to appreciate how much he differs from the others of his generation, and yet how far removed he is from the Socialist crusader certain Marxist critics once saw in him. For what is central in Dos Passos is not merely the fascination with the total operations of society, but his unyielding opposition to all its degradations. He cannot separate the 'I' and society absolutely from each other, like Hemingway, for though he is essentially even less fraternal in spirit, he is too much the conscious political citizen. But the 'I' remains as spectator and victim, and it is that conscientious intellectual self that one hears in all his work, up to the shy and elusive autobiography in the 'Camera Eye' sections of *U.S.A.* That human self in Dos Passos is the Emersonian individual, not Hemingway's agonist; he is the arbiter of existence, always a little chill, a little withdrawn (everything in Dos Passos radiates around the scrutiny of the camera eye), not the sentient, suffering center of it. He is man believing and trusting in the Emersonian 'self-trust' when all else fails him, man taking his stand on individual integrity against the pressures of society. But he is not Hemingway's poetic man. What Emerson once said of himself in his journal is particularly true of Dos Passos: he likes Man, not men.

Dos Passos certainly came closer to Socialism than most artists in his generation; yet it is significant that no novelist in America has written more somberly of the dangers to individual integrity in a centrally controlled society. Spain before the war had meant for Hemingway the bullfighters, Pamplona, the golden wine; for Dos Passos it had meant the Spanish Anarchists and the Quixotic dream he described so affectionately in his early travel book *Rosinante to the Road Again.* Yet where Hemingway found his 'new hope' in the Spanish Civil War, Dos Passos saw in that war not merely the struggle into which his mind had entered as a matter of course, the agony of the Spain with which he had always felt spiritual ties, but the symbolic martyrdom of Glenn Spotswood, the disillusioned former Communist, at the hands of the OGPU in Spain in *Adventures of a Young Man.* Hemingway could at least write *For Whom the Bell Tolls* as the story of Robert Jordan's education; Dos Passos had to write his Spanish novel as the story of Glenn

Spotswood's martyrdom. And what is so significant in Dos Passos's work always is individual judgment and martyrdom, the judgment that no fear can prevent his heroes from making on society, the martyrdom that always waits for them at its hands. That last despairing cry of Glenn Spotswood's in the prison of the Loyalists—'I, Glenn Spotswood, being of sound mind and emprisoned body, do bequeath to the international working-class my hope of a better world'—is exactly like the cry of the poilu in Dos Passos's callow first novel, *One Man's Initiation*—'Oh, the lies, the lies, the lies, the lies that life is smothered in! We must strike once more for freedom, for the sake of the dignity of man. Hopelessly, cynically, ruthlessly, we must rise and show at least that we are not taken in; that we are slaves but not willing slaves.' From Martin Howe to Glenn Spotswood, the Dos Passos hero is the young man who fails and is broken by society, but is never taken in. Whatever else he loses—and the Dos Passos characters invariably lose, if they have ever possessed, almost everything that is life to most people—he is not taken in. Hemingway has 'grace under pressure,' and the drama in his work is always the inherently passionate need of life: the terrible insistence on the individual's need of survival, the drumming fear that he may not survive. Dos Passos, though he has so intense an imagination, has not Hemingway's grace, his need to make so dark and tonal a poetry of defeat; he centers everything around the inviolability of the individual, his sanctity. The separation of the individual from society in Hemingway may be irrevocable, but it is tragically felt; his cynicism can seem so flawless and dramatic only because it mocks itself. In Dos Passos that separation is organic and self-willed: the mind has made its refusal, and the fraternity that it seeks and denies in the same voice can never enter into it.

It is in this concern with the primacy of the individual, with his need to save the individual from society rather than to establish him in or over it, that one can trace the conflict that runs all through Dos Passos's work—between his estheticism and strong social interests; his profound absorption in the total operations of modern society and his overscrupulous withdrawal from all of them; the iron, satirical prose he hammered out in *U.S.A.* (a machine prose for a machine world) and the youthful, stammering lyricism that pulses under it. Constitutionally a rebel and an outsider, in much of his work up to *U.S.A.* a pale and self-conscious esthete, Dos Passos is at once the most precious of the lost-generation writers and the first of the American 'technological' novelists, the first to bring the novel squarely into the Machine Age and to use its rhythms, its stock piles of tools and people, in his books.

Dos Passos has never reached the dramatic balance of Hemingway's great period, the ability to concentrate all the resources of his sensibility at one particular point. The world is always a gray horror, and it is forever coming undone; his mind is forever quarreling with itself. It is only because he has never been able to accept a mass society that he has always found so morbid a fascination in it. The modern equation cancels out to zero, everything comes undone, the heroes are always broken, and the last figure in U.S.A., brooding like Dos Passos himself over that epic of failure, is a starving and homeless boy walking alone up the American highway. Oppression and inequity have to be named and protested, as the democratic conscience in Dos Passos always does go on protesting to the end. Yet what he said of Thorstein Veblen in one of the most brilliantly written biographies in U.S.A. is particularly true of himself: he can 'never get his mouth round the essential yes.' The protest is never a Socialist protest, because that will substitute one collectivity for another; nor is it poetic or religious, because Dos Passos's mind, while sensitive and brilliant in inquiry, is steeped in materialism. It is a radical protest, but it is the protest against the status quo of a mind groping for more than it can define to itself, the protest of a mind whose opposition to capitalism is no greater than his suspicion of all societies.

In Dos Passos's early work, so much of which is trivial and merely preparatory to the one important work of his career, U.S.A., this conflict meant the conflict between the esthete and the world even in broadly social novels like Three Soldiers and Manhattan Transfer. But under the surface of preciosity that covers those early novels, there is always the story of John Roderigo Dos Passos, grandson of a Portuguese immigrant, and like Thorstein Veblen—whose mordant insights even more than Marx's revolutionary critique give a base in social philosophy to U.S.A.—an outsider. Growing up with all the advantages of upper-middle-class education and travel that his own father could provide for him, Dos Passos nevertheless could not help growing up with the sense of difference which even the sensitive grandsons of immigrants can feel in America. He went to Choate and to

Harvard; he was soon to graduate into the most distinguished of all the lost generation's finishing schools, the Norton-Harjes Ambulance Service subsidized by a Morgan partner; but he was out of the main line, out just enough in his own mind to make the difference that can make men what they are.

It is not strange that Dos Passos has always felt such intimate ties with the Hispanic tradition and community, or that in his very revealing little travel book, *Rosinante to the Road Again*, he mounted Don Quixote's nag and named himself Telemachus, as if to indicate that his postwar pilgrimage in Spain was, like Telemachus's search for Ulysses, a search for his own father-principle, the continuity he needed to find in Hispania. It was in Spain and in Latin America that Dos Passos learned to prize men like the Mexican revolutionary Zapata, and the libertarian Anarchists of Spain. As his travel diaries and particularly the biographical sketches that loom over the narrative in *U.S.A.* tell us, Dos Passos's heart has always gone out to the men who are lonely and human in their rebellion, not to the victors and the politicians in the social struggle, but to the great defeated—the impractical but human Spanish Anarchists, the Veblens, the good Mexicans, the Populists and the Wobblies, the Bob La Follettes, the Jack Reeds, the Randolph Bournes, all defeated and uncontrolled to the last, most of them men distrustful of too much power, of centralization, of the glib revolutionary morality which begins with hatred and terror and believes it can end with fraternity. So even the first figure in *U.S.A.*, the itinerant Fenian McCreary, 'Mac', and the last, 'Vag,' are essentially Wobblies and 'working stiffs'; so even Mary French, the most admirable character in the whole trilogy, is a defeated Bolshevik. And it is only the defeated Bolsheviks whom Dos Passos ever really likes. The undefeated seem really to defeat themselves.

[Kazin summarizes Dos Passos's career leading up to *U.S.A.* He then quotes from 'Camera Eye' (50) of *The Big Money*.]

All right we are two nations. It is the two nations that compose the story of *U.S.A.* But it was the destruction of two individuals, symbolic as they were, that brought out this polarity in Dos Passos's mind, their individual martyrdom that called the book out. From first to last Dos Passos is primarily concerned with the sanctity of the individual, and the trilogy proper ends with Mary French's defeat and growing disillusionment, with the homeless

228

boy 'Vag' alone on the road. It is not Marx's two classes and Marx's optimism that speak in *U.S.A.* at the end; it is Thorstein Veblen, who like Pio Baroja could 'put the acid test to existing institutions and strip the veils off them,' but 'couldn't get his mouth round the essential yes.' And no more can Dos Passos. *U.S.A.* is a study in the history of modern society, of its social struggles and great masses; but it is a history of defeat. There are no flags for the spirit in it, and no victory save the mind's silent victory that integrity can acknowledge to itself. It is one of the saddest books ever written by an American.

Technically *U.S.A.* is one of the great achievements of the modern novel, yet what that achievement is can easily be confused with its elaborate formal structure. For the success of Dos Passos's method does not rest primarily on his schematization of the novel into four panels, four levels of American experience—the narrative proper, the 'Camera Eye,' the 'Biographies,' and the 'Newsreel.' That arrangement, while original enough, is the most obvious thing in the book and soon becomes the most mechanical. The book lives by its narrative style, the wonderfully concrete yet elliptical prose which bears along and winds around the life stories in the book like a conveyor belt carrying Americans through some vast Ford plant of the human spirit. *U.S.A.* is a national epic, the first great national epic of its kind in the modern American novel; and its triumph is not the pyrotechnical display that the shuttling between the various devices seems to suggest, but Dos Passos's power to weave so many different lives together in narrative. It is possible that the narrative sections would lose much of that power if they were not so craftily built into the elaborate framework of the book. But the framework holds the book together and encloses it; the narrative makes it. The 'Newsreel,' the 'Camera Eye,' and even the very vivid and often brilliant 'Biographies' are meant to lie a little outside the book always; they speak with the formal and ironic voice of History. The 'Newsreel' sounds the time; the 'Biographies' stand above time, chanting the stories of American leaders; the 'Camera Eye' moralizes shyly in a lyric stammer upon them. But the great thing about *U.S.A.* is that though it sweeps up so many human lives together and intones their waste and illusion and defeat so steadily, we seem to be swept along with them and to see each life perfectly at the moment it passes by us.

The brilliance of the structure lies therefore not so much in its external surface design as in its internal one, in the manifold rhythms of the narrative. Each of the various narrative sections has its dominant musical mode, as it were; each of the characters is encased in his characteristic prose. Thus at the very beginning of *The 42nd Parallel*, when the 'Newsreel' blares in a welcome to the new century, while General Miles falls off his horse and Senator Beveridge's toast to the new imperialist America is heard, the story of Fenian McCreary, 'Mac,' begins with the smell of whale-oil soap in the printer's house in Middletown. That smell, the clatter of the presses, the political arguments, the muddy streets and saloons, give the tone of Mac's life from the first, as his life—Wobbly, tramp, working stiff—sounds the emergence of labor as a dominant force in the new century. So the story of Eleanor Stoddard begins with 'When she was small she hated everything,' a sentence that calls up the thin-lipped rebellion and superciliousness, the artiness and desperation, of her loveless life before we have gone into it. *The 42nd Parallel* is a study in youth, of the youth of the new century, the 'new America,' and of all the human beings who figure in it; and it is in the world of Mac's bookselling and life on freights, of Eleanor Stoddard's rebellion against her father and Janey Williams's picnic near the falls at Georgetown, of J. Ward Moorehouse's Wilmington and the railroad boarding house Charley Anderson's mother kept in North Dakota, that we move. The narrator behind his 'Camera Eye' is a little boy holding to his mother's hand, listening to his father's boasts (at the end of the book he will be on his way to France); the 'Newsreel' sings out the headlines and popular songs of 1900-16; the 'Biographies' are of the magnates (Minor C. Keith, Carnegie), the wonder men of the new century (Steinmetz, Edison, Burbank), the rebels (Bryan, Debs, Bob La Follette, Big Bill Haywood).

We have just left the world of childhood behind us in *The 42nd Parallel*, but we can already hear the clatter of the conveyor belt pushing all these lives along. Everyone is sparring hard for position; the fences of life are going up. There is no expectancy in this youth, not even the sentimental poetry of adolescence. The 'Newsreel' singing the lush ballads of 1906 already seems very far away; the 'Biographies' are effigies in stone. The life in the narrative has become dominant; the endless pulsing drowns everything else out. Everything is hard, dry, and already a little outrageous. Johnny Moorehouse falls in love only to learn that the socially prominent girl whom he needs for his ambition is a whore. When Eleanor Stoddard's father announces his plan to marry again, he tells her it will be to a 'Mrs. O'Toole, a widow with five children who kept a boardinghouse out Elsden way.' Mac, after his bitterly hard youth, leaves the Wobblies with whom he has found comradeship and the joy of battle to marry a girl who drives him almost insane; then leaves her and is thrown into the Mexican revolutions of the period. Janey Williams's life has already taken on the gray color of the offices in which she will spend her life. There are no refuges in this world, no evasions, and above all no second starts. The clamps have been laid down early, and for all time.

Yet we can feel the toneless terror of all these lives, the oppression and joylessness that seem to beat down upon us from the first, only because every narrative section is so concrete and every sentence, as Delmore Schwartz pointed out, 'can expand in the reader's mind to include a whole context of experience.' U.S.A. is perhaps the first great naturalistic novel that is primarily a triumph of style. Everything that lives in the book is wound up on the spool of that style; from the fragments of popular songs in the 'Newsreel' and the clean verse structure of the 'Biographies' down to the pounding beat of the narrative, the book seems to be propelled by the dynamic rhythm. The Dos Passos prose, once so uncertain and self-conscious, has here been whittled down to a sharpness that can kill; but it has by no means lost its old wistful rhetoric in U.S.A., which is particularly conspicuous in the impressionist 'Camera Eye' sections, and generally gives a kind of secret and mischievous color to the severely reportorial prose. Scrubby, slangy, with a kind of grim straightforwardness, it is the style of a very cunning artisan who seems to be working in these human materials as another might work in stone or wood—forever carving away, forever whittling, but never without subtle turns and a loving sense of design. It is never a 'distinguished' style, beautiful in its own right; never as prismatic as Fitzgerald's or as delicately molded as Hemingway's, and there is always something fundamentally mechanical about it. But it is the style Dos Passos needs to turn the motor of the conveyor belt; it is the reportorial and satiric style needed to push along and circumscribe all these lives. With The 42nd Parallel we have entered into a machine world in which the rhythm of the machine has become the primal beat of all the people in it; and Dos Passos's hard, lean, mocking prose, forever sounding that beat, calling them to their deaths, has become the supreme expression of his conception of them.

Perhaps nowhere in the trilogy, save in the descending spiral of Charley Anderson's life in the first half of *The Big Money*, is Dos Passos's use of symbolic rhythm so brilliant as in the story of Joe Williams in *1919*. For Joe, Janey Williams's sailor brother, is the leading protagonist of the war and the early postwar period, as J. Ward Moorehouse's ambitiousness marked the pattern of *The 42nd Parallel*. Joe's endless shuttling between the continents on rotting freighters has become the migration and rootlessness of the young American generation whom we saw growing up in *The 42nd Parallel*; and the growing stupor and meaninglessness of his life became the leit-motif of the waste and death that hold everyone in the book as in a ghostly vise. The theme of death, of the false optimism immediately after the Armistice, are sounded immediately by the narrator behind his 'Camera Eye' reporting the death of his mother and the notation on the coming of peace— 'tomorrow I hoped would be the first day of the first month of the first year.' The 'Biographies' are all studies in death and defeat, from Randolph Bourne to Wesley Everest, mutilated and lynched after the Centralia shootings in Washington in 1919; from the prose poem commemorating the dozens of lives the Unknown Soldier might have led to the death's-head portrait of J.P. Morgan ('Wars and panics on the stock exchange,/machinegunfire and arson/ ...starvation, lice, cholera and typhus'). The 'Camera Eye' can detect only 'the almond smell of high explosives sending singing éclats through the sweetish puking grandiloquence of the rotting dead.' And sounding its steady beat under the public surface of war is the story of Joe Williams hurled between the continents—Joe, the supreme Dos Passos cipher and victim and symbol, suffering his life with dumb unconsciousness of how outrageous his life is, and continually loaded and dropped from one ship to another like a piece of cargo.

Twentyfive days at sea on the steamer *Argyle*, Glasgow, Captain Thompson, loaded with hides, chipping rust, daubing red lead on steel plates that were sizzling hot griddles in the sun, painting the stack from dawn to dark, pitching and rolling in the heavy dirty swell; bedbugs in the bunks in the stinking focastle, slumgullion for grub, with potatoes full of eyes and mouldy beans.

All through *1919* one can hear death being sounded. Every life in it, even J. Ward Moorehouse's, has become a corrosion, a slow descent. Richard Ellsworth Savage goes back on his early idealism and becomes a cynical but willing abetter in Moorehouse's schemes. Eveline Hutchins and Eleanor Stoddard lose all their genteel pretense to art and grapple for Moorehouse's favor. 'Daughter,' the Texas girl Savage has betrayed, falls to her death in an airplane. Even Ben Compton, the New York radical, soon finds himself rotting away in prison. The war for almost all of them has become an endless round of drink and travel; they have brought nothing to it and learned nothing from it save a growing consciousness of their futility. And when they all slip into the twenties and the boom with *The Big Money*, the story of Charley Anderson's precipitate rise and fall becomes the last mad parable of their existence, a carnival of greed and corruption. Beginning with Dick Savage's life on ambulances and trains over France and Italy in *1919*, the pace of the trilogy has become faster and faster; now, as the war world empties into the pleasure world of *The Big Money*—New York and Detroit, Hollywood and Miami at the height of the boom—it has become a death ride. There is money in the air, money and power for Charley Anderson and Margo Dowling and Dick Savage; but as they come close to this material triumph, their American dream, the machine has begun to spin them too rapidly. Charley Anderson can kiss the bright new century notes in his wallet, Margo can rise higher and higher in Hollywood, Dick Savage, having sold out completely, can enjoy his power at the hands of J. Ward Moorehouse; the machine has begun to strangle them; there is no joy here for anyone. All through *The Big Money* we wait for the balloon to collapse, for the death cry we hear in that last drunken drive of Charley Anderson's and his smashup.

What Waldo Frank said of Mencken is particularly relevant to Dos Passos: he brings energy to despair. Not merely does the writing in the trilogy become richer and firmer as the characters descend into the pit, but Dos Passos himself seems so imbued with an almost mystical conviction of failure that he rises to new heights in those last sections of *The Big Money* which depict the last futile efforts of the liberals and radicals to save Sacco and Vanzetti, and their later internecine quarrels. The most moving scene in all of *U.S.A.* is the scene in which Mary French, the only counterpoise to the selfishness of the other characters in *The Big Money*, becomes so exhausted by her labors for Sacco and Vanzetti that when she goes to bed she dreams that her whole world is forever coming apart, that she is climbing up a shaky hillside 'among black guttedlooking houses pitching at crazy angles where steelworkers lived' and being thrown back. The conflicting hopes of Mary French, who wanted Socialism, and of Charley Anderson, who wanted the big money, have brought two different kinds of failure; but it is failure that broods over them and over everyone else in *U.S.A.* in the end—over the pompous fakes like J. Ward Moorehouse, the radicals like Ben Compton, the grasping little animals like Eleanor Stoddard and Eveline Hutchins, the opportunists like Richard Ellsworth Savage. The two survivors are Margo Dowling, supreme for the moment in Hollywood, and the homeless boy 'Vag,' who stands alone on the Lincoln Highway, gazing up at the transcontinental plane above winging its way west, the plane full of solid and well-fed citizens glittering in the American sun, the American dream. *All right we are two nations.* And like the scaffolding of hell in *The Divine Comedy*, they are frozen into eternity; for Dos Passos there is nothing else, save the integrity of the camera eye that must see this truth and report it, the integrity and sanctity of the individual locked up in the machine world of modern society.

With *The Big Money*, published at the height of the nineteen-thirties, the story of the twenties comes to a close; but even more does it bring the story of the lost generation to a close, that generation which has stood at the peak of modern time in America as no other has. Here in *U.S.A.*, in the most ambitious of all its works, is its measure of the national life, its conception of history—and it is a history of struggle that is vain, of failure that is irrevocable, and of final despair. There is strength in *U.S.A.*, Dos Passos's own strength, the strength of the craft that can weld so many lives together and make them live so intensely before us as they pass. But for the rest it is a brilliant hecatomb, and one of the coldest and most mechanical of tragic novels. By the time we have come to the end of *U.S.A.* we begin to feel what Edmund Wilson could detect in Dos Passos before it appeared, that 'his disapproval of capitalistic society becomes a distaste for all the human beings who compose it.' The protest, the lost-generation 'I,' has taken all of them into his vision; he has given us his truth. Yet if it intones anything affirmative in the end, it is the pronouncement of young Orestes Brownson—'There is no such thing as reforming the mass without reforming the individuals who compose it.' It is this conviction, rising to a bitter crescendo in *Adventures of a Young Man*, this unyielding protest against modern society on the part of a writer who has now turned back to the roots of 'our story-book democracy' in works like *The Ground We Stand On* and his projected life of Thomas Jefferson, that separates Dos Passos from so many of the social novelists who follow after him in the thirties. Where he speaks of sanctity, they speak of survival; where he lives by the truth of the camera eye, they live *in* the vortex of that society which Dos Passos has always been able to measure, with hatred but not in panic, from the outside. Dos Passos is the first of the new naturalists, and *U.S.A.* is the dominant social novel of the thirties; but it is not merely a vanished social period that it commemorates: it is an individualism, a protestantism, a power of personal disassociation, that seem almost to speak from another world.

NUMBER ONE

March 1943

---

53. Stephen Vincent Benét, review, *New York Herald Tribune Books*

7 March 1943, 3

Benét (1898–1943) was an American poet, essayist, and short-story writer, and the author of *John Brown's Body* (1928), a long narrative poem which won him a Pulitzer Prize. The review praises the novel for exposing a dangerous flaw in American democracy.

This is the story of Homer T. Crawford—'Chuck' Crawford—that plain man from the plain people who got to the United States Senate by the grace of a theme-song, a spell-binding voice and a hillbilly band, and as soon as he got there, started sprouting pinfeathers of fascism. This is the story of the Honorable Homer Crawford, who started by attacking the 'interests' and ended by attacking 'Jew peddlers' and 'visionary social workers'—the Honorable Homer T. Crawford who would sell his grandmother's bones for five minutes in the political spotlight, the tribune of the people who sells out the people, our home-grown, home-cured product, the most dangerous factor in our political scene. If you think he doesn't exist, all you have to do is to take a look at the files of the 'Congressional Record,' past and present. And in *Number One*, John Dos Passos has done his story with brilliant impressionism.

The story is largely told through Tyler Spotswood, Crawford's *fidus Achates*, fixer, errand-boy and contact man. It is a good method, because Spotswood at once sees through Crawford and still believes in something in him—the uncomfortable bond between the two is very well drawn. So are all the personages of the Crawford gang and the various political figures met along the way,

236

from Steve Baskette, the cautious Governor who played them close to his chest and didn't want to bet on the wrong horse, to the Reverend Chester Bigelow, that sub-Savonarola of white, Protestant, Americanism. Here are likewise tough bodyguards, the loyal secretaries, the dubious backers, the disillusioned, routine politicians, the Federal Attorney out to make a name. In fact, here are the works.

Nor is Homer Crawford exactly Huey Long—in spite of the fact that his platform is 'Every Man a Millionaire.' He is a Southwesterner from Texarcola and he talks his own lingo. 'While Fatty Galbraith stands up there perjurin' his soul before God an' man to vilify my character, to tell you how I stole the state funds when I was on the Utilities Commission an' public property in the shape of flowerin' plants an' weeds from the park commission an' wash-towels when I was in the Legislature an' used to stay at ole Miss Mulligan's boardin' house...'—yes, that is the authentic twang. No less authentic is the Crawford able to quote Henley and Goldsmith, to drop vulgarity when vulgarity doesn't pay dividends, and to get off quotable lines like 'Society's got to be reformed by practical politicians who keep track of it from day to day. If you want to raise a crop of corn you go out an' hire you a good tenant farmer, you don't engage a cryptogamic botanist.' For a line like that will go anywhere and please every one who finds thought an uncomfortable process.

A brilliant portrait, as I say—particularly in its sketch of a political convention, with the various stresses and strains involved, and in the compensatory panel of the tough party at the local night club that nearly got Crawford some bad publicity. Dos Passos has a beautifully accurate ear for American speech and an interest in how things go on that never gets stale. *Number One* is not a *Forty-Second Parallel* or a *Nineteen Nineteen*. It lacks the depth and range of those books—it lacks something of their solidity. The last section couldn't be better observed, but it doesn't quite hitch in—perhaps because we haven't had quite enough time to get used to Crawford in Washington. For once, a book should have been longer—a hundred and fifty pages more wouldn't have hurt. But if you'd like to know so that you can recognize the particular kind of fascism we could breed in these States, you had better read this story of 'Chuck' Crawford, and check certain public utterances by it. It isn't just the ache of Tyler Spotswood's hangover or the smell of the dead cigars in the conference room. Nor is it just high spirit, hill-billy clowning—though some of the shrewdest operators have known how to clown. It is something pretty nasty and pretty dangerous. And it is our responsibility—for it is we, the people, who elect the 'Chuck' Crawfords.

54. Alfred Kazin, 'Where Now Voyager?', *New Republic*

15 March 1943, vol. cviii, 353–4

Number One, the second volume in Dos Passos' new series of American portraits, takes up the story of the doomed Spotswood family at home where *Adventures of a Young Man* left it in a Spanish prison. It seems that Glenn Spotswood, who died a martyr to democratic socialism, had an elder brother, Tyler, who early in life had determined never to be a martyr to anything. Where the father, a disappointed Wilsonian, became a worker for the League of Nations and Glenn died, as he had lived, for communal and democratic ideals in an age of power politics and authoritarian revolutionists, Tyler became a press agent and contact man for an ambitious fascist hill-billy, Senator Homer T. (Chuck) Crawford. Glenn reacted against his father's Fabianism by becoming a Communist; but the point of *Adventures of a Young Man* was that he had to return in the end to something like his father's democratic integrity, or to the simple tradition of conscience—the familiar *kann nicht anders!*—followed by all the Dos Passos artist-heroes. The point of *Number One* is that even Tyler Spotswood, a genial political crook who had been impatient with his father's 'preachiness,' must find his way back to the people, back to a conscious democratic faith. '*The people is everybody, and one man alone,*' we read in the last of Dos Passos' prose-poems here; '*weak as the weakest, strong as the strongest,/the people are the republic,/the people are you.*'

But the point is made as homily, not as an effect of the

imagination, and though *Number One* is striking enough in places, particularly as a colorful description of the rise of Huey Long, it is an unsatisfying book. Dos Passos has been giving us such homilies ever since *U.S.A.*, and they evidently answer to some deep personal need. It is not that he has gone back on the trilogy; he has simply been dismantling it, stripping it of its external devices and of its cold hopelessness, going over its foundations as if to recover the individuals who were trapped in it. It appears that the trilogy spoke too quickly for him, or said too much. Its tragedy was too dense, the theme was too tonal a disgust; history emerged in it only as a brazen Aztec god on whose altars everyone was broken and sacrificed. The only triumph of the individual there was to register his protest as he went down into the maw of the machine age (and his sacrifice was his distinction; he was too good). Here the sacrifice is uplifting; it has an aura of responsibility. The individual now has to be saved; he has to complete—hopefully—his relation to society, as Dos Passos has to complete his relation to his own thought. There is a ground for Americans to stand on after all, it seems; the *mal du siècle* of the lost generation is at last played out.

Or has turned back on itself. For essentially these latest books have been about no one but Dos Passos himself; and it is their notebook character that explains why they have been so spasmodic in their brilliance, so nervous and uncertain and lame. They are the records of Dos Passos and his own voyaging, the voyage of one of the most conscientious, ardent and scrupulously moral of all American writers; and the story they tell is of the battle Dos Passos has been waging with himself to recover something of the life he once condemned so absolutely. To recover, abover all, that central self who in *U.S.A.* was only the arbiter of life's disasters, the sensitive recording instrument who once survived only as an instrument, as an artist; but who must now be brought back as a human soul, as that 'number one' in each of us with which society begins and ends. But brought back how? and into what world? Dos Passos is not sure of that, for Jefferson or no Jefferson, the world of *U.S.A.*, the only American world that Dos Passos has ever completely imagined, still stands in all its rigid ugliness and horror. What he is sure of is his need for certainty now, his belief in some possible contemporary salvation now; but it has leaped ahead of itself, ahead of its materials. The voice that speaks to us in the book speaks, in the end, only of Dos Passos' search and of his need.

It is here that one can see why *Number One*, for all its powerful scenes, its familiar technical expertness, seems like an array of scenes and effects under a sprig of homily. The philosophy of *U.S.A.* was taut, as the book itself was taut. Everything in it echoed its mass rumble, and the far-reaching tactile success of the book came out of that massed power, the heaping together of so many lives in symmetrical patterns of disaster. Dos Passos' effects have always depended on a violence of pace, on the quick flickerings of the reel, the sudden climaxes where every fresh word drives the wedge in. No scene can be held too long; no voice may be heard too clearly. Everything must come at us from a distance and bear its short ironic wail; the machine must get going again; nothing can wait. But here Dos Passos is no longer driving his characters to a hecatomb; he is leading one man up to self-knowledge and conversion. Here the story simply cries out for something local and deep, for something more reflective than the naturalist machine can provide. But the habits of the past, the full force of those twenty years in which he never dared to release himself (except in the camera eye, and then always behind it), the psychic habit of writing only through hard exteriors, have become too much for him. He has always had to write through frames and by tricks, for only thus could he save that shy romantic observer, the center of all his work, who hid in an external coarseness to keep alive. But now he has to release that central self, to give him hope where once he identified him only with a grim integrity; and he has lost him, for he has made no provision, imaginatively, for any such release and conversion. He has sacrificed him too often in the past, too mechanically, to make us believe that a fresh sacrifice can be uplifting where all the others were merely defiant.

This does not mean that Dos Passos has lost any of his expertness; it does mean that the expertness has become loose, and that all the colors in his style now run. Just as he is dismantling the structure of *U.S.A.* to tell individual stories again, so there is a kind of decomposition going on in his style: the famous hurtling effects, the tricks of pace, the words so snappily jumbled together, now seem merely scattered and startling. His extraordinary feeling for atmosphere is as keen as it ever was, perhaps even keener; but there is a nervousness about it, a staginess, that makes one think of those stilted or grandiose similes which neo-classic poets used to draw the lush classic landscape of Renaissance painting—'sweetsmelling

Jersey cows with big clean udders and large penciled dark eyes with long lashes like Hindoo ladies.' Every line is as brisk as it ever was, every word as quick in association; but where once they had an architectural fitness, leading us from character to character, from one stage in history to another, they now come at us in sudden flares, and too rapidly. It is as if Dos Passos just had to get them out, in all their full patter, for fear of losing them; but now they just seem a patter, where once they sounded time.

What this suggests, for me at least, is the tension of uncertainty—and its need of improvisation. Yet if that uncertainty is clear enough in the texture of the story, it becomes merely awkward at the end, when Tyler Spotswood sits alone in the courtroom, after being indicted for the crimes of his political gang, and suddenly has a revelation after reading a last beautiful letter from his brother Glenn in Spain. For we see then, if we have not seen it before, how much Dos Passos has been using the story, and almost fighting it, to bring us to the moment of conversion. We see then that Dos Passos has merely been using it to tell us something abstract, something in and about himself that is not in the story. It is he who has been converted, as it was he who died for a principle, for Glenn Spotswood in Spain. Yet everything else is as it ever was, everything still comes out of the American hell that was *U.S.A.*—except Dos Passos' need now to make up for it all at once, to set it right by at least one example.

THE GRAND DESIGN

January 1949

---

55. Edmund Wilson, letter to Dos Passos

27 January 1949

This excerpt from Wilson's letter to Dos Passos contains his initial response to *The Grand Design*, which was the third novel in Dos Passos's *District of Columbia* trilogy. The play Wilson mentioned he was working on was *The Little Blue Light*, first produced in Cambridge, Mass., in August 1950 and in New York in April 1951, (Edmund Wilson, *Letters on Literature and Politics 1912–1972*, ed. Elena Wilson (New York: Farrar, Straus & Giroux, 1977), 453–4).

I enjoyed *The Grand Design*—I think it is much the best of the three. It is enormously skillful in the writing (much less burdened by the naturalistic detail of which I used to complain), and in the swift and subtle presentation of social-political processes. But I do think it is true that your characters (in your words) are becoming less and less convincing as human beings. I feel that as you get older it costs you more and more of an effort to imagine the mediocrities that you insist on writing about. Everybody connected with the New Deal was not as mediocre as that, and even in the case of the ones who were, I don't think you are the person to write about them, as you haven't enough mediocrity in you to get into the spirit of the thing. I wish there were some Jeffersons, Joel Barlows, and Tom Paines in your fiction nowadays. Above all, as a brilliant conversationalist, why do you persist so in making everybody talk in clichés? Almost nobody talks like that. Sometimes you give the impression of those writers who like to show off their mastery of the idiom of some African tribe by retailing conversations with the natives. I think, though, that part of the hostility that *The Grand*

Design has aroused has been due to the fact that it has shocked people as blasphemy against the Great White Father. He was never any great hero of mine, and I am glad that you have shown up his inadequacies, but there was certainly more to those administrations than anybody could learn from your book—you hardly touch on the labor side of them, for example. The 'field' expeditions are admirable—and so are the meeting at which the old man is high-pressured into following the Communist line, and the death of Miss Washburn (though I couldn't really believe in her sleeping with that guy), and a lot of other things. I shan't reproach you with your personal tendency to represent everything in America as always deteriorating, as I am working on a play, supposed to take place in the immediate future, beside which your recent series looks like a smile by Truman.

56. Granville Hicks, 'Dos Passos and his Critics', *American Mercury*

May 1949, vol. lxviii, 623–30

Hicks had left the *New Masses* (where he had worked for five years) in 1939, the same year he resigned from the Communist Party because he disagreed with the Party's position on the Soviet–German pact. Nevertheless, he continued to believe in socialism. In this review of *The Grand Design* he reviewed what other critics had written about the novel, and concluded that political bias in reviewing was not 'a vice peculiar to the left'. Dos Passos, Hicks claimed, having lost his faith in Marxism, had found nothing to replace it with.

John Dos Passos has devoted his literary career to the examination and portrayal of life in the United States. The fact is worth recording, if only because there is no other contemporary novelist of any stature about whom such a statement could be made. From a sociological point of view, Dos Passos has chosen to be inclusive and central, whereas his contemporaries have been exclusive and often marginal. Faulkner has found his themes in a single Mississippi country, but Dos Passos has been satisfied with nothing less than the whole nation. Hemingway locates his novels in France and Italy and Spain, as if to proclaim that the specifically American has no particular interest for him. (He is, of course, as unmistakably and incurably American as Dos Passos, but that is another matter.) Wolfe is rhapsodically subjective; Dos Passos is conscientiously objective. Farrell has endlessly worked over the little area of experience that circumstances granted him; Dos Passos has deliberately broadened his range. Steinbeck has more in common with Dos Passos, being in some measure a disciple, and a couple of his novels are comparable in subject matter with what Dos Passos has done; but he has also dealt, rather more affectionately, with marginal themes.

Let it be understood that I am using 'central' and 'marginal,' 'inclusive' and 'exclusive,' as descriptive terms with no suggestion of praise or blame. In comparing John Dos Passos with his contemporaries, I am not saying that this is good and that is bad; I am merely trying to show where he stands. He is a writer pre-eminently concerned with a time and a place—that is, with the United States in the first half of the twentieth century—and he wants to know what distinguishes life here and now from life in other times and places. This means that he is directly occupied with the urban-industrial civilization that has reached its furthest development in this country. Obviously this is not the only field for a novelist to work in; it may even prove in practice to be more than commonly unyielding; but it is the field Dos Passos has chosen, and one can scarcely argue *a priori* that it is unworthy of a serious writer's attention.

Certain qualities of Dos Passos' fiction, some of which have been warmly debated in recent months, can be understood and evaluated only if one bears in mind what he has been trying to do. The charge is made that his characters are flat, and the charge is true. But Dos Passos might perfectly well reply that he intended his characters to be flat and that they had to be flat if he was to accomplish his aims. He is concerned with characters who are representative of twentieth-century America, and he is, furthermore, concerned with them in their representative aspects. As a result, there is a loss, a loss of insight into the deeper, more mysterious reaches of human personality. But let us not forget that there is also a loss when a writer chooses to portray a character as perfectly unique, for, though each of us is unique, each of us is also in some degree representative. A reader may prefer the novelist who deals with the unique, may prefer Dostoyevsky, let us say, to Balzac, but it is folly to ask Balzac to be both himself and Dostoyevsky. Another novelist would have done something different with J. Ward Morehouse and Eleanor Stoddard and Charley Anderson, and quite possibly would have made more of them than Dos Passos has, but would we then have understood, as we do now, precisely what they are in relation to the contemporary American scene?

Other consequences follow from Dos Passos' choice of theme. For one thing, he cannot possibly know the United States as William Faulkner knows Yoknapatawpha Country or as James T. Farrell knows a few Chicago blocks. He has a restless foot and a highly trained eye, and he has done as much as any human being can do, but this is a big country and it has 140 million people in it. Consequently, Dos Passos has to rely on what can only be called sociological generalizations. In other words, his conception of what is representative does depend in part on theories about the country and about this period of history. Every writer has general ideas, but not every writer has ideas about the structure of the society he lives in, and the ideas some writers have on that subject are largely irrelevant to their writings. Dos Passos' general ideas are specifically social and political, and they have to be.

I am not suggesting that Dos Passos went out and got himself a set of social and political theories so that he could write about contemporary America. The reverse would be nearer true. At the beginning of his career he hated the machine age and tried to get away from it, and one could almost say that it was because he quarreled with existing society that he made an effort to understand it. The fact remains, however, that in every book he has written, the selection of materials has been influenced by the theories he held. I hasten to add that Dos Passos has always been an extraordinarily honest observer, and in both his journalism and his fiction he has set down what he has seen whether it fitted his theories or not. Moreover, as will shortly be pointed out, he has constantly revised his ideas about society. Nevertheless, the dependence on theory has persisted because it is implicit in his aims.

In the autumn of 1945 Dos Passos was interviewed by a young radical, who asked him if the Dos Passos of *1919* wouldn't regard the contemporary Dos Passos as an out-and-out reactionary. According to his account of the incident in *Tour of Duty*, Dos Passos replied, 'No, I don't think so. I have changed and so have the times.' Precisely. Most people do change their social philosophies in the course of a quarter-century, and those who don't almost certainly should. Leaving college in a state of romantic revolt, Dos Passos was pushed in the direction of philosophical anarchism by the disillusionments of the first World War. His dissatisfactions with contemporary society hardened in the late twenties into a quasi-Communism—a belief that capitalism must be done away with and that the working class could and should establish a new society. Under the impact of the depression, he formed a close alliance with the Communist Party, though merely as a fellow-traveler and never without reservations. Disillusionment with the party set in by early 1934, and was intensified by the trials and purges in Russia. By the end of the thirties, after seeing something of Communists in action in Spain, he was an unqualified opponent of the Stalinist régime. As *The Ground We Stand On* shows, he attempted the systematic formulation of a political philosophy based on traditional American democracy. The formulation, however, refused to stick, and has undergone constant revision in the forties.

If Dos Passos were a social philosopher or were simply a journalist, the changes in his thinking would not have been embarrassing to him or surprising to his readers. Since, however, his political ideas have been part of the very fabric of his novels, and—I must say it again—necessarily so, he has had some tough problems to deal with. A shift in political thinking may do strange things to a writer, as Hemingway demonstrated during his rapid passage through the Communist orbit, and as Faulkner may be in the process of demonstrating now that he has become occupied with the Negro problem. Dos Passos wrote the first volume of *U.S.A.* when he was drawing closer to Communism, the second volume when he was deeply convinced of the imminence of revolution, and the third after disillusionment had set in. It is a miracle that the work hangs together as well as it does, but the discrepancies are quite apparent and they do detract from its force. The Spotswood trilogy is intentionally looser, and the reader is not so acutely aware of changes in the author's point of view, but he does sense that the events portrayed in the various volumes are not being judged by quite the same standards. This is a risk that Dos Passos, as a man of integrity and as an author who has chosen to portray the social scene, has had to run.

It is only against such a background that one can fairly examine Dos Passos' new novel, *The Grand Design*, and the controversy it has aroused. The controversy began with the first reviews of the book, several of which announced (a) that Dos Passos had become a reactionary, and (b) that he had written a bad novel. The counter-attack was led by J. Donald Adams of the New York *Times*, hitherto not conspicuous as an admirer of Dos Passos' work, who insisted that the attacks on Dos Passos were political in their motivation. Mr. Adams was seconded by Isabel Paterson, who pointed out that she had always condemned Dos Passos for the faults that the pro-New Deal reviewers had perceived for the first time in *The Grand Design*. John Chamberlain, writing in the *New Leader*, was indignant about 'the barrage of dead cats that has beaten down on Dos Passos' head for daring to touch on the history of the New Deal epoch,' and argued that the author of *The Grand Design* was not only as good a novelist as he had ever been but had kept 'his faith in the human being, in the individual.'

Some observations may be made at this point. To begin with, the most political and, so far as my reading went, the least fair review of *The Grand Design* appeared in the Sunday *Herald Tribune* (Rep.), and was written by Lloyd Morris, who may be a crypto-Marxist for all I know but has thus far not given many signs of it. Mr. Morris described Dos Passos as 'a weary, cynical defender of vested interests,' which is just silly, and could find virtually nothing to admire in the novel. Maxwell Geismar, on the other hand, writing in the Sunday *Times*, and writing from what Mr. Adams doubtless regards as a leftist point of view, mingled considerable praise with his condemnation. In the second place, two reviewers who have been conspicuous through the years for their adherence to literary rather than political values—Diana Trilling and Jacques Barzun—strongly asserted what Mr. Adams *et al.* deny, namely, that *The Grand Design* is inferior to *U.S.A.* on literary grounds. I am not going to insist that the defense of Dos Passos by Mr. Adams, Mrs. Paterson and Mr. Chamberlain was inspired by their political views, but I perceive that political bias is not, as Mr. Adams assumes, a vice peculiar to the left.

Up to a point, of course, criticism of *The Grand Design* has to be political, simply because it is an intensely political book. It not only presents a series of explicit judgments on political issues; these judgments permeate the entire work. As I have already said, the kind of fiction Dos Passos writes has to have representative characters, and his conception of representativeness necessarily rests on his idea of the society he is portraying. If, then, we find Messrs. Cowley and Chamberlain engaging in an exchange of ''Tis so' and ''Tain't so,' that is not a relapse into childishness but a natural consequence of Dos Passos' methods. Even the structure of the book is determined by political considerations, for Dos Passos had to cover a period of eight years in order to portray the New Deal. This is important, for one of the major weaknesses of the novel is the way it is thrown together. The characters merely pop in and out until, on page 116, the author reaches the spring of 1940 and can get down to business.

What is Dos Passos' political position? In an interview that appeared in the *Herald Tribune* after some of the reviews were in, he expressed surprise that he was considered an enemy of the New Deal as a whole. 'I have written with enthusiasm about its early stages,' he said. The interviewer continued, 'It was Mr. Roosevelt's foreign—not domestic—policy that disappointed him.' And it is true that Dos Passos, after his disillusionment with Communism, did find something to admire in the New Deal. It is also true that in *The Grand Design* he portrays the eagerness with which his 'good' New Dealers, such as Millard Carroll and Paul Graves, entered upon their tasks. But in the novel it is apparent from the outset that the enthusiasm of Carroll and Graves is destined to be betrayed. In the background is the sinister figure of the President, and in the foreground is the character known as Walker Watson, who combines the worst features of Henry Wallace and Harry Hopkins. The reader knows well enough that the 'good' New Dealers don't have a chance; they are victims, suckers; they may be righteous, but they cannot save Sodom. John Chamberlain says that Dos Passos didn't write about the achievements of the New Deal he admires, such as TVA and SEC, because they were 'tangential to the story of *The Grand Design*, which is a story of how Big Administration stifles the creative activity of the average good-enough human being.'

But isn't this an admission that Dos Passos selected his materials in such a way as to condemn the New Deal lock, stock and barrel?

It does not follow, however, that he is 'a weary, cynical defender of vested interests.' 'Weary' may be an apt adjective, but the rest of the phrase overshoots the mark. Far from being cynical, Dos Passos has all of his old sympathy and affection for people who get pushed around. Far from defending special privilege, he is attacking the vested interests of the politicians and bureaucrats. As Chamberlain points out, Dos Passos has always been a belligerent individualist, with a persistent leaning towards anarchism. His original quarrel with capitalism, going even further back than World War I to his college days, grew out of the feeling that mass production and the profit system were crushing the individual. For a time he was able to convince himself that a socialist revolution would bring liberation, but one has only to read his contributions to the monthly *New Masses* in the late twenties and early thirties to see how much of an individualist he was even in the years when he was close to the Communist Party. Now it is simply a fact that Big Administration, to use Chamberlain's term, is a menace to individual liberty—not the only menace, maybe not the greatest menace, but a menace. During the New Deal, Big Administration may have been less dangerous than Dos Passos thinks; it may have been less dangerous than any conceivable alternative; but there were tendencies in the New Deal that were bound to disturb anyone who was watching what went on in the rest of the world. As I have said, I think that Dos Passos loads the dice against the New Deal in this book. But that scarcely makes him a reactionary.

On the other hand, I cannot go along with those who maintain that there have been no significant changes in Dos Passos. There is no point in offering another lengthy discussion of structure, characterization, style, and so on. I shall merely say that the Spotswood trilogy seems to me measurably inferior to *U.S.A.*, and I have re-read both within the past two months. Something has gone out of Dos Passos' work. Geismar speaks of 'a collapse of values,' and Irving Howe, writing in *Tomorrow*, has an even better phrase: 'the loss of passion.' I cannot imagine what Mr. Adams is thinking of when he says, 'For vitality and vividness I will stack *The Grand Design* against any one of the three panels of *U.S.A.*' The book has only a few scenes, notably the description of the Communist memorial meeting, that suggest what Dos Passos was almost constantly capable of fifteen years ago.

Furthermore, I cannot accept John Chamberlain's minimization of the changes in Dos Passos' political and social outlook. If it is narrowly partisan to call him a reactionary, it is quite false to suggest that he has remained a libertarian crusader. We are dealing here not merely with a succession of modifications in his thinking about politics, but with a fundamental shift of feeling—something that amounts to a change of heart. When it was published, *Three Soldiers* was attacked as a bitter and disillusioned book, but in his introduction to the Modern Library edition (1932) Dos Passos spoke of the great hopefulness he felt in the spring of 1919 when he wrote it. This hopefulness underlay all his bitter books—*Manhattan Transfer, The 42nd Parallel, 1919*. Even *The Big Money*, written after he had grown skeptical about revolution and therefore much bleaker in his outlook than readers had been led to expect, gives off some echo of the earlier hope. But after 1936 Dos Passos came increasingly to feel that the likeliest alternative to capitalism was something vastly worse—totalitarianism on either the Russian or the German model. In the twenties and thirties he had faced the evils of the world with confidence and passion because he believed there was a good by which they could be supplanted. Now what had once seemed a good was added to the host of evils.

It is true that scores of writers have gone through a similar experience in the past two decades and that few of them have been affected so deeply or for so long a time as Dos Passos. He was specially vulnerable because, as I have said, his aims and actions as a writer were so intimately bound up with his political attitudes. The effect of the upheaval was two-fold—intellectual and emotional. From 1919 to 1936, Dos Passos believed that the capitalist system was headed for disaster, and he further believed, with some shifts of emphasis, that a better society would come out of the cataclysm. This, as Cowley has said, was an illusion, but it proved to be what James Branch Cabell used to call a dynamic illusion. Marxism—or at any rate a concept of historical processes that owed a lot to Marx—gave Dos Passos a means of interpreting and unifying and simplifying the vast and chaotic body of material he had chosen to deal with. Since giving up Marxism, he has found nothing that would serve that purpose.

But Dos Passos lost more than a useful set of ideas. Irving Howe writes, 'It is the peculiar triumph of *U.S.A.* that when judged as a totality the weakness of its component parts seems inconsequential. The secret of this triumph is, I think, in the novel's pervasive passion, its author's uncontainable feeling rushing through it like a stream of blood.' This passion has vanished. Like most of us, Dos Passos can be passionately against something only if he is passionately for something else. He is against almost everything he writes about in *The Grand Design*, but his opposition is bewildered, ill-tempered, often petulant, never passionate. Edmund Wilson, reviewing *State of the Nation* back in 1944, felt that the world had moved away from Dos Passos and that his imagination was not involved with his material in quite the same way it once had been. The fact that many reviewers of *The Grand Design* have spoken in much the same terms is not to be brushed off as a political conspiracy.

And to what conclusions does one come? Why, simply, that Dos Passos is not what President Truman called Drew Pearson and that *The Grand Design* isn't a very good novel. One might go on and point out that it is terribly difficult to do what Dos Passos has been trying to do all his life and that he deserves more credit than he is currently receiving for such successes as he has had. Like Malcolm Cowley, I feel that Donald Adams and John Chamberlain are much too willing to proclaim that Dos Passos was never much of a novelist anyway. I hope that various other critics are equally wrong in saying that he is finished. But whether he is or he isn't, his achievement stands.

NOTE

1 Drew Pearson was a political columnist and outspoken critic of Truman, who once alluded to him as an s.o.b.

CHOSEN COUNTRY

October 1951

57. Edmund Wilson, letter to Dos Passos

27 November 1951

From Edmund Wilson, *Letters on Literature and Politics 1912–1972*, ed. Elena Wilson (New York: Farrar, Straus & Giroux, 1977), 503–40

We've just read *Chosen Country* and were fascinated. I find it rather hard—which happens rarely with me—to judge it as a book, because, knowing the originals or components of so many of your characters, I keep seeing the real people and get partly thrown off the track of what you are trying to do. What comes through to me is the Peter Pan fantasy of the Smoolies or the horrors of life with Griffin Barry, which seem to me wonderfully caught, but I can't gauge the effect of all this on a reader who hasn't known them. I will hazard, though, a few specific criticisms. Negative: colorless title—you seem to be getting addicted to them—which doesn't convey the idea you intend (till I read the book, I thought it meant *Choice Country*—i.e., country appropriate for farming or something) and isn't likely to lure the reader; dependence in conversation on clichés—you are here at last dealing with people who are supposed to be clever and charming and sometimes profound and brilliant, yet you still make them carry on even among themselves an exchange of catchphrases and platitudes. You do get away from this to some extent, and at moments very successfully, in the case of Jay and Lulie[1] and the elder Pignatelli—but I think you still a little give the impression that the guy who is writing the book is the only master of language in the United States, a country where the language of everybody else is a tissue of the ready-made phrases that go with his profession or milieu. And this brings us to the positive remarks: you have never written more beautifully or fluently—having dropped your naturalistic impediments—in evoking sensations and places. That is, I think, the real development of your latest books. You seem to be able now to turn off easily and with breathtaking rapidity—the last setting in Maine, for example—descriptions that depend for their effectiveness on an extremely subtle use of language. This makes the travels in Italy go admirably—a kind of thing that can be very boring and hold the story up. I think, though, that from the point of view of the characters, the last chapters go a little too quickly. Jay seems to be functioning in court in that Sacco-Vanzetti trial without any previous experience—and haven't you got the Communist movement getting into its overtly cynical phase a good deal too early, as well as Jay reading *Ulysses* before it came out (in 1921)?

NOTE

1 Lulie, in *Chosen Country*, was based on Katy Dos Passos.

58. Arthur Mizener, review, *New York Times Book Review*

2 December 1951, 7

Mizener (b. 1907), professor of English at Cornell since 1951, is best known for his biographies of Dos Passos's contemporaries, F. Scott Fitzgerald and Ford Maddox Ford. This review claims that *Chosen Country* might be Dos Passos's best novel because there is more feeling and pathos for the characters.

Chosen Country may well be John Dos Passos' best novel. For those who read *District of Columbia*, Dos Passos' second trilogy, as if its novels were straight narrative rather than ironic comedy and decided Dos Passos' talent was fading, this book will come as a surprise. *Chosen Country* shows that all the gifts which produced *Manhattan Transfer* and *U.S.A.* are as alive as they ever were. The reader will find the marvelous narrative gift which can marshal a whole society for us and yet keep the story moving with the pace of first-rate melodrama; the ability to sketch in swiftly and precisely the evocative details, particularly the sensory details, of experience; the immense, exact knowledge of how various kinds of Americans live from day to day. All these things are here again, as they were in *U.S.A.* Only, they are here with a new power and integrity, because Dos Passos sees what he knows with a new and more human understanding.

In Dos Passos' earlier work there always seems to be something held back, something important that is not clearly expressed. The two trilogies, for all their brilliance and power, never get into clear focus what you feel, all through them, are Dos Passos' deepest feelings about his subject. These feelings are always there, an undertone you keep straining to hear behind the political ideas of *U.S.A.* and the satire of *District of Columbia*.

Both trilogies express a horror of the betrayals of our inheritance that we Americans have been guilty of. But what gives that horror its force and impressiveness is some feeling about our inheritance and the way we must possess it which Dos Passos has never managed to express directly. You almost think that Jay Pignatelli, the hero of *Chosen Country*, is speaking for his author when he thinks to himself, 'he wanted to be telling... in words that weren't flannel in the mouth, the learning of a man who might have been a man without a country (Damn the United States: I never want to hear her name again) for the country of his choice.'

For the first time in his career, Dos Passos is now telling what that yearning is. The essential theme of *Chosen Country*, as the title suggests, is how Americans—those lonely, gregarious people—come to possess what must be for each one of them a 'new found land.' 'My father,' says Jay Pignatelli, 'was an American by choice.... I feel the same way.' But this is a choice which has to be earned, especially if your name is, as so many American names are, half Anglo-Saxon and half Latin, like Jay Pignatelli's (or John Dos Passos'). And it is not easy for anyone to earn, because it is much harder to learn to love in the right way what is good than merely to hate what is bad.

Jay Pignatelli is the illegitimate son of James Knox Polk Pignatelli, himself the son of one of Garibaldi's friends and of a New England Evangelist's daughter. He makes a great success as a railroad lawyer and dies broke, leaving Jay his complex inheritance and little else. Dos Passos' heroine is Lulie Harrington, the grand-daughter of a New England Unitarian minister and the daughter of a professor who was trained in Germany and taught all his life at a small Ohio college.

We follow the lives of Jay and Lulie through the fully realized life of America, which only Dos Passos among living novelists can give us. Always our interest is in the way these two people gradually take imaginative and emotional possession of their world. Because of what they have inherited and because of what America is, their coming to terms with America is not easy. 'If I act a little crazy,' says Lulie in a low practical voice, 'it's just to keep from going crazy.' But Jay and Lulie finally settle in their new found land. At the end of the novel they stand at the door of the old New England house where they are spending their honeymoon. 'Today we begin,' he said, 'to make...' 'The wilderness our home,' she said.

Perhaps the most impressive consequence of Dos Passos' release of these feelings about the grace and difficulty of choosing our country and making a home in the wilderness of American experience is the immensely increased range of human sympathy in this book. The rich Dos Passos panorama of American types is here, and it includes, as it always has, a great many different kinds of frauds. But because he realizes how difficult the wilderness is and how easy it is to lose one's way there, Dos Passos can extend his sympathy to them all.

Even the frauds suffer and are human in *Chosen Country*. When rich and promiscuous Molly Hobart, 'sitting up primly and modestly like a little girl taking her music lesson,' sings Bessie Smith's 'Careless Love,' we feel perhaps first the irony of the contrast between Bessie Smith and Molly Hobart. This is the kind of irony which is everywhere in *U.S.A.* But we feel, too, the pathos of that prim and modest little girl; and this is new in Dos Passos.

Jay's cousin, Nick Pignatelli (a figure very like the anarchist Carlo Tresca), is a different kind of radical from those who appear in *U.S.A.* and *District of Columbia*; Nick is tough and shrewd, like the peasant he is, but in spite of his broken accent he is a very wise American who understands completely the difficulty and danger of his choice of a country. In the end he dies for it, not, like Glenn Spotswood in *Adventures of a Young Man*, in confusion and despair but with the confidence of a man fully convinced of the rightness of his choice. His wisdom is a kind Jay only slowly learns, but learning it is a part of his choosing.

When Jay's sympathies go out to Leo Sabatini, the Italian workman falsely arrested in a labor dispute, because Leo in prison is deprived of women and books and freedom, we are in the world of the genuine but limited values of *U.S.A.*; but when Jay thinks, 'the craven craving to live,' we have, without disowning that world, moved out beyond it.

From their childhoods Jay and Lulie have passions for Malory's *Morte d'Arthur* not because Dos Passos wants to note a fact about our society (as when there is a copy of Compton Mackenzie's *Sinister Street* on a Greenwich Village table in *Manhattan Transfer*), but because the parallel between Malory's world and theirs is real. 'So Sir Launcelot rode many wide ways through marshes and many wild ways.' *Chosen Country* is Dos Passos at his best, only better.

59. Harrison Smith, 'Welding the Past and the Present', *Saturday Review*

15 December 1951, vol. xxxiv, 19–20

Smith (1888–1971) headed Jonathan Cape & Harrison Smith, Inc., an early publisher of William Faulkner and other 'experimental' writers, and was president and associate editor of *Saturday Review* from 1938 to 1966. Smith is much less enthusiastic than Mizener (No. 57).

To readers who remember *Manhattan Transfer*, and the volumes which made up his lengthy and painful study of the American social scene back in the Thirties, Mr. Dos Passos's latest novel will reveal that he has been converted to approval of this country and its people, as he first illustrated in a non-fiction book a few years ago.

Chosen Country turns out to be an old-fashioned story about two young people named Jay Pignatelli and Lulie Harrington, who fell in love when they first saw each other and married after years of separation. They were, in fact, born for each other. All the boys around the wooded lake where Lulie spent a few halcyon summers were more or less in love with her cheerful giggles, her little shrieks, and her Irish eyes. There were, among others, Georgie, Jasper, Joe, Benjie, and Zeke who married a very bad girl, and assorted elders, such as Aunt Lyde, Grandmother Waring, Doc Warner, Uncle Purdy, and many more.

Not only are there several subsidiary stories attached to his characters, but Dos Passos's passion for documentation leads him to dig back into their ancestral beginnings in Europe. Thus the table of contents lists eight chapters, interspersed with three Prolegomena ranging from 1848 to 1919, and three sections labeled Footnotes on a Vanished Culture, on Social Consciousness, and on the Practice of the Law, which extend in time from 1865 to 1930. By these the author illustrates his belief that the mating of Lulie and Jay and the behavior of Georgie, Benjie, Zeke, and their assorted relatives can only be thoroughly explained if you know all about their ancestors two or three generations back. In the process of welding the past and the present Dos Passos has written a series of what seem to be short stories, or condensed plots for separate novels. He presents the reader with an embarrassment of riches. They are excellent stories, for there can be no question of the author's ability as a teller of tales.

The first Pignatelli escaped from the Italian revolution in a rowboat and met Garibaldi at sea in a tartane. 'His face was like the face of Christ,' he remembered. His son grew up in Queen City on the Ohio River. Katherine Jay was a child in her mother's arms during the siege of Vicksburg in the Civil War and faintly remembered her bedtime stories of the dead piled in oxcarts and the wounded calling for water. Ezekiel Harrington's father, an abolitionist minister, brought his former slaves and his son back into Maryland after the war at the risk of their lives. Eliot Bradford's father was an archeologist so he was born in Asolo instead of Massachusetts, grew up among the Boston Brahmins, and returned to his father's profession in Italy.

These are the forebears of the living characters in the novel. Compared with their children, or their children's children, their lives are dramatic and colorful. The young people of the late Twenties and Thirties with whom Dos Passos is principally concerned are hardly worth writing about. None of them seems to be really grown up; their occasional returns from Chicago, where they are living, to the lake of their youthful memories is a wishful lapse into prolonged adolescences. The author does not attempt to use them either as symbols of modern American life or as the protagonists in any consecutive plot or drama. He is never able to unite them except as they flutter about Lulie Harrington. The final episode, Lulie's marriage with Jay, is as slick and as artificially embroidered as a banal love story in a mass circulation magazine.

This is a strong statement to make of a writer as distinguished and capable as John Dos Passos. The final four sentences on the three hundred and seventy-fifth and last page may make it credible. On the morning after their marriage the young couple meet at dawn on the doorstep of their borrowed seaside cabin. 'The waves breathed in the cove. "Husband," she said. "Wife," he said. The words made them bashful. They clung together in their bashfulness. "Today we begin," he said, "to make..." "This wilderness our house," she said. The sun risen over the ocean shone in their faces.'

It is possible that Dos Passos was at the last moment so pleased with getting his heroine safely married that he has confused this modern couple with an unwritten prolegomena concerning someone else's ancestors who crossed the continent in a covered wagon. Actually, Jay had a minor job in a lawyer's office in New York and neither of them had the faintest intention of making the wilderness their home.

MIDCENTURY

January 1961

60. Fanny Butcher, 'Labor Abuses', *Chicago Sunday Tribune Review of Books*

26 February 1961, 1

Midcentury undoubtedly will be one of the most talked about books of our day. It will have its passionate detractors as well as its enthusiastic praisers, both for the same reason: its forthright expose of the presence of racketeers in the labor movement and of the dissatisfaction among the 'rank and file' in labor.

The author quotes letters received by members of Congress and by newspapers asking such questions as: 'Is it freedom when a man cannot work at a job without paying a union for the benefit of doing so? Is it freedom when a man cannot work when the union says "strike"? Is it freedom when our streets are blocked, cars overturned, windows broken, buildings and homes blown up by gangs of hoodlums who call themselves pickets?... Is the right to vote any more sacred than the right to work?'

Nobody today will read *Midcentury* without being disturbed from complacency about the state of the nation and his own state of mind, heart, and soul.

Midcentury is essentially a novel about labor, but it is also about our country, today and only yesterday, a novel so interspersed with fact that the book seems less a story than history. The technique which Dos Passos chooses is the same he used in his great trilogy of the 1920s and 30s, published under the general title, *U.S.A.* It is a kaleidoscopic series of actual headlines, excerpts from advertisements and letters, short biographies of actual persons and the stories of persons who, if not real, have, in Dos Passos' pages, the forceful impact of reality.

There is no flowing continuity either to the fictional life stories or to the over-all narrative except in the brief biographies of real men and women who greatly influenced the country. Some of the fictional lives are treated as tho their story were a serial in a magazine broken off at crucial moments and later resumed, so that readers may have to go back to pick up the thread of the tale.

It is a method of novel writing characteristic of Dos Passos, who invented it, and, as used by him, it is powerfully effective. There will be readers who object to the constantly changing pattern, but they are the ones who, if they looked into a kaleidoscope, would see only confusion, not an exciting shifting of design.

Among the actual midcentury figures in the book are labor leaders Walter Reuther, Harry Bridges, Dan Tobin, Dave Beck, James Hoffa, and John L. Lewis. Here, too, are Generals MacArthur and William Dean, Eleanor Roosevelt, Senators John McClellan and the younger Robert LaFollette, scientist Julius Robert Oppenheimer, capitalist Robert R. Young, movie magnate Sam Goldwyn, and the teen-agers' idol, Jimmy Dean. All of these had a powerful influence for either good or evil on the midcentury American way of life, and Dos Passos sketches each life with a sharp pencil in memorable lines.

Equally memorable are the fictional characters, especially Terry Bryant, who was a devoted union man of good will marked for tragedy; Blackie Bowman, who believed passionately in the principles of the International Workers of the World; Jasper Milleron, an executive in the vast Abingdon-Products (dog food and milling).

Others come and go: little men of good will, others of ill will toward their fellows, promoters, financiers, a very few women, but all of them directly or indirectly affected by the labor movement.

Midcentury is not an easy book to read. It is not for those who run thru pages of a novel the way barefoot dance enthusiasts used to trip across the greensward. It is a book with a message, a warning that all of the apples in the labor barrel are not sound, that today's youth is growing soft, that there are greed and corruption abroad in the land, and that there is fundamental good in man.

61. R.A. Fraser, review, *San Francisco Chronicle*

26 February 1961, 26

R.A. Fraser was the author of *Yvette*, a novel, published in 1960 by MacGibbon & Kee in London.

U.S.A. was that rare thing, a work of art which re-created an epoch by grasping it at its twin poles, Man and society. By showing how each shapes the other, Dos Passos produced a picture of an America vitally alive, where a dynamic, idealistic struggle for a better society was being fought, and where the individual counted because he still had a role to play.

Midcentury, 30 years later, represents the frustration of almost every hope contained in *U.S.A.* The difference between the two is a comment on our times that future historians will take note of: for to say that Dos Passos' viewpoint has changed and nothing else would be to deny him the interdependence of the individual and society he so clearly postulated in *U.S.A.*

The new trilogy,[1] much shorter than *U.S.A.*, is organized in a similar manner. The personal histories of several fictitious characters of the post-war years are interwoven with biographies (General MacArthur, Harry Bridges, Mrs Roosevelt, etc.) and a telling patchwork of news quotes. Its main concern is with the world of labor, but its theme is wider. For what has happened in the generation between the two books, Dos Passos seems to be saying (without explaining why it happened), is that an authentic and passionate individualism has died in America, and with it the hope of building a society based on the needs of the individual.

In contrast to the stirring descriptions of the Wobblies in *U.S.A.* ('We wobblies used to think every man ought to think his own word up for himself'), *Midcentury* presents a view of corruption and racketeering in the trade unions which the individual worker is powerless to fight. Terry Bryant, a rubber worker, struggles to reform his union: the gangsters throw him out of the union; the

261

corporation, through complicity, fires him. Later, in another job, leaders of a rival union murder him.

But the manager's position is no better. Colonel Milliron, who tries to implement improvements for his corporation, is defeated by 'the palace guard' at head office. A love affair which threatens scandal is dangerous for the corporation's image. Finally he is forced out.

And the individual who wants to start his own business? Like Will Jenks he finds he has to fight a union and corporation monopoly, run by a gangster. When Will Jenks wins, it is a Pyrrhic victory. The monopoly suggests a merger. Unions and corporations are too big, too corrupt, to allow individual freedom.

Freedom, moreover, is not highly prized. 'Playing it cool' is more important. The Wobblies' rebelliousness with a purpose has become the rebelliousness without a cause of a James Dean whose biography here is made to contrast with that of his name-sake, General William Frishe Dean of Korea fame, a self reliant and rugged individual.

Dos Passos suggests no answer (other than to equate Harry Bridges with the new style promised land, and Sam Goldwyn with the promised land, old style). Disillusionment has crept into his writing. With one important exception the characters are paper-thin symbols: 30 years ago they were symbols too but also living people described with human warmth.

The exception, Blackie Bowman, is interesting because he provides a key to the book. He is an old-timer recalling the epoch of *U.S.A.* and just after. Dos Passos describes him with extraordinary sympathy: this working stiff and his Wobbly days show again the source of the writer's inspiration: an anarchistic, but very American, individualism, idealistic and free-ranging, that belongs not to *Midcentury* but to the early 1900s.

Whether it is Dos Passos alone who has lost his fire, or whether 30 years have made such a difference to the U.S.A., is a matter for each reader's judgment.

NOTE

1 *Midcentury* is divided in three parts. No part could stand alone, nor was there ever any effort or intention to publish them separately.

62. Harry T. Moore, review, *New York Times Book Review*

26 February 1961, 1, 51

Moore (1908–81) was an American critic and author of numerous books on D.H. Lawrence, Henry James, Steinbeck, Forster, and Lawrence Durrell, in addition to *Age of the Modern and Other Literary Essays* (1971). His review is typical of many which hailed *Midcentury* as Dos Passos's best novel since *U.S.A.* Moore highlights its implicit thesis that individualism is threatened in America by conformity in government, business, labour unions, and society-at-large. Moore claims the novel is about much more than just labour abuses.

Seldom does a writer retrieve a long-lost reputation at a single stroke, but John Dos Passos has probably done just that with *Midcentury*, by far his best novel since he completed the *U.S.A.* trilogy with *The Big Money* in 1936. It is written with a mastery of narrative styles, a grasp of character and a sense of the American scene. In its fictional passages this panoramic novel recaptures the Dos Passos verve and intensity of a quarter-century ago, while the background sections, made up of sociological tidbits and pertinent biographical sketches, show the same Dos Passos skill at manipulating the devices which helped to give *U.S.A.* originality and force.

The fictional heart of *Midcentury* contains several simultaneously developing stories. At first the emphasis falls upon three men closely involved in union activities. The garrulous Blackie Bowman, one-time Wobbly and former resident of Greenwich Village, is now confined to a bed in a veterans' hospital, where his reminiscences— vintage Dos Passos—go backward through the century. Terry Bryant, who fails to reform his union, takes to taxi driving as a last refuge of individualism. Frank Worthington collides with union troubles similar to Terry's, but surmounts them to become an official far enough removed from rank-and-file reality to fail to see the merits of Terry's case when it briefly crosses his attention.

In repeated, vigorous and one-sided attacks on labor unions, Dos

Passos hammers away at racketeering of the kind we all know exists. He hardly suggests that there are good as well as evil unions. About three-fifths of the way through the volume, when the anti-union poundings threaten to become tiresome, he introduces two new and interesting characters, Jasper Milliron and his son-in-law, Willoughby Jenks, who take part in exciting battles at management levels where the villainy of unions is only incidental. In adding this dimension, Dos Passos proves again that he can write about business—which doesn't have to be a dull subject—better than anyone since Theodore Dreiser. The sequences concerned with it in *Midcentury* are worth a dozen gray-flannel-suit and executive-suite novels. Here the author gives fictional life to some of the phases of American civilization recently noted by popularizing sociologists, but he does so with pronounced individuality and the stamp of authority. If the sociologists look at outwardly-directed and herd-motivated men with a scientific eye, Dos Passos regards them with deep pessimism and gloom—here projected fictionally in the downfall of Jasper Milliron and in the ensnaring of Will Jenks in an unhappy compromise.

Not that Dos Passos has ever been a cheerful writer. He began his career in the early Nineteen Twenties with two despairing war books, long before such novels became fashionable. In 1925 his *Manhattan Transfer* displayed a gallery of unhappy city dwellers, but readers hardly noticed the mood of the book as they admired its cinematically shuttling episodes. This technique was elaborated in the 'collective' novels comprising *U.S.A.*, which perhaps didn't really champion the masses so much as this author's enthusiasts of the time thought they did, but rather celebrated individualism.

With his next trilogy, *District of Columbia*, completed in 1949, Dos Passos suffered a loss in critical reputation and, presumably, in readers. It wasn't merely a matter of disagreement with the opinions he set forth, but rather, in most cases, with the excessively dogmatic and story-spoiling way in which he expressed them. *District of Columbia* and the novels following it lacked the concentrated power of *U.S.A.* and gave their readers almost no hint that the author had left in him the kind of imaginative energy that manifests itself in *Midcentury*.

In this volume the interstitial *U.S.A.*-style biographies reappear, beginning with one of Douglas MacArthur that is mostly favorable though acidly critical of the general's intelligence service at Clark Field and on the Yalu. Another military man, Gen. William F. Dean, is portrayed as a hero for his resistance to brainwashing while a war prisoner in Korea. Mrs. Roosevelt receives only a few ironic jabs; the picture of J. Robert Oppenheimer is largely sympathetic. What begins as a portrait of Freud becomes too much a cartoon of headshrinkers, while Sam Goldwyn when shorn of his Goldwynisms seems almost 'included out.' The sketches of two Senators involved in labor investigations, John McClellan and Robert M. La Follette Jr., point up the differences between their personalities and methods. Most of the biographies focus on labor leaders such as John L. Lewis, Harry Bridges, Walter Reuther, Dan Tobin, Dave Beck and Jimmy Hoffa, and under the circumstances a few of them seem to escape rather lightly.

In place of the inward-searching camera eye of *U.S.A.*, *Midcentury* offers seven intermittent investigator's notes, anti-union testimony delivered to a shadowy figure, and although these may reflect a good deal of truth they become rather tedious. On the other hand, the interludes which are here called documentaries recapture the liveliness of the earlier trilogy's 'newsreels' in their blaring headlines and spasmodic reflections of background events. These documentaries feature references to space travel, armament, schizoid patients and other appropriate topics which, like the biographies, give perspective to the imaginative sections.

The prose of *Midcentury* has fewer color shadings than the earlier volumes. But it is recognizably Don Passos' in its sparing use of the commas that hook a reader's eye and in its Joycean ramming together of words ('a shortnecked grayhaired man'). The writer's distinctive cadences are also noticeably present, in the choral chants of the biographies and, more emphatically, in the hard-surfaced narrative passages and in the crackling realism of the dialogue, all of it good American-built writing.

The ministerial side of Dos Passos, which never lets him tell a story for its own sake, also appears here. In the fictional sections concerned with Jasper Milliron and Will Jenks, however, the novel doesn't drum its lessons home so obviously as in the anti-union sermons, but lets the dramatization do its own work.

Jasper's entrance into the story is preceded by the biography of the railroad magnate, Robert R. Young, who, like Jasper, couldn't cope with the forces working against him. Jasper wasn't born early enough to have established a strong position in the rough-enterprise era, and in his fifties he is squeezed out of his high executive position with a milling company by men who represent the newer phase, scimitar instead of bludgeon.

Will Jenks, trying to operate a taxi company in defiance of a monopoly, has for an associate the Terry Bryant who earlier in the book became a taxi driver as a form of self-expression. Even though Terry is murdered in the cab war, Will wins it; but his victory is Pyrrhic. He can consolidate his position and go forward only by merging with his defeated rivals, subsidiary of a car manufacturer, whose monopoly he had tried to break.

In these stories Dos Passos is apparently trying to show Americans what is happening to their vaunted individualism in this age of conformity and conciliation. The man of originality, the voice of singleness, the spirit of independence—he seems to be saying—will be defeated at every level of our national activity; you no longer can fight 'em, you have to join 'em.

As if this isn't a frightening enough prospect, he ends the book with a disturbing suggestion of the future in the person of Jasper's adolescent nephew-by-marriage, a Holden Caulfield type named Stan Goodspeed, whose story is balanced by the biography of the teen-agers' fetish, the late actor, James Dean. Stan, who among other things typifies American rootlessness, is last seen on a cross-country spree, which he finances by stealing credit cards belonging to Jasper, whose days are now blurred by his heavy drinking.

Ironically, this book of wormwood and gall appears at an hour when liberalism seems to be again somewhat in the ascendant and when, despite warnings of stiff times and tight sacrifices ahead, most Americans are fairly optimistic. *Midcentury*, which by scrutinizing so many current problems and presenting them with the force of an effectively told story, provides material for some severe reflection. As a story, it has enough power to lift it above the imperatives of the moment and into consideration as serious literature, certainly as one of the few genuinely good American novels of recent years.

63. Milton Rugoff, 'U.S.A. Today: A Dos Passos Montage', *New York Herald Tribune Books*

26 February 1961, 31

Rugoff (b. 1913) is the author of *The Beechers: An American Family in the Nineteenth Century* (1981) in addition to collections of folktales and works of photojournalism. He calls *Midcentury* 'thinly disguised propaganda'.

This is a jumbled book, a montage of fiction, impressionistic biographies, brief quotations from newspapers, and an 'investigator's' interviews. Occasionally it flashes with the power that made Dos Passos' *U.S.A.* one of the richest, most original and evocative cross sections of American life; but more often it is only a hollow imitation of the earlier book—all the apparatus and techniques but little of the vision or insight. *U.S.A.* hardly overflowed with affirmation but it was not moved, as this book is, by rancor and prejudice. Under the guise of championing the old-fashioned virtues of self-determination, self-reliance and personal freedom, it is for the most part a series of case histories of corrupt labor unionists.

The book's chief bogeys—aside from racketeers—are the New Deal (and in terms of personalities, Franklin and Eleanor Roosevelt) and most liberals and intellectuals. It salutes Taft and Hoover and looks with sympathy on Joseph McCarthy and Sewell Avery. Among the fifteen figures included in its biographical sketches it finds its ideal of integrity and rugged individualism in General MacArthur, General William F. Dean (the officer who survived three years in Korean prison camps), and Senator John McClellan, whose committee has spotlighted union corruption. There are ambiguous portraits of John L. Lewis and Walter Reuther, unflattering ones of Eleanor Roosevelt and the atomic scientist J. Robert Oppenheimer, and acid etchings of Harry Bridges, Dan Tobin, Dave Beck and James Hoffa. The few non-political sketches, those of Samuel Goldwyn, Robert R. Young the financier, and Hollywood's James Dean, are a welcome relief.

It is difficult to judge even the fictional strands on fictional grounds because one finds that these—far from living up to the book's broad title—deal mostly with the relationship of individuals to unions: In one, a once ardent Wobbly, 'Blackie' Bowman, ends up ill and disillusioned in a Veterans Hospital; in a second, an idealistic union member rebels against crooked leaders and is mercilessly framed; in a third, a young businessman plunges into a fierce struggle with a competitor who is in league with crooked labor leaders and politicians. Even if readers had not been taught by a decade of headlines how racketeers take over unions and crush all opposition, the 'object lesson' quality of these narratives would rob them of much of their magic as fiction.

The story of 'Blackie' Bowman who became a passionate IWW organizer before World War I but lived to see the movement disintegrate is the most convincing narrative in the book partly because Dos Passos views that union (as he always has) as led by dedicated men who never compromised and never throttled their followers. But the IWW failed and thus never had to face the test of success—that is, the loss of purpose and drive that besets such organizations when they begin to achieve their goals.

The fictional elements in *Midcentury* are thinly disguised propaganda and they fail for the same reasons that most of the propaganda novels of the Thirties failed: the message strangles the art.

64. Gore Vidal, review, *Esquire*

May 1961, vol. lv, 57–9

Vidal (b. 1925), the prolific American writer and outspoken critic, is author of more than twenty-five books, including such historical novels as *Burr* (1973), *1876* (1976), and *Lincoln* (1984). He has been a critic for the *New York Review of Books*, the London *Times Literary Supplement*, *Partisan Review*, and *Esquire*. At the time he wrote this review he had been defeated the previous year as a Democratic candidate for the U.S. Congress.

With what seems defiance, the first two pages of John Dos Passos' new novel *Midcentury* are taken up with the titles of his published works, proudly spaced, seventeen titles to the first page, sixteen to the second: twenty-four books, the work of some forty years. The list is testament to Dos Passos' gallantry, to his stubbornness, and to his worldly and artistic failure. To paraphrase Hollywood's harsh wisdom, the persistent writer is only as good as his last decade. Admired extravagantly in the Twenties and Thirties, Dos Passos was ignored in the Forties and Fifties, his new works passed over either in silence or else noted with that ritual sadness we reserve for those whose promise has been spent. He himself is aware of his own dilemma and in a recent novel called *The Great Days* he recorded with brave if bewildered objectivity a decline similar to his own. I shall not try to ring the more obvious changes suggested by his career. Yet I should note that there is something about Dos Passos which makes a fellow-writer unexpectedly protective, partly out of compassion for the man himself, and partly because the fate of Dos Passos is a chilling reminder to those condemned to write for life that this is the way it almost always is in a society which, to put it tactfully, has no great interest in the development of its writers, a process too slow for the American temperament. As a result our literature is noted for sprinters but significantly short of milers.

Now, right off, let me say that unlike most of Dos Passos' more liberal critics, I never cared much for his early work even at its best. On the other hand, I have always enjoyed, even admired the dottiness of his politics. His political progress from radical left to radical right seems to me very much in the American grain and only the more humorless of doctrinaire liberals should be horrified. After all, it is not as if Dos Passos were in any way politically significant. Taken lightly, he gives pleasure. There is a good deal of inadvertent comedy in his admiration for such gorgeous Capitoline geese as Barry Goldwater, while page after page of *Midcentury* is vintage Old Guard demagoguery. For instance, there is that fine

Bourbon comforter 'Roosevelt's war' for the Second World War, while every now and then there is a passage which seems almost to parody Wisconsin's late wonder. For instance: 'Hitler's invasion of the Soviet Union cut off support from the Communists. Stalin needed quick help. Warmonger Roosevelt became the Communist's god.... War work meant primarily help for the Soviets to many a Washington bureaucrat.' That 'many' is superb stuff. 'I have here in my hand a list of *many* Washington bureaucrats who....' Politically, to make an atrocious pun, Dos Passos is for the Byrds.[1]

Midcentury is about the American labour movement from, roughly, the New Deal to the present, with occasional reminiscences of earlier times. The form of the book is chaotic. There are prose poems in italics. Short impressionistic biographies of actual public figures. Several fictional narratives in which various men and women are victimized by labor unions. And of course his patented device from *USA* of using newspaper headlines and fragments of news stories to act as counterpoint to the narration, to give a sense of time and place.

To deal with this last device first. In *USA* it was effective. In that book Dos Passos stumbled on an interesting truth. Nearly all of us are narcotized by newspapers. There is something in the set of a newspaper page which, if only from habit, holds the attention no matter how boring the matter. Bemused, one reads on, waiting for surprise or titillation. The success of the gossip column is no more than a crude exploitation of newspaper addiction. Even if you don't want to know what the Duchess of Windsor said to Elsa Maxwell or learn what stranger in the night was visited by Sir Stork, if your eye is addicted, numbly you will read on.

(Parenthetic note to writers-on-the-make and a warning to exploited readers: any column of text, even this one, will hold the eye and the attention of the reader if there are sufficient familiar proper names. Watch: Nat King Cole, Lee Remick, Central Park, Marquis de Sade, Senator Bourke B. Hickenlooper, Marilyn Monroe. See? I trapped a number of you who'd skimmed the dense paragraphs above, deciding it was pretty dull literary stuff. '"Marquis de Sade?" Must've skipped something. Let's see, there's "titillation"... no, "Hollywood"... no.' Also, dialogue has almost the same effect on the eye as names and newspaper headlines. In an age of worsening prose and declining concentration, most readers' attention will wander if there is too much unbroken text. On the other hand, even the most reluctant reader enjoys descending the short sprightly steps of dialogue on the page, jumping the descriptions, to shift the metaphor, as a skilled rider takes hedges in a steeplechase.)

The newspaper technique is a good one, though I don't think I'd want my sister to use it. But to work properly the excerpts ought to have some bearing on the narrative. In *Midcentury* one has the impression that Dos Passos simply shredded a few newspapers at random and stuffed them between the chapters as excelsior to keep the biographies from bumping into one another. On the whole, these biographies provide what interest the book has, although the choice of subjects is inscrutable. Walter Reuther, John L. Lewis, James Hoffa are reasonably relevant to a novel dealing with organized labor, but then why include Robert Oppenheimer and Eleanor Roosevelt? And what exactly *is* Sam Goldwyn doing in the book? Or James Dean, that well-known statesman of organized labor? But, disregarding the irrelevance of many of the subjects, Dos Passos handles his impressionistic technique with a good deal of cunning. It is a tribute to his method that I was offended by the job he did on Mrs. Roosevelt. He is wonderfully expert at the precise low-blow. For instance referring to Oppenheimer's belated political awakening (and turn to the left): 'Perhaps he felt the need to expiate the crime of individuality (as much of a crime to the solid citizens of the American Legion Posts as to party functionaries Moscow-trained in revolution).' That's good stuff. Dos Passos may not make the eagle scream, but he can certainly get the geese to honking. Yet despite his very pretty malice the real reason the biographies work is again newspaper addiction: we know the subjects already. Our memories round the flat portraiture. Our prejudices do the author's work.

Finally, sandwiched meagerly among headlines, feature stories, prose-poems (*Walking the earth under the stars, musing midnight in midcentury, a man treads the road with his dog; the dog, less timebound in her universe of stench and shrill, trots eager ahead....* Dig? Not since Studs Lonigan's old buddy Weary Reilley was making the scene has there been such word-music, I mean wordmusic.), we come to the fictional characters. Excepting one, they are cast in solid cement. Dos Passos tells us this and he tells us that, but he never *shows* us anything; he has not the knack to let his characters alone to see which will breathe and which will not. The only story which comes alive is a narrative by a dying labor organizer, and one-time Wobbly. He recalls his life and in those moments Dos Passos allows him to hold the stage one is most moved. As it is, Dos Passos proves a point well made by Stendhal:

'Politics, amidst the interests of the imagination, are a pistol shot in the middle of a concert. This noise is ear-rending, without being forceful. It clashes with every instrument.'

Dos Passos ends his book with a sudden lashing out at the youth of the day. He drops the labor movement. He examines James Dean. Then he does a Salinger-esque first-person narrative of an adolescent who has stolen some credit cards (remember a similar story in *Life*) and gone on a spree of conspicuous consumption. Despite the confusion of his style, Dos Passos is plain in his indictment: doomed is pleasure-loving, scornful, empty, flabby, modern youth, product of that dread mid-century in which, thanks to the do-gooders, we have lost our ancient Catonian virtue. I found the indictment oddly disgusting. I concede that there is some truth in everything Dos Passos says. But his spirit strikes me as sour and mean and, finally, uncomprehending. To be harsh, he has mistaken the decline of his own flesh and talent for the world's decline. This is the old man's folly which a good artist or a generous man tries to avoid. Few of us can resist celebrating our own great days or finding fault in those who do not see in us now what we were or might have been. Nor is it unnatural when contemplating extinction to want in sudden solipsistic moments to take the light with one. But it is a sign of virtue to recognize one's own pettiness and to surrender vanity not only to the death which means to take it anyway, but with deliberate grace as exemplar to those younger upon whom our race's fragile continuity, which is all there is, depends.

I should have thought that that was why one wrote, to make some thing useful for the survivors, to say: I was and now you are and I leave you as good a map as I could make of my own traveling.

NOTE

1 Prominent conservative family in contemporary American politics.

65. Melvin J. Friedman, review, *The Progressive*

September 1961, 49–51

Friedman is professor of Comparative Literature at the University of Wisconsin at Milwaukee. He is author of *Stream of Consciousness: A Study in Literary Method* (1955) and numerous articles on American and European literature. He has also edited books on Flannery O'Connor, Samuel Beckett, Ionesco, and William Styron.

John Dos Passos has been almost unique among novelists in his uncanny ability to remain politically committed without compromising his devotion to fiction. Like Malraux he has managed the complete *volteface* from extreme left to extreme right; unlike him he has continued writing novels even after he has deserted his leftist phase.

This latest Dos Passos is built on the same large lines as *U.S.A.* and the *District* of *Columbia* trilogy, but it seems uncomfortably documentary even in the longer narrative sections. The accomplished story-teller and delineator of character hides behind the chronicler, the social historian. The most compelling sections of *Midcentury* are probably the profiles of distinguished Americans: Eleanor Roosevelt, Douglas MacArthur, Robert M. LaFollette, Jr., Robert Oppenheimer. The portraits of Terry Bryant, Blackie Bowman, Lorna Hubbard, Jasper Milliron, and Stan Goodspeed, which offer the uneasy literary basis for the novel, pale before their historical counterparts. (Dos Passos skillfully parallels the careers of his fictional creatures with those of celebrated contemporaries; he is especially successful with the Stan Goodspeed-James Dean juxtaposition.)

In method, *Midcentury* does not differ essentially from *U.S.A.* The narrative is made to weave in and out of the documentary with a labyrinthine complexity. The reader is expected to reconstruct the fact-fiction interplay into an aesthetic whole. The sections in *Midcentury* entitled 'Documentary' recall the tone of the 'Newsreels' in *U.S.A.* The profiles regularly alternate with the narrative and reinforce its direction. But conspicuously absent from *Midcentury* are the ingenious 'Camera Eye' notations of the earlier trilogy. With their absence of punctuation, truncated syntax, metaphorical flourishes, and verbal plays, they gave *U.S.A.* a poetic foundation. It seems clear that the enriched poetic prose of the 'Camera Eye' belongs with the tamperings with structure which *Midcentury* has already taken over from *U.S.A.* Alan Pryce-Jones made this point when he said in *Harper's*: 'Where trouble begins is in realistic fiction which makes no use of poetry yet cannot forbear to experiment with construction.'

In *U.S.A.*, Dos Passos had defined a new type of novel which satisfied the experimental vigor of the Thirties. It made its own compromise with the stream-of-consciousness novel of Joyce, Virginia Woolf, and Faulkner and went in its own original direction. *Midcentury* uses many of the same tools but for quite a different purpose. It is much more of a 'preaching novel' than the earlier trilogy. Dos Passos seems intent on disenchanting us about labor unions, strikers, 'wobblies,' and displaced Marxists. By rooting out the self-induced corruption which seems to be destroying the working class, Dos Passos is offering a thinly-veiled defense for his own conservatism. He seems to insist, by implication, that one can honorably side only with the status quo in the Fifties.

His long narrative sections read almost like sociological case histories of victimized workers. He traces Terry Bryant—one of his least convincing fictional portraits—from his release from the service through his death as a martyr for the cause of free enterprise. Blackie Bowman, who soliloquizes from a bed in a veterans' hospital, multiplies instances of the corruption of labor unions. Even the financially independent Jasper Milliron suffers from the pressures of betrayal in high positions. The 'Investigator's Notes,' which Dos Passos purposely keeps anonymous, reinforce the futility of a Terry Bryant or a Blackie Bowman when confronted by organized labor.

Midcentury thus has an organizing principle which keeps the diverse parts together and helps make possible the total symphonic effect. Dos Passos seems to be telling us that hundreds of small men are victims of debilitating forces. Only the exceptional ones can withstand the dulling effects of a wornout social system. It is not accidental that Dos Passos should be at his most poetic when he offers his profiles of these olympian figures.

66. John Gross, review, *New Statesman*

27 October 1961, vol. lxii, 614–15

Gross (b. 1912) has written several works of literary criticism, including *The Rise and Fall of the Man of Letters*, (1969) and a book on Joyce. He also edited *The Oxford Book of Aphorisms*. Gross has been literary editor of the *New Statesman*, editor of the London *Times Literary Supplement* (1974–82), and is currently an editor for the *New York Times Book Review*.

At the end of *Midcentury* a teenager steals his uncle's credit cards and sets out on the razzle, which is the John Dos Passos version of modern American history in a nutshell. Old is good, new is bad, and the unions are worst of all—for what purports to be a panoramic 'novel of our time' proves little more than a crotchety attack on labour rackets as the root of all unAmerican evil, most of it at the same level as *Time* magazine denouncing Jimmy Hoffa. This is the most controversial work from Mr Dos Passos for a long time, and it would be exciting to report that the volcano given up for extinct had started rumbling dangerously again. But it's only the growl of any bilious reactionary down at the country-club. The old Dos Passos devices—press-cuttings, pocket biographies, words run together without benefit of hyphen—are trotted out, and they give the book a surface liveliness. But the rancour, the smoking-room guffaws at psychiatry, the lump in the throat for General MacArthur! All one can do for the sake of the man who once wrote *Manhattan Transfer* and *The Big Money* is look the other way.

NOTE

1 James Riddle Hoffa (1913–?75), American Labour leader.

CENTURY'S EBB

August 1975 (posthumously)

---

67. Malcolm Cowley, review, *New York Times Book Review*

9 November 1975, 6

Century's Ebb is written in the mixture of modes that Dos Passos originated in his bold trilogy *U.S.A.* (1930–38), then modified in each of his subsequent works. Two of these are straight novels— *Most Likely to Succeed* (1954) and *The Great Days* (1958)—but the others include factual reporting, editorials, obituaries and prose poems in various dosages. Each book presents a particular phase or period of American life; for example, *The Grand Design* (1949) deals with government agencies during World War II. At some time in the 1950's, Dos Passos decided that the right name for the series was *Contemporary Chronicles*, and he rearranged it in chronological order of subject matter. Thus, *Chosen Country* (1951), an autobiographical romance about the Pignatelli (read 'Dos Passos') family, became the first chronicle, since it opens in the years before the Civil War. *Midcentury* (1961) was to be the 12th chronicle in order of subject matter, and in order of writing as well.

There followed some years devoted to historical studies and reportorial assignments, but in 1968 he wrote to his friend Bill White, 'I'm all tied up with a last (?) contemporary chronicle.' The statement is from an illuminating collection of Dos Passos's letters and diaries edited by Townsend Ludington and called, somewhat confusingly, *The Fourteenth Chronicle*. The same book contains a letter of June 25, 1970, addressed to Dos Passos's Harvard classmate Harold Weston. It says, 'I'm putting the finishing touches on a last forlorn Chronicle of Despair. The rank criminal idiocy of the younger generation in this country is more than I can swallow.'

During those last years there were many things that Dos Passos couldn't swallow. The first of them was Communism, which he detested with a hatred extending to anything that suggested a halting step in that direction. He detested liberalism, too, especially when it took the form of progressive education. He detested big government and big labor; in fact, he detested bigness in almost everything. Geography was an exception, especially if it was American geography. Despondent as he was about American culture, he was fascinated by the physical vastness and human diversity of the country, and he celebrated both of these, at times, in a fashion that suggests Walt Whitman.

The Whitmanian side of his work, not always revealed in the past, is boldly evident in *Century's Ebb*. The book opens with a biographical portrait of Whitman, sympathetic but realistic, too, and the portrait leads up to a question: 'Here, now, today, if you came back to us, Walt Whitman, what would you say?' In a sense the whole book—big, untidy, composed of disparate elements like the country itself—is Dos Passos's effort to answer that question.

The disparate elements of the book are fiction, fact and opinion, arranged in a looser pattern than in earlier chronicles (and with a few gaps in the narrative that might have disappeared in a final revision). Specifically there are a dozen biographical portraits—'obituaries,' I called them—ranging from that of Whitman, the best, to those of Lee Harvey Oswald and Malcolm X, the most perfunctory. There are three lives of invented characters, one of whom speaks in the first person: he is Danny DeLong, a rather engaging wolf cub of Wall Street betrayed by older wolves and sent to prison. There are half-a-dozen reportorial pieces that record what the author saw in his travels over the country. Finally there is the heart of the book, an interrupted series of seven long chapters called 'The Later Life and Deplorable Opinions of Jay Pignatelli.' Jay is of course the author himself transparently disguised as a lawyer. One could do without many of his opinions, but the character is fascinating: shy, persistent, often disappointed by persons he trusted, and determined to maintain a stubborn integrity. It is the picture of Dos Passos we might have gained from his previous books, but here he reveals himself candidly at moments of personal crisis.

As for his answer to the question asked of Walt Whitman's ghost, it is generally forlorn and despairing, but Dos Passos keeps finding gleams of hope. One of which is simply those individuals who work devotedly and remain honest in the midst of almost universal corruption. Another is reflected from scientific discoveries, especially when they find such applications as hybrid corn and, a strange coupling, the Apollo moonshots. A report of the first moonshot, on Dec. 24, 1968, comes at the end of the book as if chosen as a hopeful conclusion to the whole series of chronicles. 'This was the day,' Dos Passos says, 'when man proved his mastery of matter, the day he wiped out the unhappy prospects of Hiroshima.'

Dos Passos was never the most dependable of prophets or the wisest of political commentators. Whether his opinions were radical as in his youth, or Colonel Blimpish as in his later novels, he was always it seems to us now, a little credulous, a little eager to find virtue in his old or new allies and evil in his adversaries. Still, for all the faults of his 13th and last chronicle, it is easy to read and leaves us with more admiration for the series as a whole, including the later books that have been too easily rejected. The figure of Jay Pignatelli helps to bind the series together, as does the shade of Walt Whitman. 'My this is a big untidy soulstirring country we live in,' Dos Passos had written in 1943 to his Harvard friend Robert Hillyer. 'I feel myself continually tortured by curiosity about it.' That curiosity, panoramic in scope and combined with old-fashioned patriotism, is the central emotion conveyed by his contemporary chronicles.

68. Townsend Ludington, review, *New Republic*

22 November 1975, 23–5

Ludington (b. 1936), professor of English at the University of North Carolina at Chapel Hill, is the editor of Dos Passos's letters (*The Fourteenth Chronicle* (Boston: Gambit, 1973)) and author of the biography, *John Dos Passos: A Twentieth Century Odyssey* (New York: E.P. Dutton, 1980).

Three months before John Dos Passos died in September 1970, he wrote his friend, the artist Harold Weston, that he was 'putting the

finishing touches on a last forlorn Chronicle of Despair.' The book
he referred to is *Century's Ebb: The Thirteenth Chronicle*, which
brings to an end the long series of fictional chronicles he began in
1921 with the publication of *Three Soldiers*. Dos Passos' despair
resulted from his ill health, but more, from his sorrow about what
he asserted to Weston was 'the rank criminal idiocy of the younger
generation in this country.' That 'criminal idiocy' was the widespread protest against the invasion of Cambodia ordered by
Richard Nixon. By the time Dos Passos wrote *Century's Ebb*, he
was a fervent anti-Communist, an ardent supporter of Goldwater
republicanism. He had long since come to believe that the United
States—his 'chosen country' he called it in the nostalgic novel of
that title—had lost its way, had abandoned the Jeffersonian ideals
dear to him, and had become a gigantic bureaucracy controlled by
the often corrupt forces of government and labor.

The devices he used in *Century's Ebb* to reflect his sense of
American life are similar to those he used most effectively in the
trilogy *U.S.A.* In *Century's Ebb* he included pieces entitled '1937,'
'1939,' and '1948,' which serve like the 'Newsreel' sections in
U.S.A. as background to the rest of the book, and reveal his belief
that Franklin Roosevelt's New Deal was growing into a ponderous
bureaucracy while World War II loomed ever larger. As he had
before, Dos Passos turned to one of his American heroes, Walt
Whitman, to express his fears about the United States as it became a
super-nation. Four of the five parts into which *Century's Ebb* is
divided include lyric pieces by or about Whitman. But the Whitman Dos Passos called on is not the poet of 'Song of Myself' who
celebrated an exuberant, pre-Civil War America. His Whitman is
that of *Democratic Vistas*, the pained nationalist who feared that the
'fervid and tremendous *Idea*' which was our storybook democracy
had become mired in 'solid things...science, ships, politics, cities,
factories,' during the years of 'unprecedented material advance-
ment.'

To his own question, 'Are we indeed men worthy of the name,
Walt Whitman, in these "years of the modern, years of
the unperformed"?' Dos Passos' answer was both 'yes' and 'no.'
No, because he believed that America failed to meet the international challenge of communism and the domestic challenges of
materialism and violence. To show this he used biographical
sketches of prominent figures such as George Orwell, John Dewey,

Sen. Joseph McCarthy, Wendell Wilkie, John Foster Dulles, Robert Goddard, Henry Wallace, George Eastman, Lee Harvey Oswald, Malcolm X and Dr. James Watson; and several longer narratives about thinly disguised characters like Danny DeLong, modeled after Eddie Gilbert, a financial sharpie who embezzled money during the 1960s and took refuge in Brazil, where Dos Passos met him. Another narrative is about Jay Pignatelli, a lawyer whose career closely parallels Dos Passos' own. Pignatelli's narrative conveys Dos Passos' disillusionment with the left wing, particularly during the Spanish Civil War, when he felt the Communists betrayed him because of their secret involvement in the death of his close friend, José Robles.

But if there was much to cause Dos Passos to answer 'no' to his own question, he could also respond, 'Yes, something about us is indeed worthy of the name.' For him the Apollo 8 flight in December 1968, was the moment 'man proved his mastery of matter,' the moment 'he wiped out the unhappy prospects of Hiroshima.' The Apollo 11 flight was the climax. Its launching was dramatic; for him it symbolized men's ability to harness their material instincts, to control something of the forces in nature, to perform for once as he believed Whitman would have Americans perform.

Dos Passos told his friend Weston that he was putting the finishing touches on his chronicle, but he did not complete his task. The narrative about Jay Pignatelli stops abruptly, well before the end of the period (1937–1969) Dos Passos was writing about. The brief piece entitled '1948' is nothing more than a short list of events, while several of the biographical sketches, one of his most effective devices in others of his chronicles, are little more than an accounting of facts. Had Dos Passos lived, he might have been able to make the tenor of the various parts more balanced, the play of themes more subtle .in some places, more apparent in others.

Not that his intentions are obscure. We cannot mistake his belief about the direction—the ebb—of this century's tide. His fears are clearest when his hatred of communism is apparent, when he provocatively portrays Joseph McCarthy as nothing more than a country boy bewildered by the intrigues of a liberal bureaucracy; when he sympathizes so entirely with John Foster Dulles' brinksmanship that he ignores the complexities of international diplomacy; or when, detailing the career of the assassin Lee Harvey

Oswald, he describes Gen. Edwin A. Walker as 'a plainspoken man who had resigned from the Army to defend the American cause.' This description has some truth, but ignores the fact that the general was a wild-eyed radical of the far right, as much within the lunatic fringe as some of the radicals on the left whom Dos Passos had come to despise.

Century's Ebb may be unfinished, or at least unpolished, but it deserves to be published. It contains some good Dos Passos writing: the first, moving lyric about Walt Whitman, several impressionistic passages like one entitled 'Turnpike' and another about George Eastman and his Kodak camera, and parts of the long narratives. But, finally, whether *Century's Ebb* is complete and whether it stands with Dos Passos' best fiction are not the main points to be made about the book. It is the last work of one of the major American writers to emerge during the 1920s. Most important, it brings down the curtain on Dos Passos' remarkable effort throughout his literary career to convey the panorama of 20th-century society. His later novels are partly right wing polemics, but anyone wanting to dismiss Dos Passos should remember that he was not a crank, a Westbrook Pegler, but an intelligent, thoughtful man of letters who agonized about his politics. Dos Passos was not alone when he shifted from left to right, and *Century's Ebb* represents the stance of a substantial, often powerful minority of Americans. Furthermore his sorrow about his chosen country is akin to that of literally millions of his countrymen who have despaired about this story-book democracy. A sense of hopelessness is abroad in the land; many Americans fear they can do little or nothing to stem technological growth; and the government, which they once believed *was* them, now seems impersonal and unresponsive. Meanwhile the industrial machine surges ahead, having wreaked havoc on Vietnam, and continues to expend sources of energy throughout the world, in the process fouling the environment.

In the context of our contemporary dilemmas, *Century's Ebb* appears as more than a right wing diatribe. It is a poignant statement by an American who devoted his career to observing his country, hoping to awaken other Americans with his words. And if, like his earlier chronicles, it often paints a dark, even savage picture, it also reflects Dos Passos' pleasure and amusement in his fellow men, who may scurry about foolishly and self-importantly, but who have as well their moments of tragedy, of compassion and of greatness. His 13th chronicle rounds out his vision of our life and marks the end of his lover's quarrel with the world.

Select Bibliography

Biographical Studies

CARR, VIRGINIA SPENCER. *Dos Passos: A Life*. Garden City, New York: Doubleday, 1984.

LANDSBERG, MELVIN. *Dos Passos' Path to 'U.S.A.': A Political Biography 1912–1936*. Boulder: Colorado University Press, 1972.

LUDINGTON, TOWNSEND (ed.). *The Fourteenth Chronicle: Letters and Diaries of John Dos Passos*. Boston: Gambit, 1973.

——*John Dos Passos: A Twentieth Century Odyssey*. New York: E.P. Dutton, 1980.

General Studies (Literary)

ALDRIDGE, JOHN W. *After the Lost Generation: A Critical Study of the Writers of Two Wars*. New York: McGraw-Hill, 1951.

BEACH, JOSEPH WARREN. *American Fiction: 1920–1940*. New York: Macmillan, 1941.

COOPERMAN, STANLEY. *World War I and the American Novel*. Baltimore: The Johns Hopkins Press, 1967.

COWLEY, MALCOLM. *Exile's Return: A Literary Odyssey of the 1920's*. New York: W.W. Norton, 1934.

HOFFMAN, FREDERICK. *The Twenties: American Writing in the Postwar Decade*. New York: Free Press, 1965.

KAZIN, ALFRED. *On Native Grounds*. New York: Harcourt, Brace & World, 1942.

——*An American Procession*. New York: Knopf, 1984.

MILLGATE, MICHAEL. *American Social Fiction: James to Cozzens*. Edinburgh: Oliver & Boyd, 1964.

General Studies (Political)

AARON, DANIEL. *Writers on the Left: Episodes in American Literary Communism*. New York: Harcourt, Brace & World, 1961.

BUCKLEY, WILLIAM F., JR. *Up From Liberalism*. New York: McDowell, Obolensky, 1959.

DIGGINS, JOHN P. *The American Left in the Twentieth Century.* New York: Harcourt, Brace, Jovanovich, 1973.

————*Up From Communism: Conservative Odysseys in American Intellectual History.* New York: Harper & Row, 1975.

GILBERT, JAMES BURKHART. *Writers and Partisans: A History of Literary Radicalism in America.* New York: John Wiley, 1968.

GUTTMAN, ALLEN. *The Conservative Tradition in America.* New York: Oxford University Press, 1967.

LASCH, CHRISTOPHER. *The Agony of the American Left.* New York: Knopf, 1969.

PELLS, RICHARD H. *Radical Visions and American Dreams: Culture and Social Thought in the Depression Years.* New York: Harper & Row, 1973.

WEINSTEIN JAMES. *Ambiguous Legacy: The Left in American Politics.* New York: New Viewpoints, 1975.

Critical Studies of Works by Dos Passos

BECKER, GEORGE J. *John Dos Passos.* New York: Frederick Ungar, 1974.

BELKIND, ALLEN (ed.). *Dos Passos, the Critics, and the Writer's Intention.* Carbondale: Southern Illinois University Press, 1971.

BRANTLEY, JOHN D. *The Fiction of John Dos Passos.* The Hague: Mouton, 1968.

BUTLER, ROBERT JAMES. 'The American Quest for Pure Movement in Dos Passos's *U.S.A.' Twentieth Century Literature*, xxx (Spring 1984): 80–99.

COLLEY, IAIN. *Dos Passos and the Fiction of Despair.* Totowa, N.J.: Rowman & Littlefield, 1978.

FOLEY, BARBARA. 'From *U.S.A.* to *Ragtime*: Notes on the Forms of Historical Consciousness in Modern Fiction'. *American Literature*, 1 (1978): 85–105.

————'History, Fiction, and Satiric Form: The Example of Dos Passos's *1919'. Genre*, xii (1979): 357–78.

———— 'The Treatment of Time in *The Big Money*: An Examination of Ideology and Literary Form'. *Modern Fiction Studies*, xxvi (1980): 444–67.

GELFANT, BLANCHE H. 'The Search for Identity in the Novels of John Dos Passos'. *PMLA*, lxxvi (March 1961): 133–49.

HOOK, ANDREW (ed.). *Dos Passos: A Collection of Critical Essays.* Englewood Cliffs, N.J.: Prentice-Hall, 1974.

HUGHSON, LOIS. 'Dos Passos's World War: Narrative Technique and History'. *Studies in the Novel*, xii (1980): 46–61.

KNOX, GEORGE. 'Voice in the *U.S.A.* Biographies'. *Texas Studies in Literature and Language*, iv (Spring 1962): 109–116.

LOWRY, E. D. 'The Lively Art of *Manhattan Transfer*'. *PMLA*, lxxxiv (October 1969): 1628–38.

MAINE, BARRY. 'Representative Men in Dos Passos's *The 42nd Parallel*'. *Clio*, xii (1982): 31–43.

————'*U.S.A.*: Dos Passos and the Rhetoric of History'. *South Atlantic Review* 1 (January 1985): 75–86.

MARZ, CHARLES. '*U.S.A.*: Chronicle and Performance'. *Modern Fiction Studies*, xxvi (1980): 398–416.

ROHRKEMPER, JOHN. 'Mr. Dos Passos's War'. *Modern Fiction Studies*', xxx (Spring 1984): 37–51.

ROSEN, ROBERT C. *John Dos Passos: Politics and the Writer*. Lincoln: University of Nebraska Press, 1981.

SANDERS, DAVID. 'The "Anarchism" of John Dos Passos'. *South Atlantic Quarterly*, lx (Winter 1961): 44–55.

SEED, DAVID. 'Media and Newsreels in Dos Passos's *U.S.A.*' *Journal of Narrative Technique*, xiv (Fall 1984): 182–92.

SPINDLER, MICHAEL. John Dos Passos and the Visual Arts', *Journal of American Studies*, xv (December 1981): 391–405.

VANDERWERKEN, DAVID L. '*U.S.A.*: Dos Passos and the "Old Words"'. *Twentieth Century Literature*, xxiii (May 1977): 195–228.

WAGNER, LINDA W. *Dos Passos: Artist as American*. Austin: University of Texas Press, 1979.

WESTERHOVEN, JAMES N. 'Autobiographical Elements in the Camera Eye'. *American Literature*, xlviii (November 1976): 341–64.

WRENN, JOHN H. *John Dos Passos*. Twayne's United States Authors Series. New Haven: College and University Press, 1961.

Index

The index is divided into three sections: I. John Dos Passos's works; II. Characteristics and topics; III. Name index.

I. JOHN DOS PASSOS'S WORKS

II. CHARACTERISTICS AND TOPICS

III. NAME INDEX

Oppenheimer, Robert, 260, 265, 267, 271, 273
Orwell, George, 279
Oswald, Lee Harvey, 277, 280

Palmer, A. Mitchell, 102
Pater, Walter, 196
Pavlenco, P., 112–14
Perkins, Maxwell, 7
Pound, Ezra, 2, 183
Pritchett, V.S., 2, 92–3
Proust, Marcel, 7, 68, 106, 221

Rabelais, François, 71
Racine, Jean, 187
Reed, Jack, 100, 102, 107, 149, 180, 228
Rees, Goronwy, 13, 14, 145–6
Reuther, Walter, 260, 265, 267, 271
Robinson, Henry Morton, 20
Robles, Jose, 17, 23, 280
Rolland, Romain, 114
Roosevelt, Eleanor, 260–1, 265, 267, 271, 273
Roosevelt, Franklin, 20, 279
Roosevelt, Theodore, 88, 100, 102, 118, 180
Rosen, Robert, 7, 19, 26
Ross, Mary, 79–82, 99–101
Rugoff, Milton, 22, 267–8

Sacco and Vanzetti, 8, 9, 151, 166, 197, 233, 253
Sartre, Jean-Paul, 2, 3, 27, 167–75
Schramm, Wilbur, 18, 222–3
Schwartz, Delmore, 15, 26, 175–90, 231
Seeger, Alan, 36
Selvinsky, K., 112–14
Shakespeare, William, 187–8
Shelley, Percy Bysshe, 71
Sillen, Samuel, 18, 209–13
Silone, Ignazio, 156, 161, 217
Sinclair, Upton, 10, 87–91, 108
Smith, Harrison, 21, 256–8
Stalin, Joseph, 153
Stein, Gertrude, 7, 68, 92
Steinbeck, John, 18, 210, 244
Steinmetz, Charles, 81, 83, 150, 180, 230

Stendhal, 155, 175, 183, 214, 272
Strong, L.A.G., 110–12
Stuart, Henry Longan, 7, 64–7
Sullivan, Mark, 11, 102

Taft, William, 267
Tate, Allen, 7, 32
Taylor, Frederick Winslow, 134, 144, 180
Tolstoy, Leo, 13, 109, 183, 214
Trilling, Diana, 247
Trilling, Lionel, 2, 9, 16, 18, 154–61
Trotsky, Leon, 153
Twain, Mark, 70

Valentino, Rudolph, 180
Veblen, Thorstein, 14, 130, 134, 144, 147, 180, 200, 227, 229
Vidal, Gore, 22, 268–72
Voltaire, 71

Wallace, Henry, 280
Warren, Robert Penn, 20
Watson, James Sibley, 5
Wescott, Glenway, 104
Wharton, Edith, 8, 71
Whipple, T.K., 15, 147–52, 156, 158, 184–5
Whitman, Walt, 8, 13–14, 23, 27, 71, 73, 117, 146, 277–81
Wilder, Thornton, 86, 104
Wilkie, Wendell, 280
Wilson, Edmund, 2, 3, 11, 15, 18, 20, 21, 27, 84–7, 195, 213–15, 234, 242–3, 252–3
Wilson, Woodrow, 100, 102, 105, 107, 118, 132, 147, 180
Winters, Ivor, 185
Wolfe, Thomas, 244
Woolf, Virginia, 274
Wright, Frank Lloyd, 134, 144, 180
Wright, Orville, 144, 180
Wright, Wilbur, 144, 180

Zapata, Emiliano, 228
Zola, Emile, 106–7, 109, 196